The Justification
of Religious Violence

Blackwell Public Philosophy

Edited by Michael Boylan, Marymount University

In a world of 24 hour news cycles and increasingly specialized knowledge, the Blackwell Public Philosophy series takes seriously the idea that there is a need and demand for engaging and thoughtful discussion of topics of broad public importance. Philosophy itself is historically grounded in the public square, bringing people together to try to understand the various issues that shape their lives and give them meaning. This "love of wisdom" – the essence of philosophy – lies at the heart of the series. Written in an accessible, jargon-free manner by internationally renowned authors, each book is an invitation to the world beyond newsflashes and soundbites and into public wisdom.

For further information about individual titles in the series, supplementary material, and regular updates, visit www.blackwellpublishing.com/publicphilosophy

The Justification
of Religious Violence

Steve Clarke

WILEY Blackwell

This edition first published 2014
© 2014 John Wiley & Sons Inc.

Registered Office
John Wiley & Sons Ltd, The Atrium, Southern Gate, Chichester, West Sussex, PO19 8SQ, UK

Editorial Offices
350 Main Street, Malden, MA 02148-5020, USA
9600 Garsington Road, Oxford, OX4 2DQ, UK
The Atrium, Southern Gate, Chichester, West Sussex, PO19 8SQ, UK

For details of our global editorial offices, for customer services, and for information about how to apply for permission to reuse the copyright material in this book please see our website at www.wiley.com/wiley-blackwell.

The right of Steve Clarke to be identified as the author of this work has been asserted in accordance with the UK Copyright, Designs and Patents Act 1988.

Library of Congress Cataloging-in-Publication data is available for this book.

ISBN 9781118529751 (hardback); ISBN 9781118529720 (paperback)

A catalogue record for this book is available from the British Library.

Cover design by Simon Levy Associates

Typeset in 10.5/13pt MinionPro by Laserwords Private Limited, Chennai, India

Printed in Malaysia by Ho Printing (M) Sdn Bhd

1   2014

*Men never do evil so completely and cheerfully as when
they do it for religious conviction.*
Blaise Pascal

*To oppose the torrent of scholastic religion by such feeble maxims as
these, that it is impossible for the same thing to be and not to be, that
the whole is greater than a part, that two and three make five; is
pretending to stop the ocean with a bullrush. Will you set up profane
reason against sacred mystery? No punishment is great enough for your
impiety. And the same fires, which were kindled for heretics, will serve
also for the destruction of philosophers.*
David Hume

Will you love that man or woman well enough to shed their blood?
Brigham Young

Contents

Contents

Preface

Much has been written about the relationship between religion and violence, and much of what has been written is aimed at determining whether, how, and why religion causes violence. This book has a different goal. Followers of many different religions who commit violent acts seek to justify these by appealing to religion. I aim to understand how such justifications proceed; and how they do, or do not, differ from ordinary secular justifications for violence. I will show that religious justifications for violence generally exemplify the same logical forms as ordinary secular justifications for violence. I will also show that many religiously based justifications for violence are as acceptable as rigorous secular justifications for violence, provided that crucial premises, which religion supplies, are accepted. Religious believers are able to incorporate premises, grounded in the metaphysics of religious worldviews, in arguments for the conclusion that this or that violent act is justified. I examine three widely employed types of premises that appear in such arguments. These are: appeals to a state of "cosmic war," appeals to the afterlife, and appeals to sacred values.

The first three chapters of the book contain background material. Because my analysis is informed by recent work in psychology, cognitive science, neuroscience, and evolutionary biology, there is much ground to cover before we analyze religious justifications for violence. In Chapter 1, some violent actions that have been undertaken in the name of religion are discussed and two influential views about the relationship between religion, justification, and violence (or the lack of such a relationship) are considered and rejected. I also discuss and define the key terms "justification" and "violence," as well as examine the relationship between nature and "supernature," which underpins many of the metaphysical postulates developed by the religious. In the second chapter, I discuss influential generalizations about religion and assess which of these stands up to scientific scrutiny. I argue that religion has evolved and I consider competing views about how this has happened. I argue in favor of the view that religion is an evolutionary adaptation. I then offer a new, empirically informed, definition of religion. Chapter 3 is about morality. I consider the evolution of morality, the role of culture in shaping morality, and recent work in social psychology and neuroscience on moral judgment. All of this leads up to an overall characterization of the relationship between morality and religion. Readers who are well informed about any of the background topics discussed in Chapters 1, 2, and 3 may safely skip over the sections in which these topics are discussed.

In Chapter 4 I consider ordinary secular justifications for violence and explore how these can be reconciled with consequentialist and deontological accounts of morality. I then look at the ethics of war, just war theory, and pacifist objections to war. I also consider traditional religious justifications for war, many of which involve the supposition that a cosmic struggle is taking place between the forces of good and the forces of evil. I show that appeals to cosmic war make it easy to justify a range of behavior that would be harder to justify in conventional wars by the standards of just war theory. In Chapter 5, the role that afterlife beliefs can play in justifying religious violence is considered. I concentrate on arguments in the Christian tradition that appeal to the importance of salvation to justify violent actions directed at heretics and apostates, as well as arguments in the Buddhist tradition that appeal to beliefs about the cycle of reincarnation to justify violence. I also examine religious justifications for suicide that appeal to the afterlife. In Chapter 6, I consider the role that sacred values play in religious justifications of violence. I look at Durkheim's classic analysis of the sacred, as well as recent work in psychology and negotiation studies on sacred values, along with some contemporary work in cognitive science and neuroscience on sacralization. I end the chapter by arguing that ordinary reasoning about sacred values is a form of ordinary deontological moral reasoning.

Chapter 7 contains a series of recent case studies in which violent action has been taken, and religious justifications for this violence have been offered, either by the perpetrators, or by sympathetic co-religionists. Six case studies are examined. I look at two religious groups from the United States, *The Gatekeepers* and *Heaven's Gate*, and also a religiously inspired American anti-abortion activist, Scott Roeder. I consider a religious group based in Japan, *Aum Shinrikyo*, as well as followers of the Rabbi Meir Kahane, who have committed acts of violence in Israel. Lastly, I consider religious justifications for violence offered by representatives of the international organization *al-Qaeda*. In all six case studies, it is demonstrated that the justifications offered for violent action carried out in the name of religion appeal to cosmic war, the afterlife, or sacred values, or some combination of these three factors.

Chapter 8 is about religious tolerance. I consider what tolerance is and how religious tolerance is justified in liberal democratic states. I then examine evidence from social psychology about whether religion promotes tolerance or intolerance. I go on to consider whether promoting the value of religious tolerance could be an effective way to persuade those who believe that they are justified by their religion in acting violently to refrain from acting violently. In Chapter 9, I consider some other possible ways to persuade those who believe that violent action is justified by religion, and who are motivated to act violently, to nevertheless refrain from acting violently. I also consider whether, and to what extent, religiously tolerant liberal societies can and should tolerate religious groups that believe that they are justified in acting violently on behalf of their religion.

Throughout the book I follow a common, abbreviated way of writing and refer to attempted justifications simply as justifications. It should be clear enough, from context, when I am referring to an attempt to justify some or other doctrine, or instance of violent action, and when I am referring to justifications that meet the standards that we ordinarily accept as successfully justifying violent action. The justification of any form of violence is a controversial topic and there will be some readers who will not regard the standards that most people ordinarily accept as justifying violent action as sufficiently rigorous. Some readers will hold that we ought to apply more rigorous standards to all attempts to justify violence, including those that appeal to religion. Other readers, especially avid pacifists, will suppose that we can never offer successful justifications for any violent behaviour. Although I discuss pacifist objections to war in Chapter 4, a proper consideration of pacifist objections to the standards that most of us ordinarily apply to justifications of violence is beyond the scope of this work.

The book had its origins in a grant application, on "Science and Religious Conflict'" which I developed, together with Julian Savulescu, director of the Oxford Uehiro Centre for Practical Ethics, the Institute for Science and Ethics, in the Oxford Martin School, and the Oxford Centre for Neuroethics, all at the University of Oxford. Julian and I wanted to take recent work in social psychology, cognitive science, neuroscience and evolutionary biology and apply this to shed light on the nature of religious conflict; and also to suggest ways to reduce religious conflict. Our application was generously funded by the Arts and Humanities Research Council in the United Kingdom and ran from the beginning of 2009 to mid-2012 (Standard Grant AH/F019513/1). In addition to this book, the Science and Religious Conflict project resulted in two major international conferences, a number of academic papers, and an edited volume, *Religion, Intolerance and Conflict: A Scientific and Conceptual Investigation*, edited by Steve Clarke, Russell Powell, and Julian Savulescu (Oxford: Oxford University Press 2013). Julian and I were fortunate enough to have been able to employ Russell Powell to work on the grant. I benefited enormously from the opportunity to work with Julian and Russell, as well as the opportunity to work at the Uehiro Centre and in the Oxford Martin School. Work on the latter stages of this book was generously supported by the Centre for Applied Philosophy and Public Ethics, Charles Sturt University.

Thanks to Joanna Burch-Brown, Adrienne Clarke, Katrien Devolder, Tom Douglas, David Edmonds, Jacqueline Fox, Guy Kahane, Marguerite La Caze, Neil Levy, Morgan Luck, Kate MacDonald, Terry MacDonald, Francesca Minerva, Justin Oakley, Russell Powell, Simon Rippon, Julian Savulescu, Nicholas Shea, John Teehan, Steven Tudor, Adrian Walsh, and several anonymous reviewers for helping me to improve my draft material. Thanks also to Lindsay Bourgeois, Michael Boylan, Jennifer Bray, Liam Cooper, Jeff Dean, Allison Kostka, Louise Spencely, and Paul Stringer for their editorial help and support.

I

Justification, Religion, and Violence

September 11 (1857)

At dawn on September 7, 1857, a wagon train of emigrants camped at Mountain Meadows in southern Utah unexpectedly found themselves under attack. The emigrants – the Fancher–Baker party – were making their way from Arkansas to California. They numbered approximately 120, including men, women, and children of various ages, and they had perhaps 700 head of cattle with them. The attackers aimed coordinated barrages of gunfire at the party from different directions and their initial assault is reported to have resulted in seven deaths (Walker, Turley, and Leonard 2008, p. 158). However, that initial attack was soon repelled by the emigrant group who corralled their wagons and proceeded to fight off their assailants over the next five days. The attacking party was dressed as American Indians, and indeed some of them were Southern Paiute Indians. But the majority were white and were members of the Church of Jesus Christ of Latter-Day Saints (Mormons). There were reports of fractious interactions between members of the Fancher–Baker party and Mormons whom they had encountered when passing through Utah (Bagley 2002, p. 98; Walker et al. 2008, p. 87).[1] However, the party posed no threat to the Utahn Mormon community and were about to leave Utah for good.

In the late morning of September 11, a sub-group of the assailants removed their disguises and approached the corral, pretending to be representatives of a sympathetic local militia who could broker a deal

The Justification of Religious Violence, First Edition. Steve Clarke.
© 2014 John Wiley & Sons, Inc. Published 2014 by John Wiley & Sons, Inc.

between the emigrants and their Indian assailants. In exchange for livestock and supplies the representatives of the militia claimed that they would be able to persuade the assailants to cease hostilities and they would provide the emigrants with safe passage to nearby Cedar City. The emigrants were suspicious of the negotiating party, having seen through the disguises of their mainly white assailants; but as they were running low on water and ammunition, they felt that they had little choice but to accept the offer (Walker et al. 2008, p. 196), which was, as they feared, a "decoy." The remaining members of the Fancher–Baker party, who had managed to survive five days of besiegement, left their corral and were ambushed soon after by other members of the Mormon-led assailant group. Every adult and every child over the age of six was massacred and their bodies hastily buried. The only survivors were seventeen small children and infants, who were adopted into nearby Mormon families, under the erroneous assumption that they would all be too young to remember the shocking events that had transpired.

Historians who have examined the events surrounding the Mountain Meadows massacre disagree about whether or not Brigham Young, the then President of the Church of Jesus Christ of Latter-Day Saints, had a hand in orchestrating the massacre, but all seem to agree that at least some senior figures in the church were involved in planning the massacre and in the attempted cover-up that followed.[2] Although there were many participants in the massacre, only one man was ever convicted for his actions and this conviction occurred almost twenty years after the event. The convicted man was John D. Lee, one of the ringleaders of the attacking party. Lee considered himself to be a scapegoat for the consequences of decisions made by church leaders; and although he admitted that he had killed some of the members of the Fancher–Baker party, he did not consider that he had done anything wrong. He believed that he was following just orders given to him by legitimate religious authorities. In his words: "I was guided in all that I did which is called criminal, by the orders of the leaders in the Church of Jesus Christ of Latter-Day Saints."[3] All of this information may come as a huge surprise to the many people who are unfamiliar with the events of September 11, 1857. The Mountain Meadows massacre has been largely forgotten and Mormons are not particularly associated with violence these days.

The massacre may have had a political motive.[4] In 1857, Utah was a semi-independent territory of the USA and was majority Mormon and politically dominated by the leadership of the Church of Jesus Christ of Latter-Day Saints. As well as being President of the Church of Jesus Christ of Latter-Day Saints, Brigham Young was Governor of Utah Territory at the time. The church leaders were enmeshed in a complicated struggle to retain as much of their independence as they could from the distant, but ever-encroaching, "gentile" United States government in Washington. Some of them believed that the US government did not appreciate the role that Mormons played as protectors of the many white emigrants traveling westwards to California through partially colonized territory inhabited by potentially hostile Indian tribes. Furthermore, they believed that it would be politically advantageous to the Mormons if the government came to value this role and that an Indian massacre of white emigrants might help make their point. After Brigham Young announced that the Indians would no longer be "held back" by the Utahn Mormon community, attempts were made by some of the Mormons to encourage local Indians to conduct an attack on emigrants traversing Utah (Walker et al. 2008, p. 137); and when these were unsuccessful a plan to fake an Indian massacre was hatched (Walker et al. 2008, pp. 140). Unfortunately for the conspirators, the attempt to present the massacre that did take place as the work of local Indians was considered extremely unconvincing by the mainstream American media, who laid the blame for it squarely on the Mormon community of Utah. Some newspapers called for military reprisals against that community (Bagley 2002, pp. 190–1).[5]

Upon reading the above political explanation of the motives for the massacre, the average person is unlikely to be any less appalled than they were when first told that the massacre took place. The slaughter of over one hundred people for political advantage is appalling, not because it might fail to serve a political end, but because it seems highly immoral to most of us to kill people who pose no threat, regardless of whether this is for political gain or not. For many, the immorality of the massacre will seem all the more appalling and astonishing given that its perpetrators were deeply religious people. However, many Utahn Mormons of the period did not consider the massacre to be either immoral, or unjustified; and Lee was able to appeal to nineteenth-century Mormon theology to justify his actions. Lee and other Mormons believed that the adults of the Fancher–Baker party had committed serious sins and that they needed others to "shed their blood for the remission of their sins" (Bagley 2002, p. 321). According to the doctrine of "blood atonement," there are some sinful acts that are so serious that one cannot properly atone for them without being killed. In the words of Brigham Young:

> There are sins that men commit for which they cannot receive forgiveness in this world, or in that which is to come, and if they had their eyes open to see their true condition, they would be perfectly willing to have their blood spilt upon the ground, that the smoke thereof might ascend to heaven as an offering for their sins; and the smoking incense would atone for their sins, whereas, if such is not the case, they would stick to them and remain upon them in the spirit world.[6]

The Church of Jesus Christ of Latter-Day Saints does not appear to have maintained an official list of sins that might require blood atonement. The threat of blood atonement was made against those who kill the innocent or commit acts of heresy (Coates 1991, p. 64), as well as those who commit adultery (Walker et al. 2008, p. 25), aide apostates, or marry apostates (Coates 1991, pp. 65–6). It is not entirely clear what the adult members of the Fancher–Baker party did to warrant blood atonement.[7] One suggestion is that they may have been harboring apostates who were trying to escape Mormon Utah (Bagley 2002, p. 147). Another suggestion is that members of the party had boasted that they had been involved in the 1844 murder of Joseph Smith, the founder of Mormonism (Bagley 2002, p. 117). A third suggestion is that members of the party had murdered local Indians by poisoning them (Bagley 2002, pp. 106–8). Lee and the other perpetrators of the massacre understood that non-Mormons would not accept the doctrine of blood atonement and the doctrine was a religious one, not written into Utahn law, so there was no prospect of applying it through legal channels. By blaming local Indians for the massacre, Lee are his collaborators would have hoped to be able to "blood atone" the adult members of the Fancher–Baker party without incurring the wrath and retribution of non-Mormon American "gentiles."

The doctrine of blood atonement justifies the killing of particular people by appeal to improvements in the quality of the afterlife that those people can be expected to experience. Just like mainstream Christians, Mormons believe in an eternal afterlife. Unlike many mainstream Christians, they do not believe that only followers of the true religion will experience a good afterlife. However, only those who receive the atonement of Jesus Christ are eligible for the most desirable form of afterlife, which is to live in a state of "exaltation" with God. According to the doctrine of blood atonement, the atonement of Jesus Christ is not available to certain categories of sinners, unless they have died by having their blood spilled on the ground. If this doctrine is correct, then to kill such people is to do them a favor. It is perhaps the greatest possible favor that one could do for them. The benefits of being eligible for the atonement of Jesus Christ are extremely significant and last for ever, so these easily outweigh the harms involved in having a life violently shortened. The doctrines of the Church of Jesus Christ of Latter-Day Saints have continued to develop over the years as the church has carved out a place in mainstream America. The church formally renounced polygamy in the late nineteenth century and it repudiated the doctrine of blood atonement at much the same time.[8]

Religion and Violence

The Mountain Meadows massacre was an extremely violent, mass killing of civilians, instigated by religious believers. It is far from unique in these respects; and the resulting death toll is not particularly remarkable. The 1572 St. Bartholomew's day massacre of Huguenots in Paris by Catholic mobs led to at least 5,000 deaths. The Wadda Ghalughara – a massacre of Sikhs by Muslims – which took place in 1764, led to the death of 25,000–30,000 Sikhs. And violent killing motivated by religious conviction continues to this day. The attacks by al-Qaeda on the United States of America on September 11, 2001, resulted in the deaths of almost 3,000 people. Potentially even more deadly were the sarin gas attacks on the Tokyo subway system, which were carried out by members of the syncretist religious group Aum Shinrikyo on March 20, 1995. These coordinated attacks on commuters, during morning rush hour, were intended to kill tens of thousands of people, but due to flaws in the plan of attack they only resulted in twelve deaths, along with injuries to approximately 6,000 (Kaplan and Marshall 1996, p. 251). Most of the perpetrators of both of these recent sets of events appear to have considered them to be justified by the lights of their respective religions.

Massacres of civilians that are motivated by religion capture our attention, in part because they seem particularly hard to understand, especially if we start off with the widely accepted view that religion is generally a force for peace. But, in attempting to understand religious violence, we should not lose sight of the many forms of violent action, apart from the massacre of civilians, which have sometimes come to be seen as justified by religion.

Religion is often invoked as a justification for war. Sometimes religious leaders advise their followers that they are justified in participating in wars that have already commenced, and sometimes religious leaders agitate for military campaigns to take place, on the grounds that these are justified by the lights of their religion. The nine Christian Crusades to the Near East, between 1095 and 1291, are examples of this latter form of religiously sanctioned military campaign. Religious justifications are presented for the killing of many different species of animals as sacrifices to supernatural beings. In some cases humans have been among the species sacrificed. Religious motives are invoked to try to justify the killing of individuals because they have attempted to leave a religion (apostasy), because they have tried to revise a religion (heresy), and because they have spoken or written disrespectfully about a religion (blasphemy). Religion has been invoked, and continues to be invoked, in the Hindu tradition, to warrant the killing of brides whose husbands happen to have died before them. It has been used to justify suicide and in some instances, such as the case of the 1978 Jonestown massacre, in Guyana, where over 900 people died, to justify mass suicide. Religion has also been used to justify a variety of other forms of self harm, voluntarily accepted harm, and harm imposed against people's wishes.[9]

There have been many recent books written about the relationship between religion and violence and a debate ensues between those who argue that religion is a significant cause of violence (e.g., Avalos 2005; Juergensmeyer 2003) and those who consider that, while religion is prone to being used as a pretext for violence, it is not itself a significant cause of violence (e.g., Cavanaugh 2009; Ward 2006). This debate ranges over the appropriate interpretation of a series of historical events. Was the Spanish conquest of the Aztec and Inca empires and forcible conversion of their inhabitants to Christianity driven by religion, or by a desire for empire, or was it driven by some combination of the two? Were the Crusades primarily motivated by religious concerns, or were there broader political goals that really explain why they took place? Were the early twentieth-century European fascist movements secular movements, or were they indirectly fueled by religion? The recent upsurge in interest in the relationship between religion and violence has, of course, been provoked by the events of September 11, 2001, and a specific debate about the role that religion plays in motivating Islamic terrorism is also taking place. Some commentators, such as Pape (2005) and Goodin (2006), explain the behavior of modern Islamic terrorists in purely political terms. Other commentators, such as Lincoln (2003) and Ignatieff (2004), insist that contemporary Islamic terrorism cannot be properly understood without understanding its distinctively religious dimension.

The argument presented in this book is not directed at understanding the overall relationship between religion and violence. The target is much more specific. I seek to understand and explain the ways in which religion can be used to justify violent activities. I will not address the issue of whether particular instances of violence that are justified by religion are actually caused by religion, actually caused by political factors, or actually caused by some combination of religion and political factors. Religion can be used to justify violent actions that have various different causes and it is the justifications offered in the name of religion that are the subject of investigation here. Insofar as the argument in this book is directed against anyone, it is directed against scholars such as Charles Selengut, who expresses the common view that " ... ordinary judgment, canons of logic, and evaluation of behavior simply do not apply to religious activity" (2003, p. 6). As I will show, the religious generally justify their activities in much the same way as the secular and these justifications generally follow the same canons of logic as secular justifications. Religious arguments justifying violence are structurally similar to secular ones, but the religious are able to feed many more premises into those structures than the non-religious. The religious are able to appeal, among other things, to God's wishes, God's commands, the benefits of going to heaven, the benefits of avoiding hell, the benefits of being reincarnated as a superior being, and the benefits of escaping from the cycle of reincarnation, as well as all of the justificatory sources that are appealed to by the secular.

It may be tempting to try to deploy my conclusion within the debate about whether or not religion causes violence and argue that, because the religious have more conceptual resources to draw on, when attempting to justify violence, than the non-religious, they can be expected to justify more violent acts than the non-religious; and consequently, they can be expected to cause more violence than the non-religious. But this line of reasoning is highly speculative. Being able to draw on more conceptual resources to justify violence does not ensure that the religious will attempt to justify more violent acts than the non-religious, and nor does it ensure that the religious will cause more violence than the non-religious. A further reason to resist the conclusion that the religious cause more violence than the non-religious is that religion also provides conceptual resources to opponents of violence. These include pacifist religious doctrines – which we will have more to say about in Chapter 4 – as well as doctrines that might be taken to obviate the need for violent action, such as the doctrine that God providentially guides human history to ensure that everything ultimately turns out for the best.

Are religious justifications of violence more effective than secular justifications of violence? If I am right that religious justifications of violence are structurally similar to secular justifications of violence, the answer to this question depends on one's assessment of the credibility of the premises that are fed into religious and secular arguments justifying violence. Those who accept the relevant religion are liable to find arguments that appeal to premises supported by their own religious tradition to be very credible, whereas followers of other religions, as well as atheists and agnostics, are liable to find these same arguments to be quite implausible, because they do not accept the relevant premises. When and where particular religions hold sway, arguments that appeal to premises deemed acceptable by followers of the dominant religion may well be more effective than secular arguments at justifying violence; however, at other times and in other places, secular arguments for the justification of violence can be expected to be more effective.

For convenience, I am following a common, abbreviated way of writing (and speaking) – as was mentioned in the Preface – and will refer to attempted justifications simply as justifications. I do not mean to imply that I regard all or any of these as successful justifications. Nor do I mean to imply that the justifications offered, under consideration here, are necessarily motivating of the actions that are justified, or necessarily play a role in causing actual behavior. In the remainder of this first chapter I will consider a number of conceptual and background issues that need to be clarified in order to analyze religious justifications of violence. I begin with analysis of the key terms "violence" and "justification." Neither of these is especially hard to understand, but given the centrality of both terms to this book, it is important that I am clear about how they are used here.

Violence

The exact meaning of the term "violence" is disputed. For the purposes of this discussion I will understand violence narrowly as *action which is intended to cause physical harm*. There are various ways in which this definition might be extended. Robert Audi argues that we should include mention of psychological harm in any definition of violence, alongside physical harm

(1971, p. 52). There may be good reasons for doing so, especially if we are trying to capture the general significance of harms in our definition. Some instances of psychological harm will have a deeper, more profound effect on people's lives than many instances of physical harm. If I punch you in the face, you will be physically harmed to a certain extent and perhaps you will experience indirectly caused psychological harm, alongside the black eye that I give you. If I use psychological "brainwashing" techniques to manipulate you into joining an extremist religious group and indirectly cause you to quit your job, give away all your money, and cut off all contact with your family then, all things being equal, you will suffer more deeply felt, longer lasting harm than in the punch scenario. Similarly, symbolic harms may have more of an impact on peoples' lives than some physical ones. You might be more hurt when you see me burn your national flag than you would be if I'd punched you. So, perhaps symbolic harms should be included in a definition of violence too. Selengut defines violence in a way that includes threats of harm as well as actual harms (2003, p. 9) and again there may be reasons to define violence this way. Some threats may have more of an impact on people's lives than some actual physical harms.[10] I don't have any particular objection to these extensions of the core conception of violence. However, as I want my analysis of religious violence to be acceptable to the widest possible audience, I will restrict my use of the term "violence" to refer to the class of cases that are most uncontroversially described as violent – actions intended to cause physical harm.

There are two further approaches to defining violence that I will also avoid. These are both stipulative, and are not directed at capturing the ordinary meaning of the term "violence." Neither would be helpful for my analysis. One of these broadens the concept of violence in an unhelpful way and the other restricts it, again in an unhelpful way. Johan Galtung (1969) broadens the concept violence to include "structural violence." The structures in question are institutional arrangements that operate to restrict peoples' choices, so as to lead to an absence of "social justice," which Galtung equates with an "egalitarian distribution of power and resources" (1969, p. 183). On this view all, or nearly all, contemporary societies count as intrinsically violent because they are not specifically structured so as to promote egalitarian ideals and because they allow unequal distributions of power and resources to be reproduced. Furthermore, all religious organizations that are hierarchical and distribute power and resources unequally will count as intrinsically violent – that is, nearly all religious organizations. The problem with this way of defining violence is that it posits several interlaid levels of violence, which are not distinguished from one another; and so it constantly threatens to confuse our thinking about violence. There is intrinsic institutional violence, violent law, more general violent social arrangements, and violent acts. I am interested in understanding specific relations between religion, justification, and a narrowly understood class of intended harms. Because I want to understand this specific set of relations, I need to reject this overly broad definition of one of my key terms, which can only lead to confusion.

Sidney Hook restricts the range of the meaning of the concept of violence by advocating a stipulative "legitimist" definition of violence (Coady 2008, p. 23). He defines violence as " … the illegal employment of methods of physical coercion for personal or group ends".[11] This definition is so constructed as to prevent the word violence from being used to refer to (or criticize) current institutional arrangements, even if these result in physical harms to individuals. On Hook's view, a state that employed its army or police force to hurt or kill members of religious minorities, who were in violation of laws suppressing the practice of their religion, would not be acting violently. This restriction on meaning is too limiting for my analysis. Because I am concerned to examine the relationship between religion, justification, and intended acts that physically harm people it would be very unhelpful for me to employ a definition of violence that had built into it the denial of the very possibility that some religiously motivated intentional acts which physically harm people could count as violent.

Justification

If you ask someone why they have acted in a particular way you could either be asking them for an explanation or a justification of their behavior. Usually it is clear enough, in context, whether an explanation or a justification is expected. The career bank robber Willie Sutton (1901 – 1980) is famous for a joke that plays on this ambiguity. When Sutton was asked by a journalist why he robbed banks he is said to have replied "because that's where the money is!" The joke works because we are expecting that he will try to justify his behavior – try to convince us, despite our strong feelings to the contrary, that it is acceptable for him to rob banks, or at least identify some mitigating factors, making him seem less culpable for his crimes – and instead he provides a very straightforward explanation of that behavior in terms of means – end rationality. In general, a justification is the proper grounds one has for an action or belief. When I provide a justification I am doing more than simply describing a series of thought processes that lead to a conclusion. Rather, I am selecting a reason, or set of reasons, that motivates my action, and which I believe to have sufficient normative force to warrant that action. Not all of my motives will have such normative force.[12]

Justifications need to be distinguished from excuses. When I provide a justification for a course of action, I am implying that it was an appropriate course of action to take, under the circumstances. In making this implication I also reveal that I take responsibility for the course of action in question. When I offer an excuse I do not attempt to imply that my course of action was appropriate. I concede that it was inappropriate, even though I also concede that I undertook that course of action. But in offering an excuse, I attempt to convince my audience that there are mitigating circumstances that either absolve me of responsibility for the course of action in question, or at least diminish that responsibility. If Willie Sutton had replied to the journalist by saying that a mafia boss was threatening to kill his relatives if he did not keep robbing banks, or told the journalist that he was suffering from a rare form of psychological compulsion and couldn't help robbing banks, try as he might to resist this unusual compulsion, he would be offering excuses rather than justifications for his actions.[13]

Suppose I am sunbathing at a beach and I see a man in the sea who is in danger of drowning and in obvious need of assistance; I also notice a sign put up by the local council warning of a strong undertow and forbidding swimming in the area. Suppose further that I decide, despite the risk to my own safety, to break the law and swim over to him and offer assistance. If I am asked to justify my illegal action I might say something like the following: I am under a moral obligation to attempt to save the lives of those who need immediate assistance, and I consider that the importance of this moral obligation outweighs my responsibility to obey the local law. This justifying consideration might not be my only motive. I might also think to myself that being seen taking a significant risk to save a life will help me to impress a woman who I am romantically interested in and who happens to be at the beach. While this desire motivates me, I do not consider it to be a justification for my action. I do not consider that my desire to impress a romantic interest ought to be grounds to violate the local law. An overall explanation of my behavior would include mention of this additional motive, but as I consider that it lacks normative force, I do not mention it when I am asked to justify my behavior.

Participation in the process of presenting justifications for our behavior places constraints on behavior and if we are to understand human behavior properly it is important that we understand this process. An extremely important constraint that the justificatory process imposes is a consistency constraint. If I consider it justifiable to break a local council's law and risk my own safety in order to save a life, and I swim over to offer assistance to a drowning person on one occasion, then I am logically committed to doing so on all other such occasions which involve an equivalent risk, including those that might occur when the attractive woman, whom I am trying to impress, is not present. People will tend to judge my behavior according to whether or not it conforms to this consistency constraint. When I risk my life to save another person from drowning I enhance my reputation by convincing people that I am the sort of person who will take risks to protect the lives of others. If, however, I fail to act consistently and fail to take equivalent risks to protect the lives of others on other similar occasions, then people will start to question whether I was actually motivated by the consideration that I claimed had justificatory force. If they can find another motive that explains the inconsistency in my actions, such as the desire to impress the woman I am attracted to, then they will be liable to conclude that my stated justification for action is insincere and my reputation can be expected to suffer accordingly.

Statements that people make justifying their actions and beliefs often include a rhetorical component as well as a logical one; and this rhetorical component can make their justification seem more compelling. If I claim that legal sanctions against homosexual activity are justified, and go on to explain that this is because God determines what is right and wrong, the Bible contains God's determinations and it tells us in the Bible that God considers homosexual acts to be morally wrong, then I am providing an unadorned justification of a normative claim. If I exclaim "God made Adam and Eve, not Adam and Steve!" I am effectively making much the same claim, but am doing so with a rhetorical flourish that makes the assertion much more memorable and more convincing to many.

Here I will be concerned with the logical structure of justifications of acts of religious violence, rather than the efficacy of rhetoric.[14] There is much more that could be said about the psychological effects of dressing up justificatory claims in this or that rhetorical form, as well as about the difficulties that people have distinguishing logically well-formed arguments from appeals to rhetoric. Much of this is important to appreciate if we aim at a comprehensive understanding of how religion can cause violence. For example, demonizing members of out-groups and describing them as "rats," "vermin," "parasites," "cockroaches," and so on seems to be an effective way of activating someone's sense of disgust, and encourages a propensity to think of those out-group members as a threat to the health of one's own community that needs to be removed (Navarrete and Fessler 2006; Faulkner et al. 2004). Psychological research teaches us much about these techniques; and it is important that these are well understood. But work on this important task will not be advanced here.

Another important lesson to be learned from the psychological literature – which I mention here in order to head off a common sort of misunderstanding – is that the vast majority of people who act violently do not appear to view inflicting harm on others as an end in itself and do not appear to gain particular enjoyment from harming others. Comic book villains may enjoy inflicting harm on others, but the overwhelming majority of people who act violently are psychologically unlike comic book villains. They do not laugh maniacally or otherwise express delight when harming others. Most people who commit violent acts do so reluctantly and only after they have overcome internal constraints that would ordinarily make them feel guilty about harming others. When they do act violently, they do so in the belief that what they are doing is justifiable, all things considered (Baumeister 2001, pp. 60–96). Or at least this is how most perpetrators of violent acts see things at the time that they commit those acts. There are, of course, exceptions to this generalization, especially amongst psychopaths who lack internal constraints against harming others (Hare 1999) and some sadists, whose enjoyment of hurting others leads them to overcome feelings of guilt much more easily than ordinary people (Baumeister and Campbell 1999, pp. 214–15). It is important that the psychology of these exceptional cases be well understood, but this is not the subject under consideration here.

What I am interested in identifying here is what religion adds to the process by which humans justify violence. One possible answer to this question is "anything and everything." Justification is a normative process, and whatever norms there are that can be legitimately appealed to exist because God (or some other supernatural agent or agents) created them. Morality is entirely derivative of religion, or so says the "divine command theorist." This view may seem somewhat hard to accept, because it involves accepting that if God had stipulated that it is morally obligatory to torture kittens and morally impermissible to give money to charity, then it would be morally obligatory to torture kittens and morally impermissible to give money to charity. The rightness and wrongness of particular acts do not seem to be the sort of qualities that could be dependent on the simple stipulation of God or any other supernatural agent.[15]

One does not have to be a divine command theorist, though, to hold that our moral beliefs and practices are largely the product of our religion. A convincing rebuttal of this more general view will require a deeper understanding of religion and a deeper understanding of the relationship between morality and religion. In the next chapter I will attempt to provide a deeper understanding of religion and in the following chapter I will turn my attention to morality. I will go on to argue that the tendency to hold religious beliefs and engage in religious behavior (henceforth just "religion") is something that evolved in human populations over time and that morality, or at least a certain basic sort of morality, was a necessary precursor to the evolution of religion. In order to continue to function, human communities require a certain minimal form of moral structure. The human communities in which religion evolved were moral communities in this bare sense and if, at any point, a religion which undermined that minimal moral structure became dominant in a particular community, the community in question would have collapsed, taking the support base for that religion with it. Religion might be invoked to try to justify anything and everything, but religions that do not succeed in making the justifications that they offer consistent with this minimal moral structure do not survive the test of time.

Nothing Bad

Another answer to the question of what religion adds to the justificatory process is "nothing bad." Charles Kimball assures us that authentic religion is always a force for good and only "corrupted religion" leads to violence (2008, pp. 199–200). He also tells us that:

> Whatever religious people may say about their love of God or the mandates of their religion, when their behavior towards others is violent and destructive, when it causes suffering among their neighbors, you can be sure the religion has been corrupted and reform is desperately needed. (Kimball 2008, p. 47)

Similarly, Keith Ward understands religious justifications for violent action as being based on misinterpretations of scripture which,

> ignore the weightier matters of scriptures – the love of God and neighbour, and the search for compassion and mercy – and choose texts taken out of context and applied without any sense of history or concern for general traditions of interpretation. (Ward 2006, p. 37)

Ward is more circumspect than Kimball, who seems to believe that there are no "authentic" religions in the world that justify violence. Ward restricts his claims about proper scriptural interpretation to the "major world religions" (2006, p. 40).

One problem with this answer is that it equates violence with badness, but it is not obvious that just because some action is violent that it must necessarily be bad. Many, if not most, acts of violence committed in the name of religion seem to be committed by those who believe that such action furthers the greater good; and we cannot dismiss the view that violent action is at least sometimes good without first examining the relevant evidence. Ward "reluctantly" concedes that the violent actions undertaken by al-Qaeda are directed at good outcomes (2006, pp. 30–1), although he also describes the beliefs of al-Qaeda as "unequivocally evil" (2006, p. 35). He attempts to resolve the tension between these two statements by arguing that al-Qaeda members really know that "it is wrong to kill the innocent," but that "the power of self-deception is strong" (2006, p. 31). It seems intuitively hard to accept that one would have to be self-deceived to believe that it is always morally impermissible to kill the innocent, in all possible circumstances, however. Consider the following variant of an influential philosophical thought experiment – "the ticking time bomb" scenario.[16] Suppose that a madman has strapped a radioactive dirty bomb to an innocent person in a densely populated city. The bomb is on a timer and is also hooked up to the innocent person's pulse and is due to detonate in 30 seconds, unless the innocent person dies before then. If the bomb does go off it will kill hundreds of thousands of people. You happen to be near the innocent person and you have a gun. What should you do? Consequentialist philosophers often argue that it is morally justifiable to kill the one to save the many in such scenarios. There may be room for differences of opinion about what you should do, but it is hard to take seriously the assertion that those who think that killing one innocent person to save hundreds of thousands of other innocent people are simply in the grip of self-deception.

The religious beliefs of the Aztecs of the fifteenth century put devout believers in something like the ticking time bomb scenario on a daily basis. Devout Aztecs believed that the sun god Huitzilopochtli required regular human sacrifices to prevent the sun being destroyed by the forces of darkness. It was the duty of Aztec priests to ensure that these regular human sacrifices to Huitzilopochtli took place. If the sun was destroyed then life would cease.[17] These human sacrifices were often conducted in an extremely violent ritualized manner with a small incision being made in the chest of sacrificial victims before their still-beating hearts were removed from their bodies. Their bodies were then torn to pieces, roasted and eaten (Wade 2009, pp. 242–5).[18] No doubt Ward and Kimball would see the Aztec priesthood, which conducted such human sacrifices on a mass scale,[19] as theologically corrupt and perhaps evil. However, there is a straightforward way to understand the Aztec priesthood as aiming to serve the greater good: they sincerely believed that they were sacrificing the lives of some humans to save humanity (and other species) from destruction. Reports suggest that at least some of their sacrificial victims were willing ones: true believers who were prepared to forfeit their lives for the greater good (Berdan 2005, p. 122).[20]

A second problem with this answer is that it is very hard to interpret some religious scripture as instructing us to do anything other than kill innocent people. Instructions to kill the innocent are found in the holy texts of various religions. The Koran instructs devout Muslims to kill polytheists who fail to renounce their religion:

> And when the sacred months have passed, then kill the polytheists wherever you find them and capture them and besiege them and sit in wait for them at every place of ambush. But if they should repent, establish prayer, and give zakah,[21] let them [go] on their way. (9:5)

The Hindu Puranas instruct widows to either kill themselves, or submit to being killed by others, for no other reason than that their husband has died:

> Tell the faithful wife of the greatest duty of woman: she is loyal and pure who burns herself with her husband's corpse. Should the husband die on a journey, holding his sandals to her breast let her pass into the flames.[22]

And consider the following passage from the Old Testament in which God orders the Israelites to commit genocide:

> But of the cities of these peoples which the LORD your God gives you *as* an inheritance, you shall let nothing that breathes remain alive, but you shall utterly destroy them: the Hittite and the Amorite and the Canaanite and the Perizzite and the Hivite and the Jebusite; just as the LORD your God has commanded you. (Deuteronomy 20:16–17)

The instruction to "utterly destroy" these various peoples turns out to be part of a broader imperialistic program. God commands genocidal treatment of the peoples mentioned above because they happen to reside in areas near to the Israelites. God also commands that peoples living further away are to be given an opportunity to pay tribute to the Israelites and to generally serve them (Deuteronomy 20:11). If they refuse then the Israelites are instructed to kill every adult male among them "with the edge of a sword" (Deuteronomy 20:13).

These are very explicit instructions. While it was not as urgent for the Israelites to obey them as for the Aztecs to conduct human sacrifices – the sun would not cease to shine if the Israelites failed to carry out their instructions immediately – obedience to God could not be deferred indefinitely. The Old Testament makes it clear that it is a very bad idea to fail to obey God. The Old Testament God explicitly describes himself as a "jealous God, visiting the iniquity of the fathers upon the children to the third and fourth generations of those who hate me" (Exodus 20:5) and there are many examples of God punishing those who disobey orders. One such example is that of Achan. According to the Old Testament, Achan dutifully participated in the divinely ordained destruction of the city of Jericho, along with other Israelites.[23] However, he also decided to take a few "spoils of war" for himself, in defiance of God's explicit instructions. He took " … a beautiful Babylonian garment, two hundred shekels of silver, and a wedge of gold weighing fifty shekels" (Joshua 7:21). This made God extremely angry and caused Him to threaten to abandon Israel unless Achan was put to death (Joshua 7:12). Despite a confession, forgiveness was not forthcoming, and Achan was stoned, then burned and then, for good measure, his body was covered in a large heap of stones (Joshua 7:25).

Defenders of the view that Christianity is a religion of peace face a difficult problem when it comes to explaining away Old Testament passages such as the above. One influential response to this problem is to deny that scripture should be understood as a straightforward depiction of God's engagement with the world. On a "progressive" Christian view it is stressed that the divine is very hard for humans to comprehend. God makes disclosures to us at various times, and we interpret these as best we can, and collect our best interpretations in scripture. However, we also acknowledge that scripture may be a poor representation of the actual will of God. Another response is to make a sharp distinction between the vindictive God of the Old Testament and the loving God of the New Testament (Avalos 2005, p. 176; Teehan 2010, p. 161). It is not clear that Christians ought simply to disavow the God of the Old Testament in favor of the God of the New Testament.

After all, these are supposed to be the same God. Perhaps the most plausible way to understand Christianity as a religion of peace is to combine the two responses described above and hold, as Ward does, that extremely violent Old Testament passages are very inaccurate representations of the will of God and are superseded by the New Testament, which more accurately depicts God's will (2006, p. 114). But this is far from the only way in which Christians understand the relationship between the Old and New Testaments.

It is undeniable that the New Testament is much less violent than the Old Testament, as "new atheists" Richard Dawkins (2006, p. 250) and Daniel Dennett (2006, p. 206) both concede. In the New Testament we encounter Jesus expressing pacifist sentiments, telling us not to resist violence, but to "turn the other cheek" (Matthew 5:39) and to "Love your enemies" (Luke 6:27). Unfortunately there is a propensity among those who portray Christianity as a religion of peace to cherry-pick passages from the New Testament, such as the ones cited above, and skate over more awkward material. In one notorious passage, Jesus encourages his disciples to hate[24] their (presumably non-Christian) parents, children, spouse, and siblings (Luke 14:26). In another passage Jesus specifically denies having come to earth to create peace and claims to be here to create divisions between people (Luke 12:49–53). In another passage Jesus instructs his disciples to sell some of their garments and to use the money raised to buy swords (Luke 22:36–8). In still another passage Jesus threatens those who fail to serve him sufficiently well with eternal damnation (Matthew 25:41–6). Such threatening behavior seems particularly hard to reconcile with the unequivocal advocacy of peace. I don't want to make the strong claim that Ward's (2006) or Kimball's (2008) interpretations of the New Testament God as a God of peace are implausible. I have no doubt that both of these authors would be capable of offering interpretations of the New Testament that reconcile these passages with the view that the New Testament God is a God of peace.[25] What I do want to argue is that it is not obvious that these interpretations of the New Testament are superior to alternatives, such as Avalos's (2005) and Desjardins' (1997) interpretations of the New Testament as promoting a complicated mix of peace and violence.

We cannot plausibly argue that, properly interpreted, Christianity *must* be understood as a religion of peace (or of violence), because there is no definitive interpretation of Christian scripture to be had. This should not be surprising. Christian scripture is a large complicated body of writings that are not obviously consistent with one another. The same can be said for canonical texts in other religious traditions. The Koran and other Islamic holy texts are variously interpreted because they are open to a variety of interpretations,[26] as are the Vedas and other holy texts in the Hindu tradition, and the Sutras and other core texts in the Buddhist tradition. The major religions of the world have all developed expansive, complicated bodies of scripture which lack definitive interpretations. There is no proper basis for insisting that any of these religions must be understood as "religions of peace," rather than religions of both peace and violence.[27]

Between "Anything and Everything" and "Nothing Bad"

The answer I will give to the question of what religion adds to justification falls somewhere between "anything and everything" and "nothing bad." Religion does provide additional conceptual resources for the justification of acts and procedures – including violent ones – that the non-religious do not have access to, but not everything can be justified by (established) religion. While short-lasting, obscure religions might indeed succeed in inculcating doctrines that could be used as the basis for the justification of pretty much anything and everything, religious doctrines that do not accord with ordinary morality will not survive the test of time because the religions that promulgate such doctrines will undermine the communities that practice these religions and accept such doctrines (this line of argument will be developed further in Chapters 2 and 3).

Jack David Eller has recently considered the issue of what religion contributes to the justificatory process and, like me, he takes a middle view. The gist of his view is that: "The religious contribution to legitimation is neither natural or social but, characteristically, supernatural and agentive" (Eller 2010, p. 73). This answer seems promising. What religion offers the justificatory process, which it would otherwise lack, is appeal to narratives about the intentions, needs, desires, and other mental states of supernatural agents. Religion also enables us to appeal to the existence of a deeper reality than is apparent to us, which can involve an interplay between the natural and the supernatural, and which can help us to make sense of the intentions, needs, desires, and so on of supernatural agents. The Aztecs understood this deeper reality to involve an ever-present threat of our world ending as a result of the actions of supernatural forces of darkness. Huitzilopochtli wants to fight off these forces, but can only do so if natural agents provide him with regular human sacrifices. Somewhat similarly, many fundamentalist Christians believe that there is a supernatural power struggle going on between God and Satan, which spills over into the natural world. Many also believe that their actions here in the natural world can help to shape the precise outcome of this supernatural conflict (Juergensmeyer 2003, pp. 148–66).

Eller analyzes the religious contribution to justification, or legitimation, under three headings, "models," "mandates," and "metaphysics" (2010, pp. 74–6). The metaphysically rich accounts of a deeper reality than the one that is apparent to us do appear to be distinctive of religion and do appear to be useful in justifying behavior. However, although models and mandates can play a role in justifying behavior, they do not pick out anything that is distinctive to religion, and what they do pick out are social phenomena – but Eller had earlier rejected the view that what is distinctive about the religious contribution to legitimation is characteristically social (2010, p. 73). By models, Eller means role models and indeed most major religious traditions seem to be generously endowed with role models. Christians have many role models to choose from, including saints, martyrs, the Apostles, Mary, and of course Jesus Christ. Other religions appeal to their own role models, who are to be found in both their history and their legends. Many Christians ask themselves "What would Jesus do?" before acting, taking Christ's example to be a guide to proper behavior. The devout Christian former South African cricket captain Hansie Cronje wore a wristband with the initials WWJD on it to prompt him to ask himself "What would Jesus do?" before acting. But the social practice of looking to role models for guidance is hardly distinctive of religion. Many Christian South Africans considered Hansie Cronje to be a role model because he appeared to live an exemplary Christian lifestyle; however, many secular South Africans also considered him to be something of a role model, simply because of his work ethic and success as a leader and a player on the cricket field.[28] Athletes, musicians, actors, and other celebrities are often considered to be role models by many because of their worldly successes and the ways in which they lead their – sometimes very irreligious – secular lives. Leading soldiers, scientists, and politicians are considered role models by some, and a recent Google search suggests that many atheists consider Richard Dawkins to be a role model.

Mandates are explicit orders or instructions that a particular religion may provide. These may be general rules governing behavior, such as the "ten commandments" and other instructions to be found in the Bible, or more specific rules governing standards of dress, diet, hygiene, and so on. Undoubtedly these have a very significant effect on behavior. Devout Jews and Muslims do not eat pork because Jewish and Muslim dietary laws forbid the consumption of pork. But, like models, mandates are social phenomena that are not distinctively religious. Religion offers us a variety of mandates, but so does the secular world. Bernard Gert (2004) has developed a secular equivalent of the ten commandments, arguing that there are exactly ten rules of morality which are justified by consideration of rationality.[29] He has recently been outdone by A.C. Grayling who offers us a secular equivalent of the Bible – his *The Good Book* (2011), which contains a large number of instructions for leading a good secular life. Societies mandate a variety of restrictions on dress and on cuisine, often for secular reasons. In his drive to modernize Turkey and turn it into a secular state President Atatürk banned the wearing of the Fez and the Veil in 1925. Very recently France and Belgium have banned the wearing of any clothing that covers the face in public places, for ostensibly secular reasons. Restrictions on the consumption of food are also often driven by secular concerns. These include European bans on genetically modified food, as well as various bans on "junk food" sales, which have been imposed recently in a number of local districts in both the USA and Europe.

Nature and Supernature

These days, when we think of the natural world we typically think of it as a discrete continuous spatio-temporal realm, which is ordinarily closed to external influence. If we think of supernatural beings at all, we think of them as not being part of the natural world. Either they inhabit a realm that is clearly distinct from the natural one or they lack any definite location. This way of thinking of the supernatural is a consequence of the rise of the mechanistic worldview in the seventeenth century, under which nature came to be understood as a well-ordered realm governed by universal laws of nature. We think of ourselves as living within this mechanistic system and we think that we are unable to escape from the control of its governing laws. Our understanding of the natural allows us to attach a reasonably clear meaning to the term "supernatural." If there are supernatural beings or entities, then they have origins in powers that are not part of nature. We suppose that the behavior of supernatural beings is not governed by the laws of nature, and if such beings are sufficiently powerful, as we ordinarily suppose God is, then they may be able to intervene in the natural world. Before the rise of the mechanistic worldview in the seventeenth century, however, people did not think of nature as being a discrete orderly realm. Insofar as the term "supernatural" had a clear meaning, it was used to refer to beings, entities, events, and processes that seemed particularly mysterious and powerful. The supernatural, in this older, looser, more relativistic sense, is not clearly discrete from the natural world although it is distinct from the familiar natural world.[30] But although it was harder to distinguish nature from supernature before the rise of the mechanistic worldview, it does not seem to have been particularly hard for people to distinguish gods and other supernatural beings from ordinary natural beings. Gods and other supernatural beings were said to be able to travel to postulated places that natural beings could not ordinarily go to, such as heaven and hell, and were said to possess abilities that natural beings could not ordinarily possess, such as perfect knowledge, infinite strength, and so on.

It is sometimes supposed that belief in the supernatural can only ever be grounded in religious faith and that reason could never warrant acceptance of any hypotheses that go beyond the scope of the natural. If so, then there is no place for the supernatural in a naturalistic worldview.[31] However, the primary commitment of naturalistic philosophers is to the authority of the scientific method and to the formation of beliefs on the basis of reason and evidence, and this is not obviously incompatible with belief in the supernatural. As Michael Rea points out, "naturalism, whatever it is, must be compatible with anything science might tell us about nature or supernature" (Rea 2002, p. 55). Can science warrant belief in supernatural beings and entities in the modern sense of the term "supernatural"? Not only can it do so, it has done so on several occasions. Before Darwin developed the theory of natural selection it was rational to believe that living organisms were supernaturally designed. Appeal to supernatural design provided the best available explanation of the functional organization of living organisms (Clarke 2009, p. 133; Ruse 2001, p. 113), which is why it was the dominant view of biology before the development of the theory of natural selection. Other scientific explanations that appealed to the supernatural, and were the best available explanations in their day, include Newton's argument that the stability of the planets that form our solar system is best explained by God's careful initial placement of the planets, in combination with the law of gravity (Meyer 2000, pp. 133–4); and the nineteenth-century vitalist argument that the sharp divide between the living and the non-living is best explained by supposing that living beings are imbued with a non-material *élan vital* (MacDonald and Tro 2009).[32] Science has repeatedly appealed to non-natural entities and forces in the past, so we have inductive grounds to suppose that it may do so again in the future. We have no proper basis, therefore, to rule the supernatural out of science on conceptual grounds and to insist that belief in the supernatural must be irrational, or based on faith alone.[33]

It is tempting to try to draw a sharp distinction and insist that while the religious can appeal to the justificatory resources that belief in the supernatural provides it is not possible for the secular to do the same. We should resist this temptation. There have been good secular reasons to believe in supernatural entities and processes in the past and we cannot rule out the possibility that other such reasons will become apparent in the future. Nevertheless, we can settle on something close to this sharp distinction. Science seems only ever to have warranted acceptance of conceptually austere supernatural beings and entities and, by themselves, these postulates do not seem sufficiently rich to justify violent action or, indeed, any sort of action. Seventeenth-century science seemed to warrant the inference that there was a supernatural creator who placed the planets in the solar system in orbit around the sun and who designed living beings, but it was otherwise silent about the character of this creator and also about the moral status of designed life forms. Nineteenth-century vitalist biology seemed to warrant the inference that life was imbued with a non-material *élan vital*. But even if we are warranted in holding that life is imbued with a non-material *élan vital*, we have not established that life has any kind of moral value, or that we are justified or unjustified in treating living beings in particular ways. In contrast, the rich metaphysical narratives of particular religions readily lend themselves to justificatory roles.

In the next chapter, I will look much more closely at religion. The subject of Chapter 3 is morality. In Chapter 4, I look at secular justifications for violence and I start to investigate religious justifications for violence. I continue the investigation of religious justifications for violence in Chapters 5 and 6. In Chapter 7 a series of case studies of violent actions carried out in the name of religion in recent times is examined. I show that, in each case, specific religious justifications have been offered for such action and, in each case, the justifications offered are consistent with the analyses of forms of religious justifications for violence provided in Chapters 4, 5, and 6. In Chapter 8 I attend to the topic of religious tolerance, and consider our prospects for persuading those who believe that they are justified in conducting violent acts in the name of religion to behave tolerantly. In the final chapter of the book

I consider our prospects for preventing or ameliorating violent actions that particular religious individuals and groups hold to be justified by appeal to their religion.

Notes

1. Bagley cautions us to regard stories of misconduct by the emigrants in Utah with "profound skepticism," as almost all of these stories came from Utahn Mormons who were involved either in the massacre or in covering it up (2002, p. 99).

2. Mormon scholars, including Walker et al. (2008) and Brooks (1950), concede that officials of the Church of Jesus Christ of Latter-Day Saints were involved in orchestrating the massacre, but deny that there is compelling evidence that Brigham Young was involved. Bagley argues that Brigham Young was heavily involved and shared moral responsibility for the massacre (2002, p. 380).

3. Cited in Bagley (2002, p. 311).

4. However, some commentators argue that the massacre was the consequence of a series of mistakes and miscalculations, as attempts by local Mormons to conduct lower-level violent actions against the Fancher–Baker party got out of hand. See, for example, Bowman (2012, pp. 121–3).

5. The *San Francisco Bulletin* went as far as to call for volunteers to help exterminate the Utahn Mormons (Bagley 2002, p. 191).

6. Cited in Coates (1991, pp. 64–5).

7. Children under the age of eight are not considered to be responsible for their actions by Mormons and hence it was not usually supposed that the doctrine of blood atonement could be applied to them (Bagley 2002, p. 51). This consideration may help explain why children under the age of seven were spared in the massacre, although there remains a slight discrepancy to be accounted for between the maximum age of the children spared in the massacre and the Mormon age of accountability.

8. The doctrine of blood atonement was formally repudiated by the Church of Jesus Christ of Latter-Day Saints in 1889.

9. Forms of harm particularly associated with religion include cicatrization, circumcision, crucifixion, flagellation, infibulation, and subincision.

10. There are also metaphorical uses of the term "violence" that go beyond the narrow range of cases that we will consider here. For example, an actor might be said to do violence to Hamlet, meaning not that he has attempted to kill the mythical Danish prince, but that he has played the role of Hamlet in a film or a play in an extremely unconvincing way.

11. Quoted in Grundy and Weinstein (1974, p. 12).

12. In the analysis that follows I will avoid the technicalities involved in formal treatments of the logic of justification. Examination of these is not necessary

for my purposes. Readers interested in investigating formal treatments of the logic of justification could start by looking at Artemov and Fitting (2011).

13. The classic philosophical discussion of the justification/excuse distinction is to be found in Austin (1956–7). Here I am following Austin's way of distinguishing between these two terms.

14. For a detailed examination of the psychological appeal of the rhetoric of violence, as well as an evolutionary account of why humans are particularly susceptible to the influence of this rhetoric, see Smith (2007).

15. This is the much discussed "Euthyphro problem" in philosophy. Here I am following Hoffman and Rosencrantz (2002, pp. 143–6).

16. For recent discussion of this thought experiment, see Breecher (2007).

17. See Carrasco (1998, pp. 57–8, 82).

18. There were various Aztec human sacrificial practices and not all were intended to ensure the continuing existence of the sun. However, many of these were held by the Aztecs to have effects on the natural world. For example, crying children were sacrificed on an annual basis to ensure rains (Berdan 2005, p. 121). For an extended discussion of Aztec sacrificial practices, see Carrasco (1998, pp. 183–207).

19. According to Wade, a reasonable estimate is that approximately 15,000 people were sacrificed per year in Central America in the late fifteenth century (2009, p. 243). Berdan offers a somewhat higher estimate: approximately 20,000 per year (2005, p. 123).

20. An important additional incentive for them was provided by the widespread Aztec belief that sacrificial victims would become gods in the afterlife (Berdan 2005, p. 121).

21. An annual tax collected for the poor.

22. Cited by Eller (2010, p. 130). The burning of widows has been a persistent practice in Indian Hindu communities, despite having been outlawed in India in the early nineteenth century.

23. "And they utterly destroyed all that was in the city, both man and woman, young and old, ox and sheep and donkey, with the edge of the sword" (Joshua 6:21).

24. However, the Ancient Greek word usually translated as "hate" is sometimes translated as "love less."

25. Ward considers some examples of Jesus apparently acting in a somewhat violent and intolerant fashion, which he explains away in a plausible enough manner (2006, pp. 121–4).

26. For a discussion of disputes between interpreters of Islam as a religion of peace and as a religion of both peace and violence, see Avalos (2005, pp. 283–99).

27. Teehan argues similarly (2010, p. 146).

28. Or at least they viewed him this way until April 2000 when it became clear that he had been involved in match fixing.

29. Some of these are modern versions of biblical commandments and some are new.
30. For more on the natural/supernatural distinction, see Clarke (2007).
31. Some naturalistically inclined philosophers have lent support to this view, stipulating that a naturalistic philosophical outlook is incompatible with belief in supernatural entities (e.g., Pettit 1992, p. 245; Stroud 2004, p. 23).
32. Vitalism was the dominant view in chemistry and biology throughout much of the nineteenth century. While some vitalists seemed to think that the *élan vital* was an emergent natural property, many vitalists, including Van Helmont and Stahl, took the view that it was a non-natural substance (MacDonald and Tro, 2009).
33. For further defence of this claim see Clarke (2009).

2

Religion

Generalizing about Religion

The religions of the world are extremely diverse and many of the generalizations that are made about them do not stand up to serious scrutiny.
For example, it is often claimed that religion provides people with a source
of comfort, helping them to set aside their various anxieties, at least
temporarily (e.g., Freud 1927). But this is not really plausible if it is meant
to be understood as a cross-cultural and cross-temporal generalization
about actual human religions. The Aztec religion, as we saw in the previous
chapter, left those who accepted it in a permanent state of anxiety about
the possibility of their imminent death, as well as the imminent death of
everyone around them. Also, many religions posit the existence of large
numbers of anxiety-producing witches, evil spirits, demons, and so on
(Boyer 2001, pp. 22–3). Advocates of the view that religion is a source of
comfort may respond to these counterexamples by pointing out that many
religions, including the Aztec religion, at least provide adherents who lead
miserable lives with the comforting promise of a better time of it in the
afterlife. But not all of the afterlives on offer seem particularly pleasant
(Wright 2009, pp. 24–5); and even when a pleasant afterlife is on offer,
there is not usually a guarantee that it will be provided to any particular
individual. Indeed, in standard salvific religions, including most variants
of Christianity and Islam, the comfort of hoping that one may end up in
heaven needs to be weighed against the discomfort of fearing that one
may end up in hell. According to a study by Exline et al. (2000), religious
people who regard themselves as alienated from God, as a result of feelings

The Justification of Religious Violence, First Edition. Steve Clarke.
© 2014 John Wiley & Sons, Inc. Published 2014 by John Wiley & Sons, Inc.

of religious guilt or sin, experience heightened feelings of depression and suicidality.[1] In many cases these feelings will be accompanied by anxiety-producing thoughts of a possible future in hell.

Another popular view, which was extremely influential in the nineteenth century and which also fails to stand up to serious scrutiny, is the view that religions provide their adherents with coherent proto-scientific explanations of the origins of the world and its components (e.g., Tylor 1871). Indeed, the various myths associated with religions around the world can have the appearance of providing such explanations, usually telling stories about how particular people, animals, and aspects of nature came into existence. But many of the accounts developed are highly idiosyncratic, and are much less compelling than explanations of other aspects of the natural world that people are generally inclined to accept (Wilson 2002, p. 41), often presuming the existence of unlikely prior states of affairs that themselves stand in obvious need of explanation. Consider, for example, the Klamath people's explanation of the origins of the west wind: the west wind is emitted by a flatulent female dwarf (Wright 2009, p. 18). Or consider the Klamath's story about their own existence: they were created by Kmukamtch, a god who inhabited the sun, from a single purple berry (Wright 2009, p. 19). Neither of these stories seems very explanatory and both raise obvious questions about the prior state of affairs appealed to. Why is there a flatulent female dwarf located to the west of Oregon where the Klamath live? Why did Kmukamtch pick out a particular purple berry and transform it into the Klamath? But peoples, such as the Klamath, who accept these creation myths, often seem quite uninterested in seeking out these further explanations; a state of affairs that adds weight to the nowadays common view that such stories are not primarily directed at explanation (Boyer 2001, pp. 14–17).[2]

A generalization that does stand up to scrutiny is one that is so obvious that it is often overlooked: religion is ubiquitous. In every known human culture, both now and in the past, at least one religion has been practiced (Winzeler 2008, p. 3; Wade 2009, p. 40). Although there are many atheists and agnostics found all over the world, in almost all cultures atheism and agnosticism are minority positions. Three further generalizations are substantiated by cross-cultural studies of religion. First, all known religions postulate supernatural beings (Boyer 2001; Atran 2002). Most religious believers hold that these postulated supernatural beings exist, and are as real as ordinary natural beings. Second, participation in every religion involves participation in ritual activities (Whitehouse 2004; Wade 2009; Winkelman 2010). Third, every known religion helps to shape the moral beliefs and behavior of its practitioners, although the ways in which different cultures relate morality to religion seem to vary significantly (Boyer 2001, pp. 27–8, 192–8). We will discuss the first two of these points now. Discussion of the third will be deferred until Chapter 3.

Supernatural Beings

The claim that supernatural beings are postulated in all known religions seems open to apparent refutation. Buddhism is often described as an atheistic religion, as is Jainism; so, it may seem that Buddhists and Jains do not postulate supernatural beings. But the depiction of these religions as atheistic is misleading. While it is true that Buddhists do not accept the existence of a supreme being, it does not follow that Buddhists do not accept the existence of supernatural beings. Practicing Buddhists generally believe in a large number of "devas," or supernatural beings that are more powerful than humans, but less powerful than a supreme being (Sadakata 1997). Similarly, practicing Jains usually accept the existence of a variety of minor deities (Dundas 2002, pp. 212–14).[3] Many Buddhist and Jain theologians do not want us to take claims about such supernatural beings literally. But in trying to understand the nature of religion it is important that we do not worry overly about the niceties of theological interpretation and that we attend to the detail of actual religious practices and beliefs. Many ordinary religious beliefs, as Justin Barrett notes, are not "theologically correct" (2004, pp. 10–11). Believers have a tendency to ignore official doctrine and are apt to adopt belief in supernatural beings in an indiscriminate manner (Boyer 2001, pp. 322–3). This is as much a problem for monotheistic religions as it is for Buddhists and Jains. In many parts of the world, Christian ministers face an uphill battle in trying to persuade their parishioners not to believe in ghosts, ancestor spirits, witches, and deities from other religions. And many imams face similar problems trying to convince practicing Muslims not to believe in djinns, ifreets, and other supernatural beings.

An influential explanation of the general human disposition to believe in supernatural beings, propounded by Justin Barrett (2004), is that the human mind is predisposed to believe in "minimally counterintuitive" beings. Many of our beliefs are intuitive in the sense that we hold them implicitly and do not require reflection to elicit them (Barrett 2004, p. 22). If I ask you whether the parents of koalas are also koalas, it is unlikely that you will have to agonize long over the answer. Probably, like most people, you simply assume that animals have parents that are of the same species as themselves.[4] You might have first learned to make this generalization in biology class at school, but more likely you had already acquired the general principle at work here, without being consciously aware of having acquired it. You heard about instances of animal reproduction and perhaps you saw instances of animal birth; and, without realizing it, you formulated an implicit generalization about animal parentage.

Over time we generate a great number of implicit generalizations about the world around us that help to shape our expectations. We come to expect that solid unsupported objects will fall towards the surface of the earth, that day is preceded by night, that summer is preceded by spring and spring by winter, that water is wet, and so on.[5] If I am told, for example, that you have a lemon tree in your back yard and that it is producing lemons then, all things being equal, I will find this claim easy to believe as it does not contradict any of my expectations about the world. If you tell me that you have a giant, talking lemon tree in your back yard that changes color regularly, produces watermelons instead of lemons, and travels in the astral plane at night, then I will find this claim very hard to believe, as it contradicts a great many of my implicit assumptions about the nature of the world. Not only will I find the story hard to believe, I will also find it hard to transmit accurately, as I will have difficulty remembering all the details of the story.

But what if you simply tell me that you have a talking tree in your back yard? This claim violates many fewer of our implicit assumptions than the aforementioned more complicated story, so it is much less hard to believe. It is also easier to remember, and so easier to transmit. And people appear to be highly motivated to transmit stories of the minimally counterintuitive. As David Hume recognized in the eighteenth century:

> The passion of *surprize* and *wonder*, arising from miracles, being an agreeable emotion, gives a sensible tendency towards the belief of those events, from which it is derived. And this goes so far, that even those who cannot enjoy this pleasure immediately, nor can believe those miraculous events, of which they are informed, yet love to partake of the satisfaction at second-hand, or by rebound, and place a pride and delight in exciting the admiration of others. (Hume 1748, p. 175)

Hume was making a point about miracles and most miracle stories involve the minimally counterintuitive: statues that bleed, bodies of water that part, books that are written by the illiterate, incurable medical problems that are suddenly cured, and so on. The great propensity of people to transmit stories about the minimally counterintuitive may more than compensate for the difficulties involved in overcoming people's resistance to believing stories that violate their implicit assumptions about the world; and so, over time, belief in minimally counterintuitive entities tend to become entrenched in the cultures of human social groups.[6]

Why do those minimally counterintuitive conceptions that become entrenched in the cultures of human social groups so often seem to be conceptions of supernatural agents? Why do so many of us believe in gods, spirits, and ghosts and not in abstract supernatural forces, powers, and machines? Barrett's answer to these questions appeals to a postulated cognitive structure: the "hypersensitive agency detection device" or HADD,[7] a "mental tool" that enables us to detect the presence of other agents in the world, be they other humans, threatening predators, poisonous reptiles or potential high-protein meals (Barrett 2009, pp. 85–7). This device is not always accurate. The practicalities of evolution mean that we cannot expect that it would be entirely accurate. Evolutionary theory requires a trade-off between the accuracy of a mental tool that produces representations of parts of the world, on the one hand, and the speed of operation, as well as the resources demanded to develop and operate that mental tool, on the other (Perlman 2002, p. 272).

The inevitable errors that the device makes could be distributed in different ways. We might end up with many false positives – agency attributed to the world where there no agents – and few false negatives – agency that is present going undetected – or many false negatives and few false positives, or an even mix of false positives and false negatives. When we consider our actual attributions of agency to the world, it becomes obvious that we have taken the first path and have evolved to tolerate many false positives and allow few false negatives. We "see" faces in clouds, on the moon, in rock formations, and so on. When we hear unfamiliar rustling noises in the grass, we immediately become alert to the danger of snakes and other threats, rather than simply dismissing such noises as the effect of the wind. It is not surprising that we do all of this. The evolutionary costs of over-attributing agency to the world are low, but the evolutionary costs of failing to identify poisonous reptiles, hungry predators, and hostile people are extremely high. According to Barrett (2004; 2009), our general disposition to over-attribute agency to the world means that we are much more likely to accept that there are supernatural agents, rather than mindless supernatural forces or powers, intervening in the world.

A possible objection to the above line of reasoning is that many religions appear to endorse belief in supernatural beings that are more than minimally counterintuitive. The Christian God is often said to be immortal, all powerful, all knowing, and not constrained by space and time. All of these qualities are violations of intuitiveness. A minimally counterintuitive concept is normally understood as having one or two counterintuitive aspects only (Barrett 2009, p. 84), so it seems that the Christian God is not minimally counterintuitive. But it is important to distinguish between the gods of theologians and those accepted by ordinary religious adherents. While ordinary Christians may learn to endorse the official account of the Christian God, as having all of the aforementioned qualities, it seems that their actual thinking about God is typically not guided by the belief that God possesses all of these qualities.

Consider, for example, the assertion that God stands outside of space and time. If a God who stands outside of space and time can intervene in the spatio-temporally bounded universe at all, then that God can perform multiple actions in the universe at the one time. If people's thinking is guided by belief in such a God, then assertions that God performed multiple actions at once should be easy for them to comprehend. In a clever experiment, Justin Barrett had his research subjects read a story in which God intervened in the world in two different ways, at the very same time, saving a man's life and helping a woman to find her lost purse.[8] When subjects were asked to repeat the story, they typically misrepresented it in a systematic and illuminating way. They typically re-described the story as one in which God performed one action and then performed the other action immediately afterwards; and they typically did this even when they continued to endorse the official view that God's actions are unconstrained by space and time. It seems that while people learn to endorse official theological doctrines, their thinking is actually guided by an implicit "folk" conception of a god who is constrained by space and time. It is important to note, though, that ordinary thinking about God does seem to involve God having at least one counterintuitive quality. As we will see in the next chapter, people have no difficulty conceiving of God as all-knowing, a highly counterintuitive quality that no adult human would ordinarily attribute to another human.

Ritual

All religions conduct ritual activities (Whitehouse 2004; Wade 2009; Winkelman 2010). These are extremely diverse and can include praying, singing, chanting, clapping, and dancing. Often ritual activities are combined into elaborate rituals or ceremonies. Those who organize religious rituals commonly employ props to heighten the sensory experiences involved. These can include incense, fire, masks, music, ceremonial costumes, ceremonial weapons, and sacrificial animals (sometimes humans). Usually rituals invoke supernatural agents in some way or other. A god may be asked to legitimize ceremonies conducted within a community – such as weddings, funerals, and coming of age ceremonies; asked to provide benefits for members of the community; or thanked for providing benefits to members of that community. Rituals are typically conducted in designated places. These include special buildings primarily devoted to the performance of religious ceremonies, such as churches, mosques, and temples, as well as pieces of land that are designated as sacred sites.

Participation in religious rituals helps create a sense of solidarity with other participants. It serves to indicate to them that you identify with your religious community and are willing to devote significant amounts of time and energy to the ends of that community (Atran 2002, p. 173). Many of the strenuous activities involved in rituals, including singing and dancing, are particularly good ways of prompting the body to release endorphins, which create a sense of contentedness and seem to facilitate social bonding (Dupue and Morrone-Strupinsky 2005; Machin and Dunbar 2011). When people perform these strenuous activities, in time and step with others, social bonding is considerably enhanced (Ehrenreich 2006). This may be because people's brains release significantly larger endorphin surges when they perform strenuous activities in unison than are released when they perform the same activities in isolation (Cohen et al. 2010).[9] It is plausible to think that the heightened sense of community, which participation in religious rituals promotes, helped early humans to better cope with day-to-day social friction and also helped to motivate them to continue to contribute to the general welfare of their community, rather than seek to benefit from membership of that community without making an appropriate contribution to its welfare – to deter them from becoming "free-riders," in other words.[10] It thereby enabled early humans to maintain larger communities than they would otherwise be able to maintain. These communities were significantly larger than the communities maintained by other hominids, none of which appear to have conducted religious rituals.[11] This overcoming of the "social group size barrier" appears to have been a crucial step in the development of subsequent large-scale human civilizations (Dunbar 2013).

Whitehouse (2004) distinguishes between two fundamental types of religious rituals: those in the "doctrinal mode," and those in the "imagistic mode." Rituals in the doctrinal mode include most of the rituals that are regularly conducted within the major religions of the world today. These are relatively high frequency, relatively mundane events, weekly church services being an obvious example. In typical doctrinal-mode format, expert religious leaders transmit information to a community verbally and repeat this reasonably often, encouraging memorization of official doctrine. These high-frequency events generally promote religious orthodoxy. Rituals in the imagistic mode are not particularly directed at transmitting religious dogma, although they may involve the transmission of some information. These are typically low-frequency events which induce high states of arousal. Pentecostal Christian baptism ceremonies, in which participants perform acts of glossolalia (more commonly known as "speaking in tongues"), are a good example of a modern imagistic religious ritual. These are ceremonies in which people "speak," or sometimes sing, in apparent gibberish, which Pentecostal Christians generally believe to be "heavenly language." Ceremonies in which this activity takes place are generally ecstatic and, even though they have a loose structure, they do not have the tight structure of a conventional church service. It would be hard for them to maintain a tight structure, as instances of glossolalia can vary in length from a few seconds to an hour or more (Hine 1969, p. 212).

Before the rise of permanent human settlements that were sufficiently large and stable enough to support a caste of specialist religious leaders who could organize high-frequency, low-arousal ritual events, and encourage regular attendance at them, religious rituals only occurred in the imagistic mode.[12] And indeed, contemporary hunter-gatherer societies only conduct imagistic mode rituals and never doctrinal mode ones. The ritual activities that are practiced in such societies are usually infrequent and typically involve very high states of emotional arousal. A common form of such high arousal religious ritual is the performance of high-energy repetitive activity to induce trance states.[13] Such ritual performances will usually have a nominal leader or group of leaders – shamen. However, these nominal leaders are typically not specialist religious leaders, as a priest or imam would be, but charismatic part-timers whose leading role is conditional upon the consent of their immediate community rather than their place in an organized hierarchy. When ritual participants go into trance states their sensory awareness becomes limited. They are liable to tremble, convulse, foam at the mouth, and become temporarily paralyzed. They often have little or no memory of these occurrences afterwards (Wade 2009, p. 91). Entry into trance states is usually considered dangerous, and indeed, it carries a real risk of death or permanent insanity (Vitebsky 2001, p. 11).

Another type of high-arousal, low-frequency religious ritual is the initiation ceremony. Male initiation ceremonies take place in many, but by no means all, small-scale human societies. They are typically conducted when initiates are in their teenage years. Initiates may be subjected, among other things, to cicatrization (body scarring), exposure to fire, removal of teeth, being hung from hooks inserted in their skins, and circumcision (Sosis et al. 2007, p. 234). Often such ritual practices are secretive and the initiate, who may have been abducted by a group of adult males, is unlikely to know what to expect (Richert, Whitehouse, and Stewart 2005, p. 127). Initiates, who invariably seem to be terrified by the experience of participation, usually have no alternative but to go along with the ritual, apart from the alternative of being killed by the adults conducting the ritual (Whitehouse 2004, p. 122).

The terrifying nature of initiation ceremonies provides an effective solution to a practical problem that faces traditional small-group societies. This is the problem of enabling people who lack writing, or social structures that are sufficiently developed to enable rote learning to be organized, to recall how to conduct low-frequency rituals. The traumatizing of ritual participants tends to induce "flashbulb memory." In this state of mind, people retain a long-term clarity of memory, both as a result of being traumatized and as a result of subsequent efforts to understand hard-to-understand traumatizing events, efforts which help to cement vivid representations of the traumatic sequence of events in long-term memory (Whitehouse 2000, pp. 7–9).[14] Adults who retain vivid trauma-induced memories of having been initiated are able to help conduct initiations of the teenage boys of the future, and so complicated initiation ceremonies can be reliably reproduced over time.

The Evolution of Religion

It is often assumed that the various religions of the world are a series of more or less haphazard cultural constructs that do not form discernible lineages. But there are at least three reasons for thinking that religion is not a random assortment of cultural constructs and is something that has evolved (either via pure cultural transmission or via gene-culture co-evolution).[15] The first is the ubiquity of religion. If the religions of the world were merely a series of haphazard cultural constructs then it is very hard to understand why some or other religion should be present in each and every society, and should have been present in all known human societies that have preceded us over the course of tens of thousands of years.

The second is the very strong underlying pattern of similarity in the content of the otherwise very different religions of the world. All known religions invoke supernatural beings, all involve ritual activities, and all help to shape moral beliefs and behavior; and all have done these things for tens of thousands of years. These are striking similarities and the maintenance of such a pattern of striking similarity over very long periods of time requires explanation. It might perhaps be supposed that the many religions of today derive from a common ancestor religion that just happened to invoke supernatural beings, involve ritual activities, and help to shape morality, and that the spreading of religious culture from this one common source accounts for the underlying pattern of similarity across time and place. But this supposition is extremely unlikely given the sheer diversity of human cultures, as well as the geographic isolation of some of these from the influence of other human cultures over long periods of time (Wade 2009, p. 100). It is more plausible to think that religions, which share underlying similarities, arose independently, many times, in different cultural contexts in early human societies; and on many such occasions those religions became fixed in the populations in which they arose. In addition, even if all of the current religions of the world really did share a common ancestor, this would not allow us get away from the need to appeal to evolution to explain the pattern of underlying similarities found across contemporary religions. Over the course of many generations, distinct cultures, that start out as similar to one another, will tend to drift away from that initial state of similarity, unless they are subject to the ongoing influence of some or other force, or forces, acting to prevent such cultural drift (Axelrod 1997). It is hard to see what force, or forces, might persistently act on all human societies, over very long time spans, to prevent such cultural drift, other than evolution.

The third reason for thinking that religion has evolved is that participation in religion typically involves a significant outlay of time and resources, which could otherwise be put to more obviously fitness-enhancing ends (Henrich 2009). Acceptance of a religion usually involves a commitment of time and resources to acquiring and maintaining an interlocking set of beliefs and norms, as well as participating in ritual activities. Participation in the rituals of doctrinal religions typically involves a regular commitment of time and energy. Participation in imagistic religious rituals is not so time consuming, but tends to be dangerous, often involving a significant risk of injury and a non-negligible risk of death. Evolution would not tolerate any species expending such resources and bearing such risks over the long run, without fitness enhancing ends, if these could be easily avoided. Given that *homo sapiens* evolved from species that do not practice religion, it seems plausible to think that, before religion got the grip on human societies that it currently has, there were non-religious early human (or perhaps pre-human) societies. Members of these societies would have had significantly more time and resources to devote to feeding themselves, protecting themselves from threats, and raising children than members of religious societies, who expended precious time and energy on religious activities and risked their lives participating in dangerous rituals. So why didn't such non-religious early human or pre-human societies out-compete their religious competitors?

Most evolutionary explanations of traits are selectionist, or adaptationist. They proceed by demonstrating that it is reasonable to infer that a particular trait is present because it has conferred evolutionary advantages on a given species. There are many authors who agree that religion has evolved,[16] but the view that religion evolved because it conferred evolutionary advantages upon humans and human social groups is currently a minority position. The most common view in the "cognitive science of religion" is that religion is an evolutionary by-product of our cognitive development, and that it does not confer any significant evolutionary advantages upon us (Powell and Clarke 2013, pp. 459–61). Another view, which was recently quite influential, but now seems to be declining in influence, is that religion is a series of virulent "memes" that have successfully infected human populations, in much the same way as a disease might. Like diseases, memes are generally thought to be harmful to their human hosts, only conferring evolutionary advantage upon themselves, or so say many "memeticists" (e.g., Blackmore 1999; Dennett 2006). We will now consider these three different views of the evolution of religion, beginning with the memeticist view. The upshot of the discussion in the remainder of this section is that the view that religion is an adaptation is better supported than its two rivals. Readers who are uninterested in the details of debates about competing accounts of the evolution of religion can safely skip to the next section.

Memes and Religious Memeplexes

The term "meme" was coined by Richard Dawkins, and introduced to the world in his extremely influential book *The Selfish Gene* (1976). Memes are replicators, like genes, but replicators of cultural rather than genetic information. It seems undeniable that some cultural information is replicated. Many birds replicate the songs of other members of their species and humans replicate a great many aspects of our culture. Dawkins' examples are "tunes, ideas, catch-phrases, clothes fashions, ways of making pots or of building arches" (1976, p. 192). We can adopt the "meme's eye point of view" and see these items as being in competition with one another to propagate themselves in human memories and in other hosts. Other hosts of memes include books, computer hard drives, and websites. The song "I Kissed a Girl" infected Katy Perry's head in 2008 and then proceeded to use her to replicate itself in other people's heads. It also infected many computers and websites and eventually managed to infect this book. In doing so, it outcompeted numerous other less infectious songs.[17]

Not all memes that do replicate, replicate reliably. Ideas can be misremembered, and can sometimes be transmitted unreliably, even when they are recalled accurately. I recall the chorus of "I Kissed a Girl" accurately enough, but I am unable to recall many of the other lines from the song. If I tried to reconstruct the entire song, and then pass it on, it is very unlikely that I would be able to do so accurately.[18] Sometimes ideas are deliberately transformed by their human hosts, often by being amalgamated with other ideas. Indeed, "I Kissed a Girl" has been parodied many times, and each parody involves a deliberate transformation of the lyrics of the song rather than an actual replication. It is also true that not all genes replicate reliably; but whereas genes mutate instead of replicating, perhaps only one in every million times that they are transmitted, the mutation of memes seems to be a very common occurrence. The failure of many memes to replicate reliably is pointed to by critics of memetics, such as Atran (2002, pp. 236–62) and Sperber (1996, pp. 100–6), who charge that memes do not generally form discernible lineages in the same way that genes do. A related problem is that it is often unclear how to individuate memes. The song title "I Kissed a Girl" can be viewed as a meme, as can the oft repeated line from the chorus "I kissed a girl and I liked it," as can the entire chorus, as can the entire song.

Some advocates of memetics, including Blackmore (1999) and Dennett (2006), have construed religions as complexes of memes, or "memeplexes," that have infected human societies, and which now direct our behavior in various ways. Advocates of memetic explanations of human behavior tend to emphasize the extent to which religious memeplexes, as well as other memes and memeplexes, have proliferated at the evolutionary expense of their human hosts. One way such advocates try to do this is by drawing analogies to cases in nature where a parasite causes behavior in its host that is contrary to the evolutionary interests of that host. Dennett (2006) cites two such cases. One is a case where the lancet fluke hijacks the brain of an ant and causes the ant to position itself where it is most likely to be eaten by sheep or cattle. This benefits the lancet fluke, which aims to end up in a sheep or cow's stomach, an ideal environment for it to reproduce. But this benefit to the lancet fluke is gained at the evolutionary expense of host ants, which do not survive long in animals' stomachs (Dennett 2006, pp. 3–4). The other is a case where the parasite *Toxoplasma gondii* infects rats and interferes with their nervous systems, making them hyperactive and reckless. This makes it significantly more likely that infected rats will be located and then eaten by cats, an outcome that benefits *Toxoplasma gondii* but is disastrous for the infected rats (Dennett 2006, p. 63).

Memeticists sometimes write with the assumption in mind that we are simply passive hosts of both diseases and memes. But this is not really a plausible assumption. We can take various steps to try to overcome many diseases, such as taking medication, and we can isolate ourselves to prevent spreading infectious diseases.[19] In the case of religion we can do the equivalent of both of these things. We can read anti-religious literature to try to combat infection, and we can refrain from proselytizing to prevent infecting others. Additionally, we can attempt to reshape the religious ideas that infect us, and thereby reduce their influence on us. Large religious organizations are often sites of ongoing struggles between reformers and conservatives regarding official doctrine. Often reformers try to reduce the demands of religion on ordinary adherents. The Second Vatican Council, 1962–1965, provides an example of a victory for such reformers, who comprehensively reshaped Catholicism, making the demands of the Catholic faith less onerous on adherents in several respects than these had been previously (O'Malley 2010).

Not all religious memeplexes prove amenable to human attempts to reform them, and infection by some of these is plainly disastrous. Attempts to reform Jim Jones' People's Temple from within were largely unsuccessful and insufficient to prevent the vast majority of members from being gripped by the idea of "revolutionary suicide"; an idea which helped drive over 900 of them to participate in a mass suicide in 1978 – the notorious Jonestown massacre (Chidester 1988). But this outcome was not simply a disaster for the members of the People's Temple, it was also a disaster for the ideas that constitute the People's Temple memeplex. Most of the hosts of these ideas are now dead and the memeplex appears to have been unable to infect new hosts since then. Memeticists depict religions as memeplexes that, when they thrive, do so at the expense of their human hosts. But this conclusion would be very difficult to substantiate. As we will go on to discuss, there is mounting evidence that religion generally is conducive to increased human survival and reproduction. For this reason Susan Blackmore has now recanted on her earlier view that religion is a "virus of the mind" (2010). Other advocates of memetics may well follow her lead.

Religion as an Evolutionary By-product

Currently the most influential account of the evolution of religion has it that religion is an evolutionary by-product of our cognitive development. According to Pascal Boyer:

> Religious concepts are widespread the world over, not because they are an adaptation of human minds, but because they are an optimally salient and inferentially rich *by-product* of normal brain function. (Boyer 2005, p. 5)

This account is often referred to as "the standard model" and, as its name suggests, support for it is widespread, especially in the cognitive science of religion, where it is currently the predominant view. Its advocates include Boyer (2001), Atran (2002), McCauley and Lawson (2002), and Barrett (2004), as well as the evolutionary biologist Richard Dawkins (2006).[20] It may seem surprising that Dawkins (2006) is an advocate of the standard model, as he is very well known for having endorsed a memetic approach to religion in his *The Selfish Gene* (1976, pp. 198–9). However, in *The God Delusion* (2006), Dawkins explicitly advocates explaining religion as an evolutionary by-product (2006, pp. 179–90).[21]

What does it mean to say that religion is an evolutionary by-product of our cognitive development? The core idea here is that our cognitive structures have evolved in ways that bias our reasoning and dispose us to commit certain sorts of systematic errors. Natural selection tolerates these errors because, overall, their evolutionary cost is outweighed by the evolutionary benefits of possessing particular cognitive structures. Religion is said by advocates of the standard model to be the result of a combination of such cognitive biases and is not understood by them as being something that was subsequently co-opted by evolution and which has gone on to make any significant contribution to the survival and proliferation of humans (Powell and Clarke 2012). In Jesse Bering's words:

> all but a handful of scholars in this area regard religion as an accidental by-product of our mental evolution. Specifically, religious thought is usually portrayed by scholars as having no particular adaptive biological function in itself, but instead it's viewed as a leftover of other psychological adaptations (sort of like male nipples being a useless leftover of the default human body plan). (2011, p. 6)

The human mind is often said to have evolved a systematic bias in favor of attributing agency to the world. As was mentioned earlier in this chapter, a mind that contains a hypersensitive agency detection device (HADD), and which is also systematically disposed in favor of belief in minimally counterintuitive agents, is particularly liable to believe in gods, spirits, demons, and so on, according to advocates of the standard model. The urge to participate in repetitive religious rituals can also be understood as an evolutionary by-product; a by-product of planning functions of the brain systematically malfunctioning in ways that may be related to the ways in which these appear to malfunction in cases of obsessive–compulsive disorder (Boyer 2001, pp. 273–4).[22] And the fact that the participants in rituals, such as rain-dances, which are directed at requesting supernatural assistance, generally seem to believe that these rituals are effective, may be explained by invoking the cognitive biases that habitually affect lay interpretations of statistical information (Sperber 1996, pp. 50–2). In a somewhat similar vein, Richard Dawkins suggests that natural selection may have endowed young human minds with a disposition to obey their parents and authority figures unquestioningly, and that this disposition helps to ensure their survival. Dawkins also suggests that this disposition renders them gullible and liable to accept the pronouncements of religious leaders, without reflecting on the plausibility of these (2006, pp. 174–9). As exemplified by the above examples, the existence of religion is construed as completely dependent on the existence of cognitive functional structures of the mind that would be in place even if religion were nonexistent.

Many advocates of the standard model, including Boyer (2001) and Atran (2002), are also proponents of Sperber's (1996) "epidemiological" approach to explaining cultural transmission, which, like the standard model, is grounded in considerations of cognitive structure. On Sperber's (1996) account of cultural transmission, some cultural variants proliferate more effectively than others because the cognitive structures of our mind dispose us to recall and transmit these and not other cultural variants. We remember and transmit songs and tunes more readily than random assortments of noises because our minds are disposed to recall and transmit certain types of aural patterns much better than unpatterned assortments of noises. Similarly, our mind is not neutral in regard to possible competing religious concepts (Boyer 2001, p. 4). A mind which contains a HADD, and which is predisposed to accept belief in minimally counterintuitive agency, is much more likely to transmit a report of a supernatural agent acting in the world accurately, than a report of a non-agential supernatural cause of a natural event.

Although the standard model has garnered widespread support, it remains a speculative account of the origins of religion and it is problematic in at least four respects.[23] The first of these problems is raised by talk of "cognitive structures," "cognitive architecture," and "mental tools." A synonym of these terms that advocates of the standard model seem to avoid is the term "module." This is perhaps because the term "module" evokes controversy. There has been an intense debate in the philosophy of mind and in the cognitive sciences about the modularity, or lack thereof, of human psychological faculties, in the wake of the publication of Fodor's extremely influential book *The Modularity of Mind* (1983). Partly, this debate is about what mental modules are. Nearly all advocates of modularity of mind have backed away from the highly specific account of modularity that Fodor originally introduced (Barrett and Kurzban 2006, p. 628)[24] but they have so far failed to reach agreement about what modularity involves. At a minimum, though, acceptance of modularity of mind seems to involve acceptance of a conception of the mind as containing fast-operating, discrete specialist subsystems that are dedicated to particular purposes, and which have inner workings that are opaque to introspection and significantly insulated from central processing (Powell and Clarke 2012).[25] It seems clear enough that, in this sense of the term "module," standard model postulates, such as the HADD, are mental modules, or something very close to mental modules. The HADD is clearly meant to be a fast-operating, discrete subsystem; it has a dedicated function; and it is invariably described as being opaque to introspection.[26] Partly, debate about modularity concerns the extent to which the mind contains modular structures at all. While Sperber (1996) and Cosmides and Tooby (1994) construe the mind as being "massively modular," there is a dearth of evidence of any actual modules having evolved (Machery 2007).

Some critics of massive modularity theories concede that there is evidence of modularity in a few key components of the mind, especially those components of mind that are concerned with language and perception (Samuels 1998). But other critics, such as Prinz (2006), doubt whether even these components of the mind are genuinely modular.

What reasons are there for thinking that our minds contain a HADD? One reason that is sometimes cited is that people are highly prone to over-attribute agency, even attributing intentions, beliefs, and desires to abstract shapes, when these are seen to move around a screen and interact with other abstract shapes (Scholl and Tremoulet 2000). But we cannot reliably infer from the fact that a particular pattern of behavior is observed, that it results from the operation of a dedicated cognitive structure, which has evolved to produce that behavior (Lloyd 1999). Another commonly mentioned reason is that it would have been evolutionarily advantageous for us to have developed a HADD (e.g., Boyer 2001, p. 165). This may be true, but a demonstration that it would have been advantageous for us to have developed a HADD is not sufficient to show that we actually have evolved a HADD. These appear to be the only considerations that advocates of the HADD hypothesis have so far offered in defense of the claim that we have HADDs in our heads and it seems very clear that they do not do nearly enough to warrant this claim. Having made these criticisms, I should also acknowledge that the HADD hypothesis remains attractive because it offers a straightforward explanation of our tendency to over-attribute agency to the world and because compelling alternative explanations of this tendency are not currently available.

The second shortcoming of the standard model is that it is not only the claims about the mental structures, which it appeals to, that are speculative and underdeveloped. The postulated connections between these and the religious constructs that they are purported to account for are also speculative and underdeveloped.[27] To see this, let us return to the example of the HADD. Advocates of the standard model claim that the HADD causes us to over-attribute agency to the world and that, when coupled with our tendency to accept attributions of minimally counterintuitive agency, we have an explanation for the pervasiveness of attributions of supernatural agency. But none of this explains why we seem to have *ongoing* belief in supernatural agents. In many ordinary cases in which we over-attribute agency to the world we soon correct our initial attributions. We hear a rustling in the long grass and we jump to the conclusion that some person or animal is hiding in the grass; but if no further suspicious sounds are heard, then we are inclined to relax, and dismiss the suspicious noise as simply the sound of the grass rustling in the wind (Barrett 2004, pp. 40 – 1). So why don't we tend to correct our initial attributions of supernatural agency in the same way? Defenders of the standard model have yet to provide a satisfactory answer to this question.

The third problem for the standard model is that we are also owed an answer to another question. According to the standard model, the religious by-products of our cognitive structures make no contribution to fitness, and in many circumstances will be fitness reducing. So, why hasn't evolution done away with these byproducts, or at least minimized their influence? People with HADDs that cause unwarranted beliefs in supernatural agents are, all things being equal, evolutionarily worse off than people who have HADDs that don't give off religious by-products. A possible answer to this question is that religion is a by-product that cannot be done away with. Some by-products are the consequence of structural arrangements and are unavoidable. A classic example, made famous by Gould and Lewontin (1979), is provided by architectural spandrels. Spandrels are the roughly triangular areas that are created by resting a dome on top of contiguous arches. If you want to rest a dome on contiguous arches then you will inevitably create spandrels in the process of doing so. Gould and Lewontin (1979) argued that many biological characteristics are structural by-products of other adaptive features that cannot be done away with without compromising the functionality of those other adaptive features. Defenders of the HADD might be able to demonstrate that the attribution of religious by-products is structurally tied to the HADD, as spandrels are to a particular arrangement of arches and a dome. However, they have yet to do this, and in the absence of such a demonstration it is hard to see why we should accept the assertion that evolution could not have done away with the religious by-products of misfiring cognitive structures, or at least minimized their influence.

The claim that some key aspects of religion originated as by-products of human cognition is plausible enough. But, as we have seen, advocates of the standard model are committed to the claim that these aspects of religion have continued to be mere by-products and have never subsequently made any significant positive contribution to our evolution, and this seems much less plausible. Evolutionary by-products can be "exapted"; that is to say, although they may have first become fixed in a species because they were the by-products of adaptive traits, they can subsequently develop in particular ways as a result of being co-opted by natural selection for a function or combination of functions.[28] And this possibility leads us to the fourth shortcoming of the standard model. There is mounting evidence that religion has generally had a positive influence on human survival and reproductive fitness. Religious communities appear to out-persist non-religious ones (Sosis and Bressler 2003); the religious generally enjoy better mental and physical health than the non-religious and generally produce more offspring than the non-religious (Sanderson 2008); and they also appear to cooperate with one another more effectively than the non-religious (Sosis and Ruffle 2003; Henrich et al. 2010). It seems possible that all of this is because religious by-products of our cognitive development might subsequently have been exapted when they began to promote particular aspects of religion that had positive consequences for us, reinforcing those particular aspects of religion.[29] But advocates of the standard model claim that, while the cognitive structures of our mind that give off religious by-products have contributed significantly to human survival and reproduction, their religious by-products have remained mere by-products, and have not contributed in any significant way to human survival and reproduction (Powell and Clarke 2012). And this looks like an implausibly strong claim to insist on, given available evidence.[30]

Religion as an Evolutionary Adaptation

As well as the possibility that religion is composed of evolutionary by-products, some of which may have been exapted, we need to consider the possibility that religion is a direct evolutionary adaptation, or series of adaptations. A trait of a given organism is an adaptation if it has proliferated under cumulative selection because of a tendency to produce an effect, or effects – its function, or functions – which increased the chances that the organism's ancestors would survive and reproduce. Adaptation can occur, at least in theory, at a number of levels of biological organization. These include genes, cells, organisms, cultures, and social groups (Lewontin 1970). A trait that is adaptive at one level of biological organization may be either adaptive or maladaptive at other levels of biological organization.

Human cultural adaptations need not involve genetic adaptation. The ability to control fire and cook food gave some individuals and social groups a crucial evolutionary advantage over other individuals and social groups (Wrangham 2009), as did the ability to construct reliable seafaring kayaks (Richerson and Boyd 2005, pp. 159–61). All of this can be understood without positing fire-starting genes or kayak-building genes. However, some cultural adaptations surely do have a genetic component and are instances of "gene-culture co-evolution." A clear case is the evolution of adult lactose tolerance amongst members of cattle-herding communities (Richerson and Boyd 2005, pp. 191–3). Most people have diminished ability to digest lactose (a sugar found in milk) when they reach adulthood. But a minority retain their childhood ability to digest lactose as adults. Their ancestors were found clustered in certain areas, especially in northern Europe and parts of Africa, and they were mostly cattle-herding peoples. Mutations that allowed individuals within early cattle-herding communities to consume milk as adults gave those individuals a persistent competitive advantage over members of their own groups, as they had an extra supply of food. As these mutations spread, those groups whose members generally possessed the relevant genes enjoyed a significant competitive advantage over other groups, whose members generally had a diminished capacity to digest lactose when adults.[31] This advantage was reinforced by subsequent cultural adaptations, such as the making of cheese, which enabled some individuals and groups to store their extra supply of food for longer periods and consume it when they most needed it.

As already noted, both individuals and social groups appear to benefit from religion. Members of religious groups appear to cooperate with one another more effectively than members of non-religious groups; members of religious groups appear to produce more offspring than members of non-religious groups; and religious groups appear to out-persist non-religious groups. For all of these reasons, it is very plausible to think that religious societies outcompeted non-religious societies a long time ago, and that is why we no longer encounter non-religious societies. Many of the proponents of the view that religion is an adaptation of groups,[32] including Haidt (2012), Harris and McNamara (2008), and Johnson and Bering (2006), suggest that it is a genetically mediated adaptation. The roles that religion can play, as a group-level adaptation, are to facilitate in-group cooperation, strengthen in-group, ties and enhance the tendency of religious groups to compete aggressively with out-groups. It can play these roles in various ways, including enforcing social norms by suppressing free-riding (Bering and Johnson 2005), serving as a hard-to-fake indicator of group membership (Sosis 2005), and producing credible signals of cooperative intent (Henrich 2009).

I have been discussing appeals to group selection (alongside appeals to individual selection) and doing so sympathetically. However, such appeals are somewhat controversial in biology. Appeals to selection at the group level were very common in evolutionary biology up until the 1960s, and, indeed, Darwin appealed to group selection to explain the evolution of human morality (Wilson 2002, p. 9).[33] However, many such appeals were made without due consideration of the ways in which group selection can fail to occur. These issues were highlighted in George Williams's influential work *Adaptation and Natural Selection*, published in 1966. Appeals to group selection all but disappeared from reputable science for the next quarter of a century or so, in the wake of the influence of Williams and other scholars, before making a recent comeback (Godfrey-Smith 2009, p. 143).

A key difficulty with appeals to group selection is that group processes can be, and often are, undermined from within. Lower-level units of selection have their own evolutionary interests and these will often come into conflict with the interests of a group. It is in the interest of society that working individuals pay taxes, as this enables society to pay for the maintenance of roads, schools, hospitals, and so on. It is also in the interest of working individuals that others pay their taxes, as their contributions are necessary for the maintenance of the roads, schools, and hospitals that they benefit from, but it is not in their own interest to pay taxes, as doing so deprives them of money. Furthermore, the contribution to the national tax base of any given individual is minimal and the quality of the roads, school, and hospitals in their society will be much the same whether they pay taxes or not. The best outcome, from an individual's (strictly self-interested) point of view, is that everybody else pays their taxes, but they do not, and that they continue to reap the benefits of the public goods that are enabled by other people paying taxes. In other words, the best outcome from their (strictly self-interested) point of view, is that they "free-ride" on the efforts of others. From the point of view of every strictly self-interested individual, it is best to be a free-rider. But if sufficiently many people are free-riders then social institutions will collapse.[34] If free-riding cannot be prevented, or at least significantly restricted, then group-level processes are undermined by the individuals that comprise social groups and there can be no successful group selection.

A second problem with appeals to group selection is that, as Williams (1966) pointed out, many of the examples that the biologists who came before him had used as examples of individual animals acting for the good of their social group, or perhaps acting for the good of their species, are better understood as examples of individual animals acting in their own interests and producing accidental benefits for their group, or species, in doing so. Apparently as earthworms feed they make improvements to the soil around them. The collective effect of many earthworms feeding in the same soil, over many decades, is to make that soil better able to support plant growth, which other earthworms depend on for food. It also makes that soil a more suitable location for worm burrows. So, we can develop a group selectionist explanation of the earthworm's feeding behavior. But, Williams argued, it is a mistake to think that we need to appeal to group selection to explain this behavior (1966, pp. 18–19). The earthworm's feeding behavior is sufficiently explained by appealing to the earthworm's need to feed, and it is unparsimonious to also appeal to the benefits its feeding confers on groups of earthworms when explaining its behavior.

Despite articulating the above lines of criticism, Williams (1966) did not deliver a knock-out conceptual blow to group selection (and he did not claim to do so). His view was that individual self-interest can be relied on to undermine any significant instances of group selection and that explanatory appeals to group selection are typically redundant anyway; he did not insist that group selection is impossible. He argued that group selection is possible in principle but inconsequential in practice.[35] However, group selection has enjoyed something of a revival in the biological sciences in recent times (e.g., Wilson and Wilson 2007, 2008; Godfrey-Smith 2009). The lines of criticism of loose appeals to group selection, developed by Williams (1966), point the way to a more rigorous approach to group selection. To demonstrate that group selection can occur, we need to demonstrate that a selective process between groups takes place and demonstrate that it operates more strongly than any forces of selection between individuals, within the relevant groups, which might serve to undermine this between-group process. In the case of group selection amongst humans, this will principally involve demonstrating that particular human groups can curtail free-riding by individuals (and sub-groups) effectively enough to enable groups to operate efficiently, and so compete with other groups. Group selection does not support claims that our actions can function for the good of an entire species, except in very rare cases where an entire species operates as a group. Group-level adaptations exacerbate competition between groups that are typically members of the very same species (Wilson 2002, p. 10).

As we have seen in this section, there are good reasons to suppose that religion has evolved. Exactly how it has evolved is a matter of dispute. I have presented arguments that favor the view that religion evolved because it is an adaptation (of individuals and/or groups), rather than because it is an infectious memeplex, or because it is an evolutionary by-product of our cognitive development. Many of the empirical results that underpin the arguments presented in this section are somewhat speculative. More hard data are needed to substantiate the case for adaptationism about religion. Until such data have been located, it is best to remain open-minded about the exact nature of the processes by which religion evolved, even while acknowledging that the case for adaptationism is currently stronger than the case for the other two views discussed.

Social Solidarity and Religion

Participation in religious rituals seems to be an effective means of promoting feelings of group solidarity, as does participation in many other group activities. These include team sports, the drilling of soldiers, and various other group activities that involve practices also found in religious rituals, such as singing, chanting, and dancing. The increase in an individual's sense of group solidarity as a result of participation in these events is usually temporary, which is why such events are often repeated on a regular basis.[36] We can also experience spontaneous surges in feelings of group solidarity on occasions when we sense that a group with which we identify is under threat. Jon Haidt refers to this phenomenon as the "rally-round-the-flag reflex" (2012, p. 199). He recounts his own experience of this spontaneous emotional response upon learning of the events of September 11, 2001. He also reports that hundreds of Americans spontaneously decided to drive great distances to New York in the aftermath of 9/11, in the hope of being able to help their fellow Americans in a time of crisis (2012, pp. 198–9).

Haidt (2012) argues that the existence of the human disposition to feel solidarity with others is, most likely, a result of our having an evolved group-level adaptation that serves to bind individuals into social groups, motivating us to set aside individual interests and devote our energies to promoting the interest of the social groups with which we identify.[37] However, we appear to differ from other "groupish" species. The various eusocial insects appear to be unconditionally groupish, but we, in Haidt's words, are "conditional hive creatures" (2012, p. 223). We are disposed to identify with social groups under many circumstances, but we are also disposed to cease to identify with social groups if circumstances change sufficiently. In particular, if we feel that our contribution to the group is not being reciprocated by others, who are free-riding on the efforts of the group, and if we are convinced that group efforts to prevent such free-riders are not going to be effective, then we will be less inclined to continue to identify with the group. Consequently, we will be more likely to leave the group or, ironically enough, become free-riders ourselves.[38]

Participation in religious rituals and other social events that promote group solidarity seems to be an effective way of encouraging us to remain committed to a group. One obvious concern about the existence of this effect is that group leaders may try to use it to make us feel so loyal to a group that we are unable to consider leaving that group, regardless of circumstances. They can then exploit our unconditional loyalty for their own personal gain, rather than for the good of the group. It also makes us more likely to go along with leadership decisions that we would otherwise judge as being contrary to the long-term interest of the group. Haidt is alert to these concerns. He discusses the case of early twentieth-century fascist leaders, such as Mussolini and Hitler, who employed mass rallies and other rituals to encourage followers to obey them unquestioningly (2012, p. 241). Clearly, these leaders were highly effective at directing their followers to participate in activities – notably, the violent persecution of rival groups and the conduct of wars of aggression – that were not consistent with the moral codes that many of these followers had accepted before becoming bonded into highly cohesive fascist groups, and which turned out not to be in the long-term interest of either the followers of fascist leaders or of those fascist groups themselves.

Haidt points out that fascist rallies were unusual events, and were unrepresentative of ordinary human rituals in that they did not involve expressions of joy and humor (2012, p. 242). He depicts early twentieth-century fascist groupishness as being quite exceptional, and most unlike the overwhelming majority of actual instances of groupish behavior, which he portrays as persistently beneficial to both individuals and groups. But there are a great many examples, quite apart from the examples of early twentieth-century fascism, where individuals remained unquestioningly obedient to group leaders, even when these groups were led to behave in ways that were disastrous for both individuals and groups; and religion provides a significant proportion of these examples. The 1978 Jonestown massacre was the consequence of a religious group operating in ways that were disastrous for the individuals that comprised the People's Temple as well as for the People's Temple itself (Selengut 2003, p. 124). The Aztec religion succeeded in binding large numbers of individual Aztecs to a culture of large-scale human sacrifice, and condemned them to live in a state of permanent fear of their imminent demise. It was disastrous for many individual Aztecs, and also contributed to the inability of the Aztec civilization to defend itself against the Spanish conquistador Cortés and a force of less than a thousand soldiers in the early sixteenth century (White 1996; Levy 2009).

Defining Religion

I have said a lot about different aspects of religion but I have yet to say exactly what religion is. This is no accident. It is notoriously difficult to define religion (Whitehouse 2013, pp. 36–7), and the case for the definition I will offer rests heavily on the preceding discussion in this chapter. In defining religion I will try to capture the three invariant characteristics of religion that have already been discussed. None of these is exclusive to religion: (1) All religion involves the postulation of supernatural beings; however, there are postulated supernatural beings that are widely discussed in fictional contexts, and perhaps occasionally believed in, that do not seem to feature in religions.[39] (2) Full participation in religion involves participation in rituals; but there are plenty of non-religious rituals that people also engage in. (3) All religions appear to have a role in buttressing morality; however, there is plenty of moral behavior that is motivated by sources other than religion. What does seem to be exclusive to religion is a combination of the postulation of supernatural beings, participation in ritual, and relevance to morality. Religion and only religion seems to be found at the intersection of these three, otherwise very distinct aspects of human behavior.

Some definitions do not refer to any of these aspects of religion. One such definition is due to Scott Appleby, who defines religion as "the human response to a reality perceived as sacred" (2000, p. 8). Other definitions of religion only touch on one of these aspects of religion. For example, Daniel Dennett defines religions as "social systems whose participants avow belief in a supernatural agent or agents whose approval is to be sought" (2006, p. 9), which fails to mention rituals or morality.[40] However, there is one definition of religion which comes close to touching on all three aspects of religion discussed here. This is a famous definition of religion due to Durkheim.[41] It will serve as a useful starting point for us. As will soon become apparent, though, I will move a long way from this starting point.

According to Durkheim:

> a religion is a unified system of beliefs and practices relative to sacred things, that is to say, things set apart and surrounded by prohibitions – beliefs and practices that unite its adherents in a single moral community called a church. (Durkheim 1912, p. 46)

One thing missing from this definition is the stipulation that the relevant beliefs include belief in supernatural beings. Durkheim considered including this stipulation in his definition, but decided to exclude it on the grounds that "there are great religions in which the idea of gods and spirits is absent, or plays only a secondary and unobtrusive role" (1912, p. 32). The "great religions" that Durkheim mentions are Buddhism and Jainism (1912, pp. 32–4). Durkheim is aware, though, that practicing Buddhists and Jains often do postulate supernatural beings.[42] However, he sees such practices as a corruption of "theologically correct" religion. I am concerned to describe religion as it is actually practiced, without reference to theologically driven attempts to reform religion, or otherwise restrict what counts as genuine religion, so I will disregard Durkheim's reasoning and refer to the supernatural in my definition. I will also add a reference to ritual in the practices that form a religion, as ritual is invariably a part of at least some of the practices of any and every religion. I will omit reference to a *unified set* of beliefs and practices as it is not obvious that religious beliefs and practices are unified in any significant way. If we look at beliefs about the pantheons of gods of many polytheistic religions, it is often hard to discern any strong unifying principle, other than that they are all supernatural and all agents. Also many religious ritual practices are highly idiosyncratic. Often the only feature that they share is that they all arouse our senses and contribute to the atmosphere of a religious ritual. I will also drop reference to a church in my definition. Although all religions have some influence on moral beliefs and behavior, not all of them appear to exert the sort of influence that results in the formation of "a single moral community called a church." In particular, imagistic religions typically do not seem to have this sort of effect.

Durkheim (1912) refers to the sacred in his definition of religion, which is a concept that he contrasts with the profane. We treat a religious artifact, agent or rite as sacred, according to him, when we hold an attitude of reverence towards it. This involves attributing value to it beyond mere considerations of utility.[43] By contrast, to treat an object, agent or procedure as profane is to treat it as a matter of mere utility. Actual religions, according to Durkheim, form churches that seek to organize moral behavior, seek to ensure an attitude of appropriate reverence for the sacred, and seek to prevent the sacred from being intermingled with the profane. Durkheim's use of the concept "the sacred" and his distinction between the sacred and the profane has proved to be extremely influential in both sociology and anthropology (Stirrat 1984). However, the claim that the concept of the sacred is a cultural universal does not look sustainable. There appear to be some cultures that make no use of it (Goody 1961). We will return to the concept of "the sacred" in Chapter 6, because, as we will see, it plays a crucial role in many justifications of religious violence. However, because it does not appear to be a cultural universal, it should not appear in the definition of religion.

Taking into account the various amendments to Durkheim's definition of religion that we need to make, to address the above issues, we arrive at the following definition, which coheres with the best evidence we have about religion:

> a religion is a collection of beliefs, always including beliefs in supernatural agents, and practices, always including ritualistic practices, that a community have in common and which help to shape the morality of that community.

One influential line of criticism of available definitions of religion, which has been forcefully made by Cavanaugh (2009), is that they do not succeed in capturing the many different ways in which the term religion has been used at different times and across different cultures. The definition provided here is different from many other definitions of religion on offer because it is not intended to reflect the many different ways in which the term "religion" has been used, at different times and in different places. Instead, it is directed at cohering with our best evidence about religiosity. As the term "religion" has often been used without proper regard to evidence about religiosity, it is only to be expected that this definition will not be compatible with many such previous uses. The definition's relationship to other definitions of religion is equivalent to the relationship between the dihydrogen oxide definition of water and earlier definitions of water. According to the dihydrogen oxide definition of water, water is the liquid form of a molecule composed of two hydrogen atoms bonded to one oxygen atom (H_2O). This definition is a modern Western one and was not endorsed by Westerners before the late eighteenth century (and the rise of Daltonian atomic theory) or by people from non-Western cultures (Needham 2002). It would not be a good objection to proponents of the dihydrogen oxide definition of water to point out that the term "water" has been used in very different ways at different times and in different places. Regardless of how exactly the term was used in different times and at different places, there was a phenomenon, which was present in all of these times and places, that earlier uses of the term "water" more-or-less managed to refer to, and which we now believe to be the liquid form of dihydrogen oxide. The dihydrogen oxide definition of water has replaced these other definitions because it coheres with the available evidence about water that we have better than competing definitions of water.

I doubt that Cavanaugh would be satisfied with my response to his line of criticism. He asserts that "It is a mistake to treat religion as a constant in human culture across time and space" (2009, p. 61); and he takes it that he has shown that "there is no transhistorical and transcultural essence of religion" (2009, p. 59). But what Cavanaugh has actually shown is that the term "religion" has been used in different ways at different times and in different places. Available evidence suggests that there is a phenomenon, described by my definition, which is found in all cultures, and which has been present in all of these for tens of thousands of years. Not all previous uses of the term "religion" have picked out instances of this phenomenon. On some occasions the term "religion" has also been used to refer to phenomena that only partially resemble, or are only loosely related, to the phenomenon that I have defined as "religion."

Notes

1. Exline et al. do not insist that the experience of such negative feelings is always bad for us. They suggest that experiences of "Godly sorrow" can sometimes lead to "spiritual maturity" (2000, pp. 1493–4).

2. Or consider the Navajo origin myth: the winds (who are holy people) dried the earth and created a sweat house. First Man entered the sweat house and unwrapped a medicine bundle that he had taken from the underworld. The medicine bundle contained precious stones, which First Man used to create key features of the world (Bellah 2011, p. 167). Again, at least as many questions are raised as are answered by this origin myth. What is the origin of the winds? What motivated the winds to dry the earth and create a sweat house? What is the origin of First Man? Why did First Man leave the underworld and enter the sweat house; and why did he create the features of the world that were created, rather than some different set of features?

3. I haven't mentioned Confucianism here, which is often categorized as an ethical system rather than a religion. It is worth noting that ancestor worship among Confucians is very widespread, along with the concomitant belief that ancestors can survive death and become supernatural beings that influence worldly affairs (Rainey 2010, p. 4).

4. The example is from Barrett (2009, p. 78).

5. It is possible that an innate disposition to acquire "folk physics" assists us in forming some implicit generalizations about the world and makes us less likely to acquire others.

6. Experimental evidence in favor of the high rate of transmission of minimally counterintuitive representations is provided by Boyer and Ramble (2001) and Barrett and Nyhof (2001).

7. Sometimes the acronym is said to stand for *Hyperactive* Agency Detection Device.

8. From Barrett's unpublished thesis. Cited by Boyer (2001, p. 102).

9. Rowers in crews, who Cohen et al. (2010) studied, experienced double the size endorphin surges that solo rowers received.

10. To benefit from membership of a community without making an appropriate contribution to the welfare of that community is to "free-ride" on that community. There are many contexts in which a collective action, undertaken by members of a community, can end up being less effective than it might otherwise be if some individuals enjoy the benefits of that collective action but do not contribute to it. For further discussion, see Hardin (2003). Concerns about difficulties involved in overcoming the "free-rider problem" will come up again later in this chapter, as well as in the next.

11. However, there is some evidence to suggest that the now extinct Neanderthals conducted religious rituals (e.g., Brockway 1978).

12. Dunbar (2013) dates this transition to somewhere between 9500 and 7700 BP (BP stands for "before present," where present = 1 January, 1950).

13. A recent survey of nearly 500 small-scale societies revealed that at least 90 percent of them practiced forms of rituals that prompted some participants to enter trance states (Bourguignon 2004).

14. This is a somewhat controversial thesis. For discussion of some of the controversy surrounding the "flashbulb memory" thesis, see Whitehouse (2004, pp. 106–11).

15. For discussion of the various routes to cultural evolution, see Richerson and Boyd (2005).

16. Including Guthrie (1993), Blackmore (1999), Boyer (2001), Atran (2002), McCauley and Lawson (2002), Wilson (2002), Barrett (2004), Whitehouse (2004), Dawkins (2006), Dennett (2006), Wade (2009), Wright (2009), Teehan (2010), and Haidt (2012).

17. According to Perry, "'I kissed a girl' was born as an idea in my head. The chorus actually popped into my head when I woke up." When she repeated the chorus to her producer Dr. Luke, he insisted that they turn it into a song on her first album on the grounds that "it's so catchy because it won't get out of our heads." See BBC News, August 26, 2008, http://news.bbc.co.uk/1/hi/entertainment/7581625.stm (accessed August 18, 2011).

Religion

18. Misheard or mistranscribed song lyrics are so common that there is a term for these: "mondegreens."
19. We can also vaccinate ourselves to prevent various diseases from infecting us in the first place.
20. Boyer elaborates on the standard model, describing a large number of views that its proponents also typically endorse (2005, pp. 4–7).
21. Although he still wishes to preserve a role for memetics in shaping the details of particular religions (Dawkins 2006, p. 190).
22. Also, in a highly speculative discussion, Atran suggests connections between the evolution of autism and the urge to participate in religious rituals (Atran 2002, pp. 192–5).
23. These problems are discussed in greater length in Powell and Clarke (2012).
24. Including Fodor himself. See Fodor (2001).
25. Informational encapsulation is often also considered to be a property of mental modules. However, see Barrett and Kurzban (2006, pp. 631–2).
26. My prime example of a mental module, which advocates of the standard model appeal to, is the HADD. I do not mean to suggest that all scholars working in the cognitive science of religion who endorse the HADD hypothesis are advocates of the standard model.
27. This is also a problem for any adaptationists who happen to accept claims about relations between particular cognitive structures, such as the HADD, and religious by-products.
28. A trait that is produced by natural selection for one function but is subsequently adapted for a different function is also an exaptation.
29. Haidt (2012) and Pyysiäinen and Hauser (2010) both defend the view that religion is an exaptation.
30. Why can't advocates of the standard model simply concede that some by-products may well have been exapted, while still remaining advocates of the standard model? In part this is a terminological issue. Classically, advocates of the standard model have denied that religion has adaptive value, whereas adaptationists have never denied that some adaptations can start out as by-products, which are subsequently exapted. The concession that some adaptations may have started out as by-products is no concession at all to adaptationists. However, the concession that some by-products may well have acquired adaptive value deprives the standard model of what makes it distinct from adaptationism, so it is a major concession.
31. For information on the genes involved in the evolution of adult lactose tolerance, see Tishkoff et al. (2006) and Ingram et al. (2009).
32. Note, however, that the view that religion is a purely individual-level adaptation has been defended by a few scholars, including Richard Alexander (1987).
33. However, Dawkins disputes the common interpretation of Darwin as an advocate of group selection (2006, pp. 171–2).

34. Surowiecki (2011, p. 38) suggests that the recent financial crisis in Greece may be substantially explained by a failure of the Greek state to prevent free-riding tax evaders.

35. Dawkins (1976) argues similarly.

36. Participation in "imagistic rituals" seems to cause much longer term increases in feeling of group solidarity than the listed examples (Whitehouse 2000, 2004).

37. According to Haidt (2012, pp. 233–4), the hormone and neurotransmitter oxytocin is highly likely to be the key component of this functional system. While other studies have appeared to demonstrate that oxytocin straight-forwardly increases trust in others, Haidt draws on recent work by De Dreu et al. (2010), which suggests that oxytocin promotes positive sentiments towards in-group members, as well as negative sentiments towards out-group members.

38. Haidt (2012, p. 236), drawing on recent work by Singer et al. (2006), speculates that mirror neurons may play a key role in the brain neurophysiology of our conditional groupishness.

39. These include Superman, Spiderman, the Goose that Laid the Golden Eggs, and Santa Claus. Santa Claus has a historic connection to Christianity. However, he is not an official figure in any variant of Christianity and the Santa Clause myth, which has pagan origins, has survived by virtue of a parasitic relationship with Christian culture.

40. The action of seeking divine approval is suggestive of a concern for morality. Dennett may perhaps be assuming that divine approval is typically sought when people behave in ways that are consistent with the demands of morality.

41. It is a "famous definition" according to Jack Goody (1961, p. 144). It has recently been endorsed by Jon Haidt (2012, p. 248).

42. He discusses the case of Buddhists who treat the Buddha as a god, and Jains who worship a creator god, or *Jinapati* (Durkheim 1912, pp. 32–4).

43. This use of term "sacred" remains current in sociology (Nisbet 1993, p. 6).

3

Morality

Introduction

The subject of this chapter is morality. I consider the evolutionary origins of human morality, as well as the role that culture plays in shaping morality, with a particular focus on Jonathan Haidt's "moral foundations" theory. Recent work on the neuroscience of moral cognition, conducted by Joshua Greene and his collaborators, is also considered.[1] Greene's approach to understanding moral cognition is relevant to discussion of the sacred and the role it plays in justifying violence (see Chapter 6). I then examine recent work in moral psychology, especially Haidt's account of moral judgment (2001; 2012). In the final section of the chapter the relationship between religion and morality is discussed.

Although this chapter is about morality, I will not address questions of philosophical ethics, properly understood. Philosophical ethics is a normative rather than a descriptive discipline. It aims, among other things, to determine what the right things to do are, regardless of whether or not people generally believe that these are the right things to do. The question of whether we consider particular practices to be morally acceptable, or unacceptable, is logically distinct from the question of whether or not the practices that we regard as morally acceptable (and unacceptable) really are morally acceptable (and unacceptable). Questions about the true nature of morality, questions about the proper interpretation of moral truth claims, and questions about how one might go about finding out about the true nature of morality, and how one might go about determining the most appropriate way to interpret moral truth claims, are other questions that are

The Justification of Religious Violence, First Edition. Steve Clarke.
© 2014 John Wiley & Sons, Inc. Published 2014 by John Wiley & Sons, Inc.

investigated in philosophical ethics. They are all going to be side-stepped here, as the focus of this book is on trying to understand some actual moral judgments that people make.

Evolved Morality

The case for thinking that morality has evolved mirrors the case for thinking that religion has evolved, which was discussed in the previous chapter. Like religion, morality is ubiquitous. There is no known human society, either today, or at any time in recorded history, whose members have not exhibited at least some forms of moral behavior. Also paralleling the case of religion, there are underlying similarities in the patterns of moral behavior exhibited across different human societies. Members of all known human societies distinguish morally right actions from wrong ones (Brown 1991), express moral sentiments (Brown 1991), endorse moral norms, which they distinguish from merely conventional norms (Turiel 1983), and make moral judgments (Joyce 2006). And, like religion, morality is costly for individuals. The energies that individuals devote to moral cognition could be employed in other ways that would be more obviously fitness-enhancing. Also, adherence to moral codes of behavior often involves forgoing opportunities to acquire resources, and sometimes involves forgoing opportunities to reproduce.[2] It is extremely unlikely that evolution would tolerate a significant waste of energies and opportunities in the long run, especially if this wastefulness could be avoided. It is much more plausible to think that, despite appearances, morality is not wasteful from the evolutionary point of view, and is in fact a result of our evolutionary history.

As we have seen, the currently dominant account of the evolution of religion has it that religion is an evolutionary by-product. While it might be argued that human morality is an evolutionary by-product, or even an evolutionary accident (Machery and Mallon 2010, p. 22), the dominant view, amongst those who argue that morality has evolved, is that morality is an evolutionary adaptation (e.g., Joyce 2006; Haidt 2012; Boehm 2012). Humans have evolved to live in communities in which individual behavior is guided by moral considerations, and the basic evolutionary benefit conferred on individuals living in these "moral communities" seems clear enough. If I am a member of a well-functioning moral community, then other members of my community will be disposed to help me when I need help, and will be disposed to avoid harming me. The support of community members, who will help me when I need help and who avoid harming me, enables me to survive and to reproduce much more easily than would be possible otherwise. It also enables me to benefit from access to collective goods that can only be created by cooperating communities.

Other members of my community might perhaps sometimes help me without intending to do so, but if they are going to help me persistently, then this is presumably because they care about my welfare, as well as the welfare of others. It is because they have evolved altruistic attitudes and sentiments towards members of their own communities (and perhaps also members of other communities).[3] Without such attitudes and sentiments there would be little or no human moral behavior. The existence of altruistic attitudes and sentiments presents us with an evolutionary puzzle. If people act on these, and devote time and resources to helping others, then they do not use that time and those resources to further their own ends. It looks like they thereby fail to maximize their own evolutionary fitness. The theory of natural selection – a key component of the theory of evolution – is premised on the assumption that there are variations between different members of the same species, some of which are inherited, as well as the assumption that it is the members of a given species whose variations best adapt them to their surroundings ("the fittest") that are the members of that species most likely to survive and proliferate (Rosenberg 1985, p. 123).

The puzzle we are presented with is to explain how altruism could be adaptive when it seems to be the sort of trait that detracts from individuals' ability to maximize their own evolutionary fitness. It might perhaps be supposed that the solution to this puzzle lies in pointing out that in a moral community, in which people are disposed to help one another, the benefits I receive from the help of others will typically outweigh the costs of my helping others, so it is in my interests to continue to participate in a moral community, all things considered. But this is only an apparent solution, because it fails to address the free-rider problem, which came up in the previous chapter. Even if I am better off participating in a moral community than not participating, the best thing for me to do, from a strictly self-interested point of view, is to accept the help of others while failing to provide help to others – to free-ride on their altruistic efforts. Free-riders get to use their own time and resources to maximize their evolutionary fitness and they also benefit from the time and resources devoted to their ends by others. So, how could altruism have evolved, when it appears that the behavior of rational self-interested free-riders would have outcompeted altruistic behavior and would have undermined any moral communities that might have started to develop?

A complete answer to the above question will need to draw on several sources, all of which provide us with reason to think that individual inclinations to free-ride will be suppressed, at least under some circumstances. One such source is kin selection (Hamilton 1964). By helping those who are our kin we are partially advancing our own evolutionary interests. On average I share 50 percent of my genetic material with a sibling, 25 percent with a nephew or niece and 12.5 percent with a first cousin. By helping these kin I advance my own evolutionary interests, in proportion to the extent to which they share my genetic material.[4] In small tribal communities, in which the majority of people are partially related to one another, kin selection can do much to explain why it will often not be in my evolutionary interest to free-ride on the efforts of other members of my community. Kin selection may be invoked to explain some helping behavior towards non-kin too. If my means of distinguishing kin from non-kin is limited, and in small tribal communities this may often be the case, then the best way to ensure that I help kin may well be to help all of the people with whom I frequently interact (Joyce 2006, p. 21). Of course kin selection does not promote helping behavior towards strangers, whom I have no reason to regard as my kin.

A second source is reciprocal altruism (Trivers 1971). If I act to help you when you need help, on the understanding that you will help me in return, when I need help, and you actually do help me in return, then my helping behavior can indirectly result in benefits to me. There is a danger that you may fail to help me when I need help and free-ride on my helping behavior. But there are at least some circumstances in which it will not be in your interest to free-ride. If you and I are going to have the opportunity to help one another on multiple occasions in the future and you know that I will withhold my help in the future if you fail to reciprocate, then it may not be in your long-term interest to free-ride on my helping behavior. Indirect evidence that this logic of "reciprocal altruism" may have played a role in the evolution of human altruism is provided by the occurrence of patterns of reciprocally altruistic behavior in many other species (Teehan 2010, p. 25).[5] One striking example of such behavior is found in interactions between small "cleaner fish" and larger species of fish. Larger fish allow the smaller cleaner fish to come very close to them and eat (and thereby remove) parasites attached to their bodies, sometimes even allowing the cleaner fish to enter their open mouths. The larger fish could easily attack and try to eat the cleaner fish during, or at the conclusion of, the cleaning process. However, they invariably seem to forgo the possible short-term payoff of a nutritious meal in the expectation that they will have parasites removed from their bodies by the cleaner fish on future occasions (Trivers 1971).

A third source is "indirect reciprocity" (Alexander 1987). If I complete a cooperative venture with a member of my community, I indirectly advertise my propensity to cooperate with other members of my community. I enhance my reputation as a good cooperator and consequently I am more likely to be sought out by others for cooperative ventures in the future. Conversely, if I enter into a cooperative arrangement with someone and fail to cooperate, and instead "defect," or free-ride on their efforts, then I damage my reputation, advertising to others that I am not someone who can be trusted to cooperate. As a result I will be less likely to be sought out by others for future cooperative ventures. An indirect benefit of cooperation is the increased social status that comes from building up a good reputation as a reliable completer of cooperative ventures. The thinking of others is tilted in favor of high-status individuals. High-status individuals are in a position to do more damage to the reputations of defectors than are members of the community of a lesser status, and so the potential costs of defecting on a high-status individual are greater than they would be when one is involved in a cooperative venture with a lesser-status individual.

A fourth source is group selection, which was discussed in the previous chapter. Just as religion may be a group-level adaptation, the same may well be true of morality (Sober and Wilson 1998; Haidt 2012). It seems plausible to think that societies whose altruistic members acted to advance one another's interests would have outcompeted societies whose members were less altruistic and therefore less cooperative. More cooperative hunter-gatherer societies would, all things being equal, have been better at acquiring food and other resources and would, therefore, have enabled their members to reproduce more frequently than members of less cooperative hunter-gatherer societies (Haidt 2012, pp. 217–18). More cooperative hunter-gatherer societies can also be expected to have outcompeted less cooperative ones militarily, coordinating activities to kill or enslave members of nearby societies, as well as damaging infrastructure. It may seem counterintuitive to think of human cooperation – and by implication morality – as being advanced by military activity. However, the idea is not inconsistent with much of what we know about early human life. The majority of hunter-gatherer societies seem to have devoted considerable energy to forming raiding parties to attack rival societies, sometimes killing members of those societies, sometimes enslaving them. Incessant low-level warfare between well-coordinated war parties from rival tribal groups seems to have been the norm amongst pre-state human societies (Keeley 1996).[6]

Group-level processes can only operate effectively if individual free-riding is sufficiently restricted. Free-riding is extremely well suppressed amongst the various eusocial insects, which include some species of ants, bees, and wasps.[7] These are species in which reproduction is usually the preserve of a small number of fertile "queens," with the vast majority of female "worker" insects forgoing opportunities to reproduce. Some (but not all) eusocial insect species have actually evolved to a state where their workers are sterile. This counterintuitive arrangement can make evolutionary sense in species of hymenoptera, such as ants. In such species, female sibling workers ants have a very high degree of genetic relatedness to one another, so by advancing their mother queen's reproductive interests, worker insects can propagate their own genes very effectively.[8] Eusocial insect species have been known to create highly complex, cooperating communities that can include vast numbers of individual members. Ant colonies have been found that have up to 20 million ants living in them (Beckers et al. 1989).

Human communities are not usually as successful at suppressing free-riding as eusocial insect communities. Humans have altruistic motives, but they also have selfish motives, and the temptation to disregard altruistic motives and act on competing selfish motives is a constant of human life. A disposition to behave altruistically evolved, in human communities, in part because free-riding was restricted to a sufficient degree to enable moral communities to flourish. An adaptation that also seems to have been important in suppressing free-riding, and thereby ensuring the flourishing of moral communities, was the development of a capacity to recognize, abide by, and enforce moral norms.[9]

All human societies, both now and throughout recorded history have accepted norms or rules of proper conduct, which are applied, sometimes explicitly, sometimes implicitly, to regulate communal behavior (Machery and Mallon 2010, p. 13). These are typically rules that everyone is expected to abide by. Some norms are pragmatic (e.g., "always put the milk back in the refrigerator after you have used it, otherwise it will go off"), some are aesthetic (e.g., "avoid overusing fake tan"), and some are matters of convention (e.g., "set the table with the fork on the left of the plate and the knife on the right"). A class of norms that is particularly relevant to our investigation is the class of moral norms. Many moral norms are ones that seem designed to enhance cooperation and prevent free-riding. Common examples include "do not lie," "do not steal," "repay debts on time," and "keep promises." All societies appear to have such norms and all appear to enforce them in some or other ways. Some moral norms (such as prohibitions against stealing and failing to repay debts) are enshrined in law in typical modern societies and enforced by the police and the legal system. Other moral norms are not enshrined in law. Compliance with these is usually enforced by expressions of social disapproval, and by the threat of social sanctions. Persistent failure to adhere to moral norms can lead to a variety of social sanctions, including temporary or permanent exclusion from one's community (Posner and Rasmusen 1999).

Many of our emotions appear to be structured in such a way as to encourage compliance with moral norms. People are inclined to feel and express a variety of negative emotions in response to violations of moral norms, including anger, disgust, and contempt. Expressions of such emotions have the effect of regulating the behavior of other people, as most people do not wish to be the targets of the anger, disgust, and contempt of others.[10] People are also inclined to feel shame or guilt when they knowingly violate norms; and most of us are strongly motivated to avoid experiencing feelings of shame and guilt. According to Robert Frank, there is an underlying logic that may explain the evolution of shame and guilt, which is that these emotions function as a form of assurance of commitment. If you promise that you will do something for me later, if I do something for you now, I will want reason to believe that your promise is credible before agreeing to the arrangement. One reason I might have to think that you will keep your promise is a conditional one: if you are psychologically normal, then you will experience discomforting sensations of shame or guilt if you do not keep your promise. The prospect of experiencing such discomforting sensations is a deterrent to promise-breaking (Frank 1988).[11] So, as well as being enforced from without, by formal and informal punishments and by the emotional responses of others, moral norms are enforced from within, by our own emotions. These considerations, together with the observation that normative reasoning is universal, across cultures and throughout recorded human history, support the conclusion that our abilities to comprehend norms, be motivated by norms, and judge whether or not norms are being complied with, are a suite of evolutionary adaptations (Machery and Mallon 2010, pp. 13–16).

Our moral reasoning is not exhausted by the ability to apply norms. There are circumstances that we may find ourselves in, in which we need to make moral decisions that cannot be made simply by applying moral norms. One such set of circumstances occurs when we find that two of our moral norms are in conflict with one another, and when we lack clear rules telling us which norm is the more important to adhere to. Suppose that I have promised to lend you money at the same time that I am due to make a repayment on a loan. If my financial circumstances suddenly and unexpectedly change then I may be unable to both keep the promise and make the repayment. I will have to either violate the norm that I should always keep my promises, or violate the norm that I should always repay my debts on time; but it is not clear which norm I should violate and I will need to exercise judgment in order to decide what to do. When humans develop new ways of living, as a result of developing new technologies, their lives often acquire aspects that are not clearly governed by well-established norms. Do the same norms regarding privacy, consent, and respect for autonomy that we generally apply in public places also apply on the Internet? The answer to this question is unclear, because strong, stable norms regulating behavior in this relatively new domain of human interaction have yet to be established (Clarke 2010). Again judgment is required to guide action.

Another context in which we may need to exercise judgment in moral decision making is when we are considering whether or not to disregard a norm. We sometimes disregard moral norms for selfish reasons, but we can also do so for moral reasons. Our sense of sympathy for someone who violates a moral norm, when their circumstances make it particularly hard for them to adhere to that moral norm, may lead us to decide not to enforce that norm on particular occasions. People who accept a proscription against the intentional killing of others can be willing to allow an exception, when others are in intense pain, for example (e.g., Angell 1982). Whether we should or should not override moral norms on moral grounds, on a given occasion, is a matter of judgment. It may be that when making such judgments, we rely on a general capacity for rational judgment, or it may be that our capacity to make moral judgments is a distinct evolutionary adaptation.[12]

Morality, Evolution, and Culture

Although all human societies are moral societies, the actual practices that are considered to be morally acceptable, or unacceptable, in different societies and at different times, vary significantly. Institutionalized slavery is considered to be obviously immoral in most, if not all contemporary societies, and indeed, the Universal Declaration of Human Rights, which was adopted by the United Nations General Assembly in 1948, prohibits all forms of slavery. However, institutionalized slavery has been practiced in many different societies, at many different times, and has often attained widespread acceptance (Drescher 2009). In the USA, institutionalized slavery was practiced well into the nineteenth century, only ending at the conclusion of the US Civil War (1861–1865). In China it was not abolished until the early twentieth century, and in Saudi Arabia it persisted until the 1960s. Slavery was condemned by many in these countries well before it was abolished; but one can also find many people arguing that particular forms of institutionalized slavery are consistent with the demands of morality.

The former Vice-President of the United States of America (1825–1832), John C. Calhoun, was a noted defender of slavery, repeatedly arguing in its defense in the US Senate. In his words, it is "folly and delusion" to regard slavery as a moral evil. Not only is slavery not immoral, according to him it is actually a cause of much good, as it is " … the most safe and stable basis for free institutions in the world."[13] Debates about the morality of this or that practice have also played out in recent times and some of these debates have led to dramatic shifts in received opinion about what is and is not considered morally acceptable. In the mid-twentieth century, consensual homosexual acts were considered to be patently immoral by all but a very small minority of people in most Western countries. Half a century later we find the situation reversed, at least among educated Western populations, who increasingly consider it to be glaringly obvious that there is nothing immoral about homosexual acts between consenting adults.[14]

What is considered moral and immoral can vary greatly at different times and places, but the range of variation is not infinite, because societies that endorse some particular moral codes do so at the expense of their own long-term survival. One claim sometimes made about slavery is that it is an economically inefficient system, in part because slaves lack a strong interest in ensuring productivity (e.g., Genovese 1967). If this is so, then slave societies will be outcompeted by more efficient non-slave societies over the long-term – at least when slave societies face competition from more efficient non-slave societies. In part, this may be why institutional slavery is no longer with us. Also no longer with us is the practice of institutionalized human sacrifice which, as we saw in Chapter 1, was employed on a mass scale in the Aztec empire of the fifteenth to sixteenth centuries. Not only was this practice incredibly wasteful, it also undermined a sense of allegiance to Aztec society amongst the many Aztecs who considered themselves to be potential sacrificial victims. It also alienated nearby tributary states that were required to provide regular sacrificial victims. When Cortés and less than one thousand Spanish conquistadors allied themselves with some nearby tributary states, as well as some minor states that had hostile relations with the Aztecs, his forces destroyed the very large and apparently very powerful Aztec empire, with surprisingly little effort (White 1996; Levy 2009).

It is not clear exactly where the limits to the moral beliefs and practices that a society can maintain over the long term are, but it is clear that there are such limits. Human societies face the challenge of ensuring that their own members cooperate with one another, as well as the challenge of seeing off competition from rival societies. A society that failed to significantly restrict free-riding by its members would soon fall apart, if it were not destroyed by rival societies first. There is no known case of a human society succeeding in significantly restricting free-riding amongst its members without upholding moral norms that serve to prevent free-riding. Moral practices may vary in many ways in particular societies, over the course of time, but if they start to vary in ways that significantly undermine the functioning of those societies, then those practices will not survive in the long run, because those societies will not survive in the long run.

I have related the evolution of morality to the challenge of overcoming the free-rider problem, as have several other authors (e.g. Joyce 2006; Teehan 2010). But, although it is necessary to overcome the free-rider problem for a society to continue to function, there is clearly more to the evolution of morality than just overcoming this problem. Haidt (2012, pp. 125, 172–3) relates the evolution of morality to the overcoming of six "adaptive challenges." As well as needing to overcome what he calls the challenge of "forming partnerships with non-kin to reap the benefits of reciprocity" and the challenge of "forming coalitions to compete with other coalitions" (both of which required us to overcome the free-rider problem), we have needed, according to Haidt, to overcome the challenges of "caring for vulnerable children," "keeping oneself and one's kin free from parasites and pathogens," "negotiating status hierarchies" (p. 125), and "living in small groups with individuals who would, if given the chance, dominate, bully, and constrain others" (p. 172). As Haidt acknowledges, these last two challenges are in tension with one another. We are prepared to accept some forms of authority as legitimate, but are usually also inclined to monitor the behavior of our chosen leaders, remaining wary of the propensity of leaders to become tyrants if they are given the opportunity to do so.

Haidt suggests that we have evolved six "cognitive modules" that enable us to address the six aforementioned adaptive challenges (2012, p. 123). He further suggests that these modules are the cognitive bases for six "moral foundations" that are present in all cultures, but which make contributions of varying importance to the overall morality of different cultures (p. 124). These six moral foundations are at the heart of his "moral foundations theory" of the cultural variability of morality, and they correspond to the six adaptive challenges mentioned above. They are the "fairness/cheating" foundation, the "loyalty/betrayal" foundation, the "care/harm" foundation, the "sanctity/degradation" foundation, the "authority/subversion" foundation, and the "liberty/oppression" foundation. Each foundation is associated with characteristic emotions and these are liable to be triggered in ways that are sometimes only loosely connected to the original target of evolutionary adaptation. For example, according to Haidt, the moral emotion of compassion evolved – as a component of the care/harm foundation – to ensure that parents and other carers were acutely sensitive to the needs of the children in their care (2012, pp. 131–4). However, compassion can be triggered by stimuli that bear only a loose relation of similarity to human children, including infant members of other species and cute cartoon characters. Exactly what we respond compassionately to, and how compassionate we are disposed to be, in particular contexts, varies considerably across cultures.

To try to capture the relationship between nature and culture in generating morality, Haidt endorses an analogy, which he credits to Gary Marcus (2004): "The brain is like a book, the first draft of which is written by the genes during fetal development," with culture and individual experience filling in the details (Haidt 2012, p. 130). Haidt (2012) appears to have done a good job of capturing both the range of subjects considered to be components of morality across cultures, and also of accounting for the capacity of culture to shape morality. But there is reason to hesitate before endorsing Haidt's (2012) account of the generation of morality. Haidt does not appear to have provided sufficient evidence to demonstrate that the particular cognitive modules that he postulates actually exist.[15] There might of course be evolved moral modules in the human mind, as Haidt suggests, but it could also turn out that much human moral cognition is generated by central processing, rather than by the activity of discrete modules.[16] Nature may have provided us with a first draft of our morality as Haidt (2012), following Marcus (2004), suggests, but it may well have been a very rough first draft with much left for culture and individual experience to fill in.[17]

The sanctity/degradation foundation, which is related to the emotion of disgust, is of particular relevance to us because, according to Haidt (2012), it has a close connection to religion. Early human societies faced the challenge of avoiding pathogens and parasites, many of which were not visible. Having an evolved disgust response to common sources of pathogens and parasites, including rotten food, diseased people, carcasses, feces and other waste products, helped our ancestors avoid pathogens and parasites and was a crucial step in our evolutionary history. It seems that the disgust response is a component of a flexible emotional system that is highly responsive to cultural influences; influences that can cause people to find particular activities and objects disgusting, which they would not find disgusting otherwise (Kelly 2011).

Conservatives who consider homosexual activity to be morally objectionable do not merely think of homosexual activity as immoral; they often also experience the sensation of disgust at the thought – not to mention the sight – of homosexual activity (Gervais and Norenzayan 2013). Such reactions can vary over time, often reducing in intensity in response to repeated exposure to a source of disgust (Clarke and Roache 2012). The well-known conservative bioethicist, Leon Kass, reports experiencing disgust at the sight of people eating in public. He is especially disgusted by the sight of people licking ice cream in public (1994, pp. 148–9). Kass, who was born in 1939, grew up in a conservative society in which well-bred people tried hard not to be seen eating in public spaces and were particularly careful to not be seen licking ice cream in public places. These days it is very common to see people walking down the street eating snacks (including ice cream). For most people of Kass's generation, the disgust response that they might well have experienced fifty years ago, at the sight of others eating in public spaces, has faded into insignificance, or has completely disappeared. Younger people who have grown up used to seeing people eating in public, experience no equivalent disgust reaction at all, unless perhaps a person seen eating in public is doing so in a particularly messy way.

Religious organizations are often good at organizing and promoting moral rules associated with sanctity and the avoidance of degradation, and they are often also concerned to enforce these rules. Many religions have developed elaborate rules of conduct governing the handling and consumption of food, the cleaning and clothing of the body, participation in sexual activity, and the proper treatment of the sick and the dead (Graham and Haidt 2010, p. 144). The Hebrew Bible, one of the sources of modern Western morality, stipulates a great many rules regarding sexual conduct, hygiene, menstruation, the handling of corpses and so on (Haidt 2012, p. 13). In modern Western cultures people are often ignorant of many of these rules, or treat adherence to them as optional, or sometimes deliberately flout them. However, in many non-Western societies an attitude of respect for, and adherence to, the religiously prescribed rules of their own tradition is typical, and there is often a high social cost associated with failing to adhere to such rules. One way in which religions are particularly effective in enforcing moral rules is by relating these to the concept of the sacred (Haidt 2012, p. 149). If particular behavior is judged by religious authorities to violate sacred prohibitions, then followers of a religion who recognize these authorities as legitimate will consider such behavior to be unacceptable, regardless of attempts to justify it. As we will see in Chapters 6 and 7, the concept of the sacred plays a key role in many religious justifications of violence.

Consequentialism, Deontology, and the Neuroscience of Moral Cognition

Our evolved disposition to behave altruistically towards others and our evolved disposition to uphold moral norms come into tension with one another in situations where adherence to moral norms would lead us to act in ways that harm, rather than help, others. This tension is mirrored in the tension between the two most influential families of theories in philosophical ethics: consequentialist theories and deontological theories. Consequentialist theories, which have been championed by Bentham (1789), Sidgwick (1907), Singer (1993), and Parfit (2011), tell us that what really matters, morally, is the overall consequences of our actions; and these are usually assessed by consequentialists in terms of the total welfare of all people. By the lights of typical consequentialist theories, it can be justifiable to harm others, if doing so leads to increases in total welfare in the long run. Deontological theories of morality have been championed by Kant (1785), Ross (1930), Kamm (2007), and Scanlon (2008). According to these theories, adherence to rules or norms, rather than consideration of consequences, is the most important component of morality and an increase in total welfare is not in itself sufficient grounds to justify the violation of established moral norms.[18]

The dispute between consequentialists and deontologists in philosophical ethics has been going on for so long that it can seem intractable. Recent work on the neuroscience of moral cognition, by Joshua Greene and collaborators, may help explain this apparent intractability. Greene's view is that our brain contains two "warring subsystems" which both contribute to moral cognition.[19] Moral philosophers may be rigorous consequentialists and rigorous deontologists, but, according to Greene, most people reason like consequentialists under some circumstances and like deontologists under others. This is because their moral cognition results from an ongoing struggle between an "inner consequentialist" and an "inner deontologist." Under some circumstances the inner consequentialist tends to prevail, but under other circumstances the inner deontologist usually comes out on top. To see why Greene holds this view we need to consider key instances of a series of thought experiments known as "trolley problems" or "trolley dilemmas." These thought experiments were first discussed by philosophers (Foot 1967; Thomson 1976) in order to try to elicit intuitions – the immediate responses we have, when thinking about a subject; or how things seem to us in advance of reflection[20] – about a series of possible scenarios that raise moral dilemmas. Trolley problems are now widely used as a basis for empirical studies of moral cognition by psychologists and neuroscientists.[21] Two key trolley problems are the "basic trolley dilemma" and the "footbridge dilemma":

1. **Basic trolley dilemma**   Suppose that you are standing by the side of a railway track and you see a runaway railway trolley careering down the track. Further down the track are five railway workers. If the trolley continues along the track it will hit them at speed and kill all five.[22] However, as luck would have it, you are standing next to a switch, which you can operate to divert the trolley down a side track. One railway worker is on the side track and will die if the trolley is diverted. Should you operate the switch, preventing the deaths of the five workers, but causing the death of one, or should you refrain from interfering and allow the five to die, but spare the life of the one worker on the side track?

2. **Footbridge dilemma**   As in the basic trolley dilemma, a runaway trolley is speeding down the track and is set to kill five workers. This time, however, you are standing on a footbridge overlooking the track. Immediately in front of you, and also standing on the footbridge, is an unusually large man. He is so large, indeed, that his body would be a sufficient impediment to stop the runaway trolley. If you push him off the footbridge and onto the track at the right moment, you will

prevent the deaths of the five workers, but your action will result in his death. Should you push the unusually large man off the footbridge, preventing the deaths of five workers, but causing his death, or should you refrain from interfering, spare his life, and allow the five to die?

The two dilemmas are very similar in structure. In each case we have an opportunity to save five lives, but if we take the opportunity to save those lives, we will cause the death of one person. It might be supposed that our moral judgments about both of these dilemmas would be consistent. If we have consequentialist inclinations, then in both cases we would judge that we should kill one to save five. And, if we have deontological inclinations, then in both cases we would judge that, because interference involves killing, we should not interfere in either case and should allow each group of five to die. However, most people's reported judgments have the appearance of inconsistency. Most people report that it is morally permissible to kill one to save five in the basic trolley dilemma, but impermissible to do so in the footbridge dilemma (Petrovich, O'Neill, and Jorgensen 1993). Can we justify, or even explain, this apparent inconsistency in ordinary moral reasoning?

One influential line of thought is that the apparent inconsistency can be justified, and also explained, by invoking the traditional deontological distinction between treating someone as a means and as treating them as an ends; and asserting, along with Kant (1785), that it is always impermissible to use someone only as a means to further the ends of others. In the basic trolley dilemma we foresee the death of the lone workman on the side track, but we do not intend his death as a means to save the five, so, arguably, we are not using him as a means. The five are saved regardless of whether or not the lone worker is on the side track. But, in the footbridge case, we clearly are using the unusually large man as a means to save the five. However, ordinary moral judgment does not appear to track this distinction, as is demonstrated by a variation on the basic trolley dilemma known as the "loop case." If the side track in the basic trolley dilemma loops back and re-joins the main track before the point where the five workers are located, then operating the switch and directing the runaway trolley down the side track can prevent the death of the five if the weight of the body of the lone worker on the side track is sufficient to stop the trolley before it reaches the five workers. When asked to consider the loop case, with the stipulation that the worker on the side track is unusually large and of sufficient weight to stop the trolley, most people report that it is permissible to switch the trolley onto the looping side track, even though the unusually large, lone worker is now being used as a means to save the five (Greene 2008a, p. 42).

Greene et al. (2001) offered a purely descriptive (rather than justificatory) explanation of these inconsistencies, which is that we have an evolved aversion to causing "up close and personal" harms to others (Greene 2008a, p 43). In the footbridge dilemma we are invited to physically push the unusually large man to his death, whereas in the basic trolley dilemma and the loop case we are invited to cause the death of the lone workman in an impersonal manner, by operating a switch some distance from him. However, Greene has since backed away from this hypothesis (2008b, p. 107). Studies of people's reactions to variations on the footbridge dilemma suggest that it is not entirely successful at explaining the apparent inconsistency in people's moral responses between the two key trolley dilemmas. Greene's more recent view is that ordinary reactions to the footbridge dilemma, and the variations on it, are best explained (but not justified) by integrating considerations of using people as a means with considerations about the use of "up close and personal" force (Greene et al. 2009; Cushman and Greene 2012).

Greene (2008a, pp. 42–3) is skeptical about the possibility of a justification being found for inconsistencies between ordinary responses to the basic trolley case and the footbridge case. But, regardless of whether or not we can find a justificatory resolution to the apparent inconsistency between ordinary responses to the basic trolley dilemma and the footbridge dilemma, there remains a question about why ordinary cognition leads us to experience some moral decisions as having the structure of a dilemma that requires resolution (Cushman and Greene 2012).[23] Greene's warring subsystems account is intended to explain this phenomenon. On this account we have an "inner consequentialist" and an "inner deontologist" and both produce recommendations to guide our actions in circumstances that elicit moral cognition. In many such circumstances they produce the same recommendations, but in some circumstances, such as the trolley dilemma cases, they produce conflicting recommendations, together with the sensation that one is experiencing a dilemma.[24]

The main evidence that Greene presents for his warring subsystems account of moral cognition is the results of functional magnetic resonance imaging (fMRI) studies that he and his collaborators have conducted. They interpret these as showing variations in patterns of neural activity when different thought experiments are contemplated.[25] fMRI studies of cognition in the basic trolley dilemma suggest that the parts of the brain associated with cool, deliberative reasoning are highly active when this dilemma is contemplated.[26] Parts of the brain that are mostly inactive when people are considering the basic trolley dilemma, and which are associated with hot emotion, suddenly "light up" when people are presented with the footbridge dilemma. Greene (2008a) construes deontological judgment as being triggered by an "alarmlike" process.[27] Attempts by the inner consequentialist to coolly contemplate the overall benefits of pushing the unusually large man off the footbridge are interfered with by a sudden "jolt of emotion" as one's inner deontologist, which monitors the outputs of the inner consequentialist, immediately announces that such action is wrong and ought not to be undertaken.

Greene and his colleagues construe ordinary moral cognition as being comprised of "two warring subsystems" and it might be wondered why these subsystems are described as "warring." Couldn't we equally describe ordinary morality as being comprised of two subsystems that mostly operate in separate domains; the deontological one operating when the right combination of "up close and personal" harm and the use of people as a means is in play and the consequentialist subsystem operating at other times? Greene's answer is no. The deontological subsystem continually monitors the outputs of the consequentialist subsystem and the consequentialist subsystem does not "switch off" when the deontological subsystem is operating either.

Just as the inner deontologist overrides the inner consequentialist under some circumstances, there are other circumstances in which the inner consequentialist overrides the inner deontologist, even when a deontological jolt of emotion has been experienced. One such class of circumstances are catastrophe situations in which people typically will allow exceptions to otherwise hard and fast deontological rules.[28] This phenomenon is nicely demonstrated in an experiment by Nichols and Mallon (2006) involving a variation of the footbridge dilemma. In this variation the runaway trolley is now a train transporting a deadly artificially produced virus, and there is a bomb that has been planted on the tracks that the train is traveling on. If the train passes over the bomb, the bomb will explode and disperse the virus into the atmosphere, killing billions of people. This time a scientist, who is aware of the deadly consequences of allowing the train to continue, is standing on the footbridge and has to decide whether or not to push an unusually large man standing in front of him onto the tracks to stop the train. The scientist decides to push. When asked whether the scientist in this hypothetical scenario did something wrong, all things considered, most people revealed themselves to be less than absolute deontologists by suggesting that it is acceptable to violate the deontological prohibition against killing one to save many, if the number of the many is sufficiently large. It seems that an overwhelming consequentialist case for pushing the unusually large man off the footbridge can be sufficient to enable cool deliberative consequentialist reasoning to override the force of the deontological jolt of emotion and lead to consequentialist action. This result lends strong support to the view that the consequentialist subsystem remains active even in what looks like the "natural domain" of deontological judgment.[29]

Reasoning and Intuiting

Greene and his collaborators take a "dual-processing" approach to understanding moral cognition. On dual-processing accounts of cognition, which are very influential across a range of areas of psychology (Chaiken and Trope 1999; Kahneman and Frederick 2002), our cognitive activities fall into two basic types: effortful, deliberative, and conscious ("reason"); and automatic, intuitive, and non-conscious ("intuition"). The rise to prominence of views like Greene's marks an important shift in the recent history of moral psychology. For most of the twentieth century, moral psychology was dominated by rationalists, such as Piaget (1932) and Kohlberg (1969), who construed all moral cognition as the product of deliberate conscious reasoning. The most influential contemporary views in this sub-field of psychology take it that intuition, and the emotions that accompany intuition, are at least as important to moral cognition as reason, if not more important (Monin, Pizarro, and Beer 2007).

For Greene, deontological moral cognition is primarily intuitive and grounded in "our deepest moral emotions" (2008a, p. 63), and instances of deliberative conscious deontological reasoning are " … a kind of moral confabulation" (2008a, p. 63). We have strong, emotionally grounded moral reactions to particular circumstances, but it is not obvious to us how to make sense of these reactions. One thing that at least some of us do is to employ *post hoc* reasoning to construct justifications for our reactions, after these have occurred. The credibility of such justificatory reasoning is bought into question by the fact that – if Greene is right – it occurs after our emotionally grounded reactions have already determined what we consider to be morally acceptable and morally unacceptable. Consequentialist moral cognition is different, though, according to Greene. In his view, consequentialist moral cognition is primarily grounded in reason, not intuition (2008a, p. 64).

Jon Haidt is another prominent author who advocates a dual-processing approach to understanding moral cognition (2001, 2012) . Haidt has developed and defended the "Social Intuitionist Model" of moral judgment (2001, 2012) (the "SIM"). Whereas Greene thinks of consequentialist moral judgment as deliberative and reason-driven, for Haidt all forms of moral judgment are primarily intuitive. Haidt does not deny that deliberative conscious moral reasoning occurs, but he construes the overwhelming majority of actual instances of it as *post hoc*. According to him, the *post hoc* character of some such reasoning is revealed by studies of "moral dumbfounding" (Haidt 2012, pp. 36–44). Because many of the reasons that people provide to back up their moral judgments are not terribly well considered – as one might expect if these are indeed *post hoc* – they can be easily challenged. People who have their moral reasoning challenged often concede that the reasoning they have provided to substantiate a moral judgment is inadequate, while remaining firmly convinced that their moral judgment is correct, even though they are unable to provide any new reasons to back up that moral judgment. They end up being " … rendered speechless by their inability to explain verbally what they knew intuitively," which is to say that they end up morally dumbfounded (Haidt 2012, p. 25).[30]

Haidt and his collaborators have conducted a series of studies designed to elicit moral dumbfounding. In one of these studies, research subjects were asked to make a moral judgment about the behavior of a family who cooked and ate their recently deceased pet dog. While a substantial proportion of subjects took the view that, although this act is disgusting, it is not immoral, significantly many other subjects insisted that the family's action was morally wrong. When asked to provide reasons to justify this moral judgment these subjects usually struggled, but would sometimes suggest that the family might get sick from eating dog meat. When the research subjects who produced this line of reasoning were asked to consider a variation on the thought experiment, where it was stipulated that the dead dog was thoroughly cooked and no germs were present in the dog meat, they often continued to insist that the family's action was immoral, even though they were unable to provide additional reasons to justify their claim (Haidt et al. 2000).

For Haidt, the sort of reasoning that is shown up by instances of moral dumbfounding is just ordinary moral judgment at work, in situations where its *post hoc* character can easily be made apparent. According to him moral reasoning:

> is usually an ex post facto process used to influence the intuitions (and hence judgments) of other people. In the social intuitionist model, one feels a quick flash of revulsion at the thought of incest and one knows intuitively that something is wrong. Then, when faced with a social demand for a verbal justification, one becomes a lawyer trying to build a case rather than a judge searching for the truth. (Haidt 2001, p. 814)

Haidt allows that it is possible for reason to override moral intuition, but claims that instances of this happening are rare (2001, p. 815). His account of moral judgment raises a challenge to ordinary assumptions about the role that moral justifications play in shaping our actions. In doing so it calls into question the importance of the project pursued in this book. Justifications of violent actions are a form of moral justification. To accept a justification of a particular violent action is to judge that action to be morally acceptable, all things considered. Justifications are a matter of great moral importance if they motivate actions. However, if justifications are usually *post hoc*, then they are usually not genuinely motivating of action. Instead, they are most often a form of propaganda; elaborate rhetorical devices that people use to defend decisions, which they would have made anyway, from criticisms that others might raise. It might be interesting to see how such rhetorical devices are employed, but, if Haidt (2012) is right about the nature of morality, then a study of justifications won't tell us anything very enlightening about what actually motivates violent actions committed in the name of religion. Furthermore, it won't be of much use in enabling us to understand how to reduce religious violence. However, if Haidt's view is mistaken, or overstated, and significantly many moral judgments are driven by reason, and are not *post hoc*, then moral justifications matter. Perhaps not all of them matter, but enough of them matter enough to make a study of some of the structures of moral justification an important undertaking.

Haidt's SIM is intended to be an abstract model of the cognitive and social processes that lead to ordinary moral judgments being formed. It is not intended to capture the exact details of the causal processes underlying moral judgments. Rather, it is intended as an outline of the most important factors contributing to overall moral judgment. On Haidt's view, the immediate causes of the clear majority of our moral judgments are our moral intuitions (2001, 2012). These are the product of various social and biological sources and are usually attuned to our particular culture, as a result of the influence of expressions of other people's moral judgments, as well as expressions of their (usually *post hoc*) moral reasoning. Having formed our own moral judgments intuitively, we go into "lawyer mode" and start generating *post hoc* reasoning to use in the public sphere, in order to persuade others of the rightness of our chosen moral positions. Haidt does allow that "reasoned judgment" is possible – that some of our moral reasoning actually leads directly to moral judgment, and is not *post hoc* – but he holds that this is a rare occurrence. He also holds that reason can be used to influence our moral intuitions in "private reflection," which then affects our moral judgments indirectly. But again he considers that this happens rarely in practice.

Haidt presents various sources of evidence in favor of the view that reasoned judgment and private reflection are relatively insignificant in moral judgment (2001, pp. 819–20). However, his case for this conclusion has been challenged on several fronts. Saltzstein and Kasachkoff (2004) point out that an argument for the conclusion that reason plays a crucial role in the formation of moral judgments need not be premised on the assumption that most of our moral judgments are made deliberatively. If a moral judgment is made on one or more occasions by rational deliberation, and as a result a moral rule is endorsed, then moral judgments that involve applying that rule can be automated by the mind and used intuitively on other occasions. Most instances of moral judgment in response, say, to evidence of dishonesty, may well be instances of intuitive judgment. However, the ultimate source of our judgments about the wrongness of dishonesty is not obviously intuition. Someone could consciously deliberate about the wrongness of dishonesty and then endorse a rule to the effect that dishonesty is prima facie morally unacceptable. That rule could then be reapplied automatically, by intuition, to a host of new situations involving dishonesty.

Pizarro and Bloom (2003) point out that the SIM fails to make a place for the conscious construal of situations, which can dramatically change how we respond morally to those situations. If a university lecturer is informed that a student has unexpectedly failed to turn up to an exam for a course that she is teaching, she may well react to the news with anger and condemn the student for being irresponsible. However, if she subsequently learns that the student had a very good reason for not turning up, such as the unexpected death of a close relative, then she will rapidly reappraise the situation and her moral condemnation will probably be swiftly replaced with sympathy and a conviction that the student's absence from the exam is justified.[31]

Another challenge to Haidt is from Cordelia Fine (2006), who argues that private reflection plays a more important role in moral reasoning than Haidt recognizes. She presents evidence for the conclusion that, in addition to sometimes affecting the formation of the intuitions that give rise to moral judgments, as Haidt allows, private reflection can disrupt the processes by which intuitions become moral judgments. We may, for example, become aware that we are making intuitive moral judgments about a group of people on the basis of culturally prevalent stereotypes. However, conscious reflection about the wrongness of cultural stereotyping as a source of intuitive judgment can disrupt, and thereby prevent, the formation of future moral judgments that would otherwise be based on such stereotypes.[32]

The significance of the objections to Haidt's social intuitionism discussed above remains unclear. Until we are clearer about their significance – perhaps clarity will result from further empirical studies – it seems best to remain open-minded about the relative contributions of reason and intuition to moral judgment.[33] But suppose that new empirical studies provided evidence demonstrating that the various objections already discussed were relatively insignificant and debate in psychology was determined decisively in favor of social intuitionism. Would that outcome doom the majority of moral justifications to the realm of the *post hoc*? I am not convinced that it would. My reasoning is as follows. Studies in psychology are typically studies of the behavior and cognition of contemporary Westerners, and we need to be very careful about generalizing from these studies across culture and across time. Indeed, by the lights of the SIM itself, we should exercise extreme care before making such generalizations. The SIM is a *social* intuitionist model and according to the SIM, the relative weight of the contributions of reason and intuition to moral judgment can be expected to vary from society to society, and vary across time, as a result of the influence of social factors. So, changes in the way that we structure our societies can increase, or decrease, the relative contribution of reason to moral judgment (Clarke 2008, pp. 812–14). Even if our society is currently one in which reason plays a very insignificant role in moral judgment, this does not mean that the role of reason in moral judgment is insignificant in other cultures; it does not mean that the role of reason in moral judgment was always insignificant in our society; and nor does it mean that the role of reason in moral judgment is doomed to remain insignificant in our society in the future.

Haidt provides a specific example of a way in which we may be able to strengthen the role of reason in moral judgment, which is to conduct "just community schooling." According to him, this has the effect of strengthening the role of private reflection in the moral judgments of students who have been educated in "just community schools" (2001, p. 829). In just community schools, students and staff jointly decide on rules to run their school, in open public forums, and in so doing they become skilled in articulating reasons in the public sphere.[34] Proponents of "deliberative democracy" also emphasize the importance of public deliberation in improving the quality of moral decision making; in addition some of these proponents emphasize the importance of deliberately designing institutions to raise the quality of public debate (Bohman 1998). Participation in the procedures of deliberative democracy in a well-designed institutional setting is, in effect, an adult version of just community schooling, and we can expect it to lead to an increased role for reasoned judgment in the moral deliberation of its participants. On similar grounds, training in logic and critical reasoning can lead to an increased role for reasoned judgment in moral deliberation. People often find it difficult distinguishing reasoned judgment from *post hoc* "lawyer mode" reasoning and rhetoric. Training in logic and critical reasoning generally leads to them becoming better at making these distinctions and, consequently, more capable of making moral judgments on the basis of reason (Clarke 2008, pp. 813–14).

I have suggested some ways in which the role of reason in individual moral judgment can be increased. Another suggestion is for individuals to outsource their moral reasoning to people who make moral judgments in ways that involve a proportionally greater role for reason than is ordinarily the case.[35] Haidt does allow that there are such people. Indeed, he identifies professional philosophers as members of this class (2001, p. 819). People rarely seek moral guidance from professional philosophers. More commonly, they seek moral guidance from religious leaders. As there are many different religious traditions it is difficult to generalize about the training that religious leaders receive. In some religious traditions, religious leaders may be trained to make moral judgments in ways that involve a proportionately greater role for reason than is ordinarily the case. However, in other religious traditions, religious leaders will not be trained to make moral judgments in ways that involve a proportionately greater role for reason than is ordinarily the case. Their moral judgments will be just as driven by emotion, all things being equal, as those of ordinary members of their community. So, even though much moral decision making involves deference to experts (especially religious experts), in our current society this may not result in much in the way of additional reason-driven moral decision making. However, the point being made here is not one about our current society, but about what is possible and how our society might develop. It surely is possible that our society could develop into one in which people defer to those moral experts whose expertise is based on their taking a reason-driven approach to moral decision making.

Morality and Religion

Religions generally promote group solidarity. They do so directly through rituals that promote a sense of solidarity among members of a religious community. They also do so indirectly by promoting morality, which involves promoting prosocial behavior and this generally strengthens group solidarity. As we noted in Chapter 1, religions often promote morality by producing and encouraging adherence to codifications of recommended moral behavior, such as the ten commandments. These don't usually do much more than codify key aspects of the morality that is already current in a society, but they do provide that morality with a clear source of authority. For many people, questions about whether or not they should behave morally can be set aside when they come to believe that moral codes are legislated by a supernatural agent (Boyer 2001, p. 194). As we also noted in Chapter 1, religions typically provide numerous morally exemplary role models for the devout to emulate. Neither the codification of morality, nor the promotion of moral role models are unique to religion, but they are both ways in which religions can and do buttress ordinary morality, and thereby help reduce free-riding and help promote social cohesion.

The moral codes that religions uphold almost invariably seem to be directed, among other things, at the promotion of prosocial behavior and the reduction of free-riding. Every major religious tradition and very many minor ones endorse some or other variant of "the golden rule" – namely, "do as you would be done by" – which forbids free-riding (Neusner and Chilton 2009; Gensler 2013).[36] There are some religions that endorse particular forms of antisocial behavior and encourage particular forms of free-riding, but these cases need to be seen in an appropriate context. Some mainstream religions allow a place for an antisocial hermitic lifestyle and many religions promote alms giving and other forms of charity, which encourages begging – a form of free-riding. However, a close look at religiously endorsed hermitic behavior and religiously encouraged begging shows that neither of these forms of behavior is considered, by advocates of any mainstream religion, to be appropriate for ordinary religious adherents.

Christianity, Buddhism, and Hinduism are all religions that have traditionally made a special place for hermits. However, in all of these religious traditions, religious adherents who live a hermitic lifestyle are understood to be exceptional people and ordinary religious adherents are neither expected, nor particularly encouraged, to live as hermits.[37] The same three religions all endorse alms giving, especially to Christian mendicants, Buddhist monks, and Hindu sadhus. However, although these religions promote the giving of alms to members of these specialist religious sub-groups, all of whom beg for food at least some of the time, none of the religions in question promotes begging as appropriate behavior for ordinary religious adherents. In any case, the giving of alms to members of the above sub-groups is often understood as a form of payment for blessings, prayers, and other types of spiritual services; it is, therefore, often not construed, by ordinary religious adherents, as a way of encouraging free-riding. Many religions also encourage acts of charity to the poor and dispossessed, which clearly does involve promoting a form of free-riding. But it would be misleading to say that any of these religions actually endorses free-riding by promoting charity to the poor. The poor are often subjected to religious indoctrination, as a condition of receiving charity, and they are often aided and encouraged to "work their way out of poverty" and become productive, contributing members of society. Their free-riding is tolerated in the short term in order to strengthen religious communities and reduce free-riding in the long term.

One further way in which religions might be seen as promoting free-riding is by promoting a tolerant and forgiving attitude. Indeed, it is often presumed that the religious are particularly forgiving (McCullough and Worthington 1999). If religions urge us to tolerate or forgive, rather than punish, free-riders, then religion can be construed as undermining of moral communities. But religions are usually not unconditional promoters of tolerance and of a forgiving attitude. The weight of available scientific evidence suggests that religions generally promote tolerance towards in-groups and generally promote intolerance of out-groups (Powell and Clarke 2013). Also, the promotion of tolerance and forgiveness within a religious community should not be construed as the promotion of unconditional free-riding. Religious communities, who are more tolerant of their co-religionists' moral transgressions than they are of the moral transgressions of out-group members, are not usually unconditionally tolerant. They do not tolerate all forms of bad behavior, they do not tolerate sustained patterns of bad behavior, and their forgiveness usually comes at a price. Co-religionists, whose bad behavior is tolerated, are usually required to seek forgiveness from religious authorities, atone for their sins, and then try to change their ways. As with the case of giving charity to the poor, free-riding is tolerated in the short term, in order to strengthen the bonds of community and reduce free-riding in the long term. We will return to the subject of religious tolerance in Chapter 8.

In addition to generally discouraging free-riding, religion may have played a specific role in enabling the free-rider problem to be overcome. It may have thereby contributed to the evolution of morality. Many (but not all) of the supernatural agents that different human cultures postulate, are said to be "all knowing"; or at least they are said to have "privileged epistemic access" to our thoughts, even if they are not reckoned to know absolutely everything (Bering and Johnson 2005, p. 118). In cultures that postulate such supernatural agents, the belief that these supernatural agents will punish people for transgressions of the prevailing moral code is often also found (Bering and Johnson 2005, p. 127). Supernatural punishments are commonly thought to take place in the afterlife, but they are also often believed to take place in this world. The various misfortunes that befall people – disease, bereavement, poor harvests, unfaithful spouses, and so on – are commonly attributed to the interventions of wrathful supernatural agents, who are believed to be punishing individuals for earlier moral transgressions (Bering and Johnson 2005, pp. 126–7). Belief in supernatural agents that can detect such transgressions, by reading our thoughts, seems to come naturally to us. Indeed, seven-year-old children find acceptance of the idea that a supernatural agent can read at least some of their thoughts to be completely unproblematic, even though they also understand that human adults are incapable of reading their thoughts (Bering 2011, pp. 92–9).

The sincere belief that a very powerful agent will punish you, if you act immorally, is a very strong incentive to avoid acting immorally. This incentive strengthens ordinary morality and also serves to extend its scope. If we are aware that others are failing to make the same contributions to the welfare of the community that we make, and which are expected of them, then we can threaten to punish them, and can threaten to exclude them from the community. But what if there are opportunities for them to free-ride that can go undetected? It is extremely difficult to prevent free-riding when it occurs without us knowing that it has occurred. And, perhaps not surprisingly, there is evidence that people act immorally more often than they would otherwise when they believe that they are not being watched (Bateson, Nettle, and Roberts 2006; Ariely 2008, pp. 195–215). The belief that we are always being watched by a god who will punish us if we act immorally provides us with an extra incentive to avoid acting immorally, even when we have good reason to believe that other members of our society will be unable to detect our immoral actions (Johnson 2005; Shariff and Norenzayan 2011). Bering and Johnson (2005) suggest that a propensity for individuals to form such beliefs may be an evolutionary adaptation. Social groups comprised of members who generally possessed such beliefs were better able to overcome free-rider problems than other groups, and so their members were able to cooperate more effectively than they would have been able to otherwise.[38] As a consequence, these groups outcompeted other groups whose members lacked belief in supernatural beings who could read thoughts and police behavior; and these group-level benefits resulted in evolutionary benefits for individual members of such groups.[39] As Bering and Johnson put it: "Those who readily acquiesced to the possibility of moralising gods, and who lived in fear of such agencies, survived to become our ancestors" (2005, p. 137).[40]

Religions can do much to shape a community's morality, but there are practical limits to how much they can do. In the previous chapter we saw that it is plausible to think that religion is an evolutionary adaptation. Morality is also very likely to be an evolutionary adaptation and, unlike religion, human communities cannot do without it. There are many controversial claims made about the evolution of human culture.[41] Some scholars, including Tooby and Cosmides (1992) and Wilson (1998), take the view that human genetics greatly constrains the scope of possible human cultures. Others, such as Kitcher (2011) and Prinz (2012), construe the connection between human nature and culture to be a loose one. If this connection is loose, as Kitcher and Prinz suggest, then evolution imposes few constraints on human culture, including religion. But even on a liberal construal of the relationship between human nature and culture there is a clear evolutionary constraint on human culture. Human communities evolved by successfully suppressing free-riding. Those human communities that did not succeed in suppressing free-riding are no longer with us. All known human communities' solutions to the free-rider problem appear to involve the maintenance of communal morality. Religions can reshape morality in many ways, but any religion that reshaped the morality of a community in such a way as to significantly diminish that community's ability to suppress free-riding would not last long, because that community itself would not last long. It would be undermined from within by the self-interest of free-riders and, unless that society was entirely isolated, it would soon be undermined from without, by competition from other societies.

Notes

1. Greene's ideas have been updated and unified in a book released in late 2013, which was unavailable at the time that this manuscript was completed. See Greene (2013).
2. A further point is that considerable energy is expended on policing the moral behavior of others and punishing those who fail to act morally.
3. Here I follow Joyce in construing altruism as "Acting with the intention of benefiting another individual, where this is motivated by a non-instrumental concern for his or her welfare" (2006, p. 14). This is a psychological sense of altruism, as opposed to a purely "evolutionary" sense of altruism, which also encompasses unintended actions that benefit other individuals. For more on this distinction, see Sober and Wilson (1998).
4. The figures given here refer to genetic material that is shared as a result of descent from a common source. This way of expressing things is conventional, but is potentially misleading. In actual fact, any two randomly chosen and unrelated humans can be expected to share over 99 percent their genetic material. This background fact is assumed here. See also Joyce (2006, pp. 232–3, note 7).
5. Skepticism is sometimes expressed about much of this evidence. See, for example, Hammerstein (2003).
6. The same seems to be true of chimpanzees (Wrangham and Peterson 1997).
7. Free-riding amongst eusocial insects does occur, though. For some recent examples, see Sumner and Keller (2008).
8. This is by virtue of their haplodiploid sex determination system. Kin selection plays a very significant role in suppressing free-riding amongst haplodiploid eusocial insects, in which female siblings share three-quarters of their genetic material, but share only half of their genetic material with mothers. In these circumstances, it is more effective, from a genetic point of view, to help rear sisters, than to reproduce. Not all eusocial insects are haplodiploid, so this consideration does not help explain all forms of eusociality.
9. For evidence that normative cognition is an adaptation, see Cummins (1996), Cosmides and Tooby (2005), and Machery and Mallon (2010).
10. For discussion of the particular roles that anger, disgust, and contempt play in the formation of moral judgments, and in regulating the behavior of others, see Prinz (2012, pp. 304–8).

11. For emotions such as guilt and shame to work as commitment devices, expressions of them must be hard to fake and hard to disguise. Frank argues that this is indeed the case (1988, pp. 96–145).

12. Joyce (2006) and Mikhail (2011) both argue for the existence of an evolved capacity specifically dedicated to making moral judgments.

13. From an 1838 speech by Calhoun, cited in West (1997, p. 33).

14. The increasing liberalization of American attitudes towards homosexuality, between 1973 and 1998, is discussed by Loftus (2001).

15. Churchland (2011, pp. 112–16) is also concerned by the thin evidential basis offered for Haidt's moral foundations theory.

16. Haidt explicitly endorses a massively modular account of the mind (2012, p. 341, note 30). As we saw in the previous chapter, there are good reasons to be skeptical about the evidential basis for the claim that the mind is massively modular.

17. Prinz (2012, pp. 293–363) argues similarly.

18. I do not mean to give the impression that consequentialist and deontological theories are jointly exhaustive of all ethical theories. Another highly significant tradition in ethical theorizing is the tradition of virtue ethics, which dates back to Aristotle. For a recent survey of ethical theories, see Hooker (2012).

19. This is not actually Greene's terminology. His view has been characterized this way by Selim Berker (2009, p. 294) and Prinz offers a similar characterization (2012, p. 297). For some recent objections to Greene, see Berker (2009) and Kahane (2012).

20. The term "intuition" is used in a variety of ways in philosophy. In construing intuitions as intellectual "seemings," I follow Levy (2006a, p. 569) and Bealer (1998, p. 207), among others.

21. Their use is sometimes referred to as "trolleyology" (e.g., Edmonds 2009).

22. Why can't the five workers get out of the way of the runaway trolley? Different presentations of the thought experiment include different stipulated conditions that are designed to exclude this possibility. The track they are working on is in a narrow tunnel, the track is passing through a steep ravine, they are looking in the wrong direction and can neither see nor hear the approaching trolley, and so on.

23. Cushman and Greene suggest that the presence of persistent philosophical dilemmas is indicative of "fault lines between psychological processes … " and " … can reveal the hidden tectonics of the mind" (2012, p. 269).

24. Another class of situations in which the inner consequentialist and the inner deontologist appear to produce conflicting recommendations are "crying baby" cases, where smothering and thereby killing a crying baby will save the lives of many (Cushman and Greene 2012).

25. Their interpretation of these studies is not accepted by all. See, for example, Klein (2011).

26. Which is not to assert that consequentialist judgment occurs without any accompanying emotional activity (Greene et al. 2009, p. 64).

27. Berker criticizes Greene's talk of an "alarmlike" process as lacking in empirical backing (2009, p. 308).

28. Not all deontologists will allow that it is permissible to admit of exceptions to moral rules in extreme cases. The most famous of all philosophical deontologists, Immanuel Kant (1785, pp. 162–6), notoriously argued that that it is morally unacceptable to lie, even in the extreme case where lying to someone intent on murdering a friend would prevent the death of that friend.

29. Similar points are made by Nichols and Mallon (2006, p. 539) and by Greene (2008a, p. 65).

30. It is possible, as Saltzstein and Kasachkoff (2004) suggest, that at least some of the morally dumbfounded do have reasons that justify their moral judgments, but that they are not good at articulating these, or at least they are not good at articulating such reasons in the context of psychological studies.

31. Haidt (2003) argues that conscious re-construals of moral situation are rare in practice and that most instances of revisions of a moral judgment are the result of social influences.

32. However, it may be that the occurrence of such disruptions is not the result of rationally governed processes (Levy 2006b).

33. Bloom (2010) argues similarly.

34. Just community schooling was an approach to schooling championed by the arch-rationalist moral psychologist Lawrence Kohlberg. According to him, the use of this approach to school management accelerates student's moral development, leading to their moral judgments becoming more explicitly reason-based (Reed 1997, pp. 163–220).

35. Levy makes a very similar suggestion (2006b, p. 102).

36. It is worth noting that on some interpretations the golden rule may permit free-riding as a direct response to earlier instances of free-riding by others.

37. For a discussion of famous hermits and hermitic movements, see France (1998).

38. Of course, a free-rider problem remains, which is that any individuals who have not evolved a tendency to believe in supernatural punishing agents will still be liable to free-ride on the group when they are not being observed by others.

39. An additional evolutionary role that belief in supernatural punishment may have played in the evolution of human cooperation is that by generally reducing free-riding it reduced the need for societies to police and punish free-riders. Societies which expended less effort on policing and punishing free-riders, yet nevertheless enjoyed reduced levels of free-riding, enjoyed a competitive advantage over rival societies (Johnson and Kruger 2004).

40. Is the disposition to believe in punishing supernatural agents an adaptation with a genetic basis? Johnson and Bering (2006) argue that it is. However, Shariff, Norenzayan, and Henrich (2009) argue that it is a straightforward consequence of cultural evolution.

41. For recent discussion of the most influential theories underwriting such claims, see Lewens (2007).

4

Justifying Violence, War, and Cosmic War

Justifying Violence

In this chapter ordinary secular justifications for violence are considered. Then a specific context in which justifications for violence are often offered is discussed: war. The followers of many different religions believe that there is an ongoing war, taking place on a cosmic scale, between the forces of good and the enemies of the good; and they are liable to appeal to the ethics of (conventional) war to justify violent action undertaken while prosecuting this cosmic war. The forces of good are typically understood by the religious to be led by God, or some other supreme good supernatural being, who is often believed to be locked in a struggle with forces led by Satan, or some other powerful evil supernatural being. Almost all of the religions that postulate an ongoing cosmic war call upon the devout to be "Soldiers of Christ" – or play the equivalent role in other religious traditions – and contribute to the war effort on behalf of the forces of good.[1]

As well as considering the tendency of religions to postulate an ongoing cosmic struggle and to try to justify violent action, undertaken in the context of this struggle, by appealing to the ethics of war, I will also consider a countervailing tendency found in many religious traditions, which is to promote peace and oppose violent solutions to conflicts. As was noted in Chapter 1, the traditions of major world religions are diverse and all possess scripture that can be used to promote peace, as well as scripture that can be used to promote violence. Most major world

The Justification of Religious Violence, First Edition. Steve Clarke.
© 2014 John Wiley & Sons, Inc. Published 2014 by John Wiley & Sons, Inc.

religions are represented by a range of clerics who advocate a variety of views. Some of these clerics will favor violence in circumstances in which the interests of their religion, or the broader society in which it is practiced, can be protected, or advanced, by violence. Other clerics, who may represent the same religion, will be opposed to violence in the very same circumstances. Most Catholic clerics in Western countries were in favor of pursuing the Vietnam War (1962–1975), at least at the time that it began. The Vietnam War pitted forces serving a predominantly Catholic elite in South Vietnam against forces led by atheist communists in North Vietnam. However, some of the most prominent opponents of Western participation in the Vietnam War were also Catholic clerics.[2]

It may seem obvious that violent actions stand in need of justification. After all, people who have undertaken violent actions often go to great lengths to attempt to justify such actions while others, who feel that such violent actions are not justified, can be forthright in their condemnation. What could be said to someone who wanted to be told why violent actions stand in need of justification? One thing that could be said is that violent actions typically cause pain and pain is generally considered to be bad. A second point is that many violent actions cause injury, placing restrictions on the ways in which the lives of the victims of such violent actions are lived. A severed limb, a punctured organ, or a disfigured face, can all stand in the way of life-plans, dramatically restricting the ways in which victims are able to shape their lives, and in some cases depriving them of the possibility of leading any type of life that they would consider to be worth living. A third point is that some violent actions result in death, cutting short the time available to victims to lead worthwhile lives.[3]

Despite the above considerations, most philosophers who have thought about the ethics of violence have considered that some violent actions are justified, at least some of the time. Many consequentialists will consider particular violent actions to be justified when they judge that the good consequences expected to flow from these actions outweigh the harms that they can be expected to cause. Deontologists will not generally accept that violent actions can be justified by appealing to their good consequences, and will generally endorse rules prohibiting specific types of violent action, such as murder and assault. Some deontologists will want to endorse a rule, or rules, prohibiting all forms of violent action. However, most deontologists have allowed that some forms of violent action are consistent with the demands of morality, and some have argued that we are morally required to act violently in at least some circumstances. For example, Kant insisted that we are morally required to apply capital punishment to convicted murderers (Rauscher 2012).

Some consequentialists, especially rule-utilitarians such as Brandt (1972), urge people to endorse moral rules prohibiting specific categories of violent action. They do so on the grounds that the benefits to humanity of establishing and enforcing rules prohibiting particular forms of violent action can reasonably be expected to outweigh the costs of disallowing instances of those particular forms of violent action. However, the rule-utilitarian faces the challenge of explaining why, as a utilitarian, she would want to disallow those instances of a particular form of action that can reasonably be expected to produce overall gains in utility. Why should rule-utilitarians not allow exceptions to such rules when there is a compelling utilitarian case to do so?[4] As we saw in the previous chapter, moral norms, including norms prohibiting particular categories of violence, are well entrenched in most societies. If Greene's (2008a) "warring subsystems" account of ordinary moral cognition, discussed in the previous chapter, is even roughly accurate, then ordinary people will generally reason about violence like deontologists, endorsing rules prohibiting specific categories of violence, but will also allow exceptions to these rules in circumstances where there is an overwhelming consequentialist case for such exceptions.[5]

Perhaps the most compelling and most widely appealed to justification for violence is self-defense. Suppose that you are walking along a quiet street one evening when you see, some distance away, a wild-eyed man sprinting towards you and brandishing a blood-stained knife. You also notice, much closer to you, a recently deceased man, who appears to have been stabbed to death, and is now lying in a pool of blood. The recently deceased man has dropped a gun in front of him. You pick up the gun and shout out to the wild-eyed man, "Stop or I'll shoot," hoping that he will be deterred from attacking you. For good measure you also fire warning shots into the air. However, he keeps running and lifts the knife above his head as he comes close, apparently intending to strike you with it. There is no time to try any further means to dissuade him from attacking you – certainly none you can conceive of – and you can tell from the speed at which he is sprinting that you will not be able to outrun him. No other person who might be able to intervene is present. Are you justified in shooting the wild-eyed man in order to try to prevent him from attacking you, even though shooting him might well result in his death? You have attempted to avoid the looming attack by non-violent means, but unfortunately these did not work; there is no untried way of fending off the attack that is apparent to you, and you do not have time to think of further possible strategies. You are effectively faced with a choice between two outcomes. Either he stabs you with his knife or you shoot him. You can try to shoot to incapacitate him without killing him; however, given the rapid speed of his approach, and given your need to prevent the attack, and your inexperience with firearms, you have to accept that there is a significant chance that you may end up killing him. But surely you are entitled to defend yourself from violent attack, even at the risk of killing an attacker.

Self-defense is one of the most established criminal defenses (Leverick 2007, p. 1), and a lot of people will say that you are morally, as well as legally, entitled to shoot the wild-eyed man in self-defense. However, some will disagree. The fact that you are willing to risk taking the life of another person, in order to try to protect your own life, suggests that you think that your own life is more worthy of preservation than the life of your attacker. But why think that your life is more worthy of preservation than his? It is widely presumed that individuals have equal moral value, and that there is an equal right to life, so it is not obvious that you are entitled to risk his life, defending yours, merely because you are being attacked (Norman 1995, p. 121). One response to this line of reasoning is a perspectival one. From an impartial point of view it is surely true that all lives have equal value. However, people are, almost invariably, partial towards themselves, and value the preservation of their own lives over the preservation of the lives of other people with whom they have no special connection. Humans can be expected to try to preserve their own lives and a moral theory that requires them to be strictly impartial, when self-preservation is at stake, seems too demanding to be realistic, or so this line of response goes.[6] A second line of response accepts that all lives have equal value, but holds that it is the assailant who is responsible for his own death, and not you, if you end up killing him while acting in self-defense. This is because he has unfairly placed you in a situation where you are forced to choose between protecting your own life and protecting his (Ryan 1983, pp. 515–16).

If you are entitled to defend yourself from unjust attack then presumably I am also entitled to assist you in defending yourself when you are unjustly attacked. If I observe you being attacked by the wild-eyed man, in the scenario described earlier, and if it is morally acceptable for you to resort to violent action to defend yourself, then surely it is morally acceptable for me to resort to violent action to assist you in defending yourself. While appeals to self-defense, and to the defense of innocent third parties, look like relatively uncontroversial justifications for violence, they are not the only appeals that people make when attempting to justify violence. Some argue that we are also entitled to resort to violence to protect significant items of property from theft, damage or trespass (e.g., Rothbard 2002, p. 77). And there are other categories of violence that are often defended as being consistent with the demands of morality. Parents are often heard asserting that they, and perhaps some other adults, such as teachers, are entitled to employ some (usually mild) forms of violent punishment to discipline their children.[7] In some contexts consensual acts of violence are often considered to be justified. Boxers are usually considered to be entitled to punch one another in a freely agreed upon and properly regulated boxing match. Until the nineteenth century, it was widely considered that consensual dueling was morally acceptable (and perhaps morally obligatory when a gentleman's honor had been seriously slighted), even if this led to the death of one or both of the duelers.[8]

All of the aforementioned forms of violence are ones that are sometimes considered justifiable for individuals to conduct in their capacity as ordinary members of a society. In most modern societies there are forms of violence that are not considered justifiable when conducted by ordinary people, but which are considered to be justifiable when conducted by people who occupy certain professional roles. In most societies people are not entitled to use coercive or violent means to arrest someone whom they suspect of having committed a crime, but police officers are entitled to use coercive and violent means to arrest someone suspected of having committed a crime – although they are required to do so in a lawfully prescribed way.[9] This entitlement is tied to the professional role of police officer. Similarly, a professional prison officer is entitled to use coercive and violent means to ensure that convicted criminals, who are incarcerated, obey the regulations imposed at their correctional facility (again, provided that they do so in a lawfully prescribed way). Ordinary citizens are not entitled to use such means to ensure that convicted criminals obey the regulations imposed at their correctional facility, even if and when these convicted criminals are on "day-release" or otherwise in contact with members of the public.

The fact that we allow some professionals to conduct some forms of violent action, while ordinary people are prevented from conducting those same forms of violent action, can be understood in social contractarian terms, in the tradition of Hobbes (1651). In forming a society that furthers our individual survival, we implicitly consent to cede certain powers to the state; and the state, in turn, establishes and maintains institutions designed to ensure our security. We give up, among other things, any entitlement to arrest suspected criminals and to enforce regulations imposed on convicted criminals by their correctional facility. More generally, we give up any right to act violently towards other members of our society, except in a carefully circumscribed range of circumstances – such as those in which we are acting in self-defense. We entrust the state, and its duly appointed officials, to ensure that our society is peaceful and to police crime and operate a judicial and penal system to reduce, and ideally remove, the threat of criminal activity. This enables us to lead prosperous lives, secure in the knowledge that the state will try to prevent attempts to deprive us of peace or property; and that, if these are not successfully prevented, that appropriate redress will be made through the legal system.

There is a particular form of violent action that the modern state typically claims an exclusive right to prosecute, which will be the subject of the next section of this chapter: this is war. Modern states typically insist that wars should only be prosecuted by designated officers of the state – namely military personnel.[10] Not only do states claim an exclusive right to prosecute wars, they also claim an exclusive right to determine when they are entitled to go to war, as well as a right to compel their citizens to pay for the upkeep of military forces that prosecute wars. Many also claim a right to conscript particular categories of their citizens to participate in wars.

Justice, War, and Just War Theory

A war is a sustained armed conflict between significant political groups or communities. A large-scale fight between two political groups or communities that did not involve the use of armaments would not ordinarily be considered to be a war, and nor would a brief armed skirmish. To be considered as participants in a war, the groups in question need to be politically oriented and significant enough in size. An armed conflict between two street gangs would not be a war both because of their lack of size and because of their lack of political identification. Most wars these days are between two or more nation states. But not all wars occur between nation states. There are civil wars, which take place within nation states, and there are wars that involve non-state actors. The nine crusades that took place between the eleventh and thirteenth centuries are generally regarded as wars. For the most part, these were prosecuted by pan-European coalitions of Christians who represented Christianity rather than any European state or states. More recently the international organization al-Qaeda, which does not represent any state or states, has been prosecuting a war against America and her allies.

There are three broad schools of thought about the ethics of war. Just war theorists hold that war is sometimes morally acceptable. They seek to articulate conditions under which it is morally acceptable to start a war, or to participate in one that has already started; and they also seek to articulate codes of conduct for the prosecution of war. Pacifists are opposed to war. They are either skeptical of the alleged benefits of participating in particular wars, or they take the view that going to war is immoral, regardless of the potential benefits of doing so. Realists hold that morality does not apply in the sphere of war. The realist position is not an influential one, in either philosophy or theology, but it has been very significant in international relations. Realists, such as Kennan (1954) and Morgenthau (1978), portray attempts to impose moral conditions on warfare as misguided and sentimental. When war is entered into, participants should abandon any concern for morality and act in the interest of their own side, or so realists maintain. The view that the demands of morality should be thought to suddenly cease to apply when wars start, even though they continue to apply in other conflict situations, seems both ad hoc and mysterious.[11] What realists may be getting at is that in war moral norms are often thought of as being conditional in nature. When one side breaks the rules in a sporting contest, we expect that the referees officiating the contest will impose appropriate penalties, to deter future misbehavior. In the sphere of international conflict there are no referees and so the only credible deterrent available, in cases when one side violates agreed upon rules of war, is for the other side to demonstrate a willingness to behave similarly.[12]

Modern secular just war theory emerges from the Christian tradition of thinking about the relationship between morality and war (Johnson 1999, p. 24). The Christian just war tradition involves a synthesis of the ideas of classical thinkers with more distinctively Christian strands of thought (Johnson 1984, pp. 176–7). Many other religious traditions have also developed doctrines regarding the ethics of war (Sorabji and Rodin, 2006). These include Islam (Kelsay 2007), Judaism (Niditch 1993), Hinduism (Rosen 2002), and Sikhism (Cole 2004). Just war theories usually involve a set of stipulations about when it is permissible to wage war (*jus ad bellum*) as well as a set of norms regarding proper conduct in war (*jus in bello*).[13] In modern just war theory it is generally accepted that war can be conducted if: (1) it is declared and waged by a legitimate authority, (2) a just cause for going to war is identified, (3) going to war is a last resort, (4) there is a

reasonable prospect of success, (5) the violence employed is proportionate
to the wrong resisted, and (6) the war is fought with the right intentions
(Coady 2008, p. 63).[14] Modern just war theory rules of conduct in war are
a little harder to spell out quite so succinctly, but include respecting the
combatant/non-combatant distinction and not targeting non-combatants,
attempting to minimize "collateral damage," avoiding the use of weapons
that are banned by international laws, and treating prisoners of war
humanely (Coady 2008, pp. 109–16; Johnson 1999, pp. 36–8).

The concept of a "just cause" is a fairly open-ended one. Defense against
unjust attack seems like a clear and uncontroversial form of just cause, as is
assisting a third party that has been unjustly attacked. Sometimes the belief
that one's group or country is about to be unjustly attacked is held to be a
just cause for a "pre-emptive strike" on one's opponents. The Boer war of
1899–1902 began with a pre-emptive strike by Boer forces against British
troops garrisoned in Natal and the Cape Colony. The Boers, not unrea-
sonably, interpreted British behavior towards them as a prelude to war and
sought strategic advantage by attacking first. On some occasions, such as the
declaration of war on Serbia by Austria-Hungary, which triggered World
War I, the assassination of an individual has been considered a just cause
for war.[15] The cause cited for the 2003 invasion of Iraq, by America and her
allies, was the (alleged) failure of Iraq to comply with UN resolutions requir-
ing the destruction of weapons of mass destruction. The mistreatment of the
citizens of a country, by their own government, is sometimes considered to
be a just cause for war. The cause cited by NATO, to justify the 1999 bombing campaign against Yugoslavia, was the ongoing violent and repressive
actions of the Milosevic government, undertaken against its own citizens,
especially in Kosovo.

Religious traditions have recognized a further range of just causes.
In the Christian tradition, Aquinas and Gratian both recognized the
punishment of heresy and sinful behavior as a just cause for military action
(Johnson 1997, pp. 52–3). Of course the aim of military action would not
merely be to punish heresy and sinful behavior, but also to re-establish correct belief and proper behavior. The seventeenth-century Christian author
Thomas Barnes argued that knowledge of the true faith permits, and indeed
requires, one to go to war against those who exhibits a variety of vices that
are condemned in the Bible. These include "monstrous pride," "insolence
against God," "tumultousnesse and rebellion," and "false-heartednesse"
(Johnson 1997, p. 59). Gratian argued that Christians were justified in
attacking "The enemies of the Church" (Johnson 1997, p. 53). In effect this

line of argument could be used to justify attacks on anyone practicing a different faith, including Christians of other denominations.[16] Nowadays, such specifically religious justifications for war are usually considered to fall outside the scope of just war theory, and appeals to them are considered to be illegitimate by modern secular just war theorists (Johnson 1984, pp. 176–7). However, historically, religious justifications for war have been considered as legitimate forms of just cause in just war theory. Just war theory has been secularized, but it has religious roots, and the distinction between a just war and a religious war is a modern one (Firestone 1999, p. 15; Johnson 1997, pp. 43–5).

Some just war theorists, including Walzer (2000, pp. 251–62) and Rawls (1999, pp. 98–9), endorse a "supreme emergency exception" to the *jus in bello* requirements of just war theory. In a situation of supreme emergency, these authors suggest, those who are under attack in a war are entitled to disregard ordinary moral norms and behave in the way that international relations realists suggest that they should have been behaving all along during war: doing whatever it takes to defend themselves. Walzer suggests that conditions of supreme emergency obtain "when our deepest values and our collective survival are in imminent danger" (2004, p. 33). The phrase "supreme emergency" was used by Churchill to describe Britain's circumstances at the beginning of World War II. Britain was then at war with a very powerful enemy that sought to take over British territory and permanently alter British life, abolishing democratic government, along with a range of individual freedoms. So, the deepest values and collective survival of the British people clearly were then in danger. However, Walzer (2000) does not consider that Britain faced an *imminent* danger at that time. Walzer does, though, hold that the successful invasion of France by Germany in May 1940 placed Britain in a state of imminent danger (2000, p. 251). At that stage Germany was preparing to invade Britain and Britain was without significant allies. The period of "supreme emergency" was over by the end of 1941, according to Walzer (2000, p. 261). By then both the Soviet Union and America had become participants in the war on Britain's side. With the entry of these two great powers into the war and the redeployment of the bulk of German forces to the eastern front, the German threat to Britain's ongoing existence was no longer imminent.

During the war, British air forces conducted indiscriminate "terror bombing" attacks on German cities, aiming, among other things, to weaken German morale by killing or injuring German civilians, or by rendering them homeless – a clear violation of just war norms of non-combatant immunity.[17] Walzer (2000; 2004) does not seek to defend the use of terror bombing tactics before the German invasion of France, or after the Soviet Union and the USA had entered the war, but he does seek to defend Britain's use of such tactics between May 1940 and the end of 1941. In that period terror bombing was believed to be the only effective means of preventing a German invasion (2000, p. 259); and its use was justified by supreme emergency considerations, or so he argues. Critics of the idea of supreme emergency, including Coady (2008) and Toner (2005), have suggested that the supreme emergency exception could easily be invoked in a much broader range of contexts than Walzer intends. Coady identifies war situations that Walzer does not want to endorse as supreme emergencies, but which look like they could well be described as such from the point of view of those under attack (2008, pp. 287–90). Toner (2005) suggests that considerations of consistency require that, if we acknowledge supreme emergency exceptions in war situations, then we should also do so when we consider conflicts between individuals that occur outside of war contexts. If we do this, then in some circumstances other than war situations, people will be licensed by considerations of supreme emergency to kill innocent individuals in order to prevent threats to their own lives.[18]

Pacifism

The term "pacifism" refers to a cluster of views. What these have in common is that they are anti-war (Teichman 1986). Absolute pacifists think that we should never go to war, regardless of the consequences of not doing so, and less-than-absolute pacifists are skeptical of the alleged benefits of going to war on any particular occasion. Pacifism has been extremely influential in recent Christian theology, but many philosophers have been scathingly critical, portraying pacifism as sentimental and lacking in intellectual rigor.[19] Pacifists have attempted to ground their views in both deontological and consequentialist ethical theories (Fiala 2010). Deontologically inspired pacifists typically assert that we should endorse a rule, or set of rules, against ever risking killing or against ever taking up arms in a war. If we were to endorse such a rule, or set of rules, then we would be prohibited from risking killing in self-defense, and prohibited from risking killing while trying to defend those who are unjustly attacked by third parties. Morality, on the pacifist view, requires us to be bystanders to immoral activity, doing nothing while the innocent are slaughtered, or so the critics of pacifism charge. The deontologist pacifist can provide a partial response to this charge, pointing out that there is much that we can do to try to protect the innocent from unjust attack, short of acting violently. We can try to help people flee from attack; we can attempt to reason with attackers; we can offer to pay attackers to refrain from attacking; and so on. But this is only a partial defense. The deontologist pacifist, if he is to be consistent, needs to be willing to say that we should stand by and let innocents be slaughtered, if there is no effective non-violent way of preventing such slaughter; and this is a conclusion that most people will find very difficult to accept.

If consequentialists are to be absolutist pacifists then they will need to find some basis for a rule against ever going to war. A rule-utilitarian form of pacifism looks useful here, but it is not clear that a strict application of such a rule, in circumstances where the possibility of war looms, would tend to produce the best consequences, as the absolutist consequentialist pacifist needs to claim. If, for example, at the outbreak of World War II, the Allied powers had not resisted the Axis powers, then it is reasonable to think that the Axis powers would have taken control of most, if not all, of the inhabited territory of world. As the Axis powers were fascist and imperialistic, they would have imposed fascist, imperialistic rule on conquered territories and, all things being equal, we would now be living in a world dominated by fascist, imperialistic governments, ruthlessly suppressing dissent, promulgating racist doctrines, and massacring races deemed to be inferior. It is very hard to believe that such a world would be better than the one we currently have, so it is very hard to see why a fair-minded consequentialist would endorse a rule that could well have led to such an outcome.

Less-than-absolutist pacifists can make the argument that we are often too ready to go to war before exploring non-violent alternatives.[20] Also, they can point to occasions where non-violent methods have succeeded, such as the non-violent struggle for Indian independence from British colonialism, spearheaded by Gandhi, which led to the Indian Independence Act of 1947, and Indian self-rule in 1950. This example seems to be a particular favorite of many pacifist authors.[21] Such examples are disputable (Churchill 2007). Critics of pacifism point out that, at the time, Britain was not in a good position to hold on to its colony, having just come through World War II. In any case, while Indian independence did come about without a violent struggle against the former colonial power, it is misleading to describe the transition from colonialism to independence as non-violent. Indian independence involved a chaotic separation of colonial India into the modern states of India and Pakistan. This involved hundreds of thousands of deaths as well as the displacement of perhaps 10 million people (Metcalf and Metcalf 2006).[22]

One further way of construing pacifism is as a call for the development of international institutions that can serve as instruments of conflict resolution, and as alternatives to war (Alexandra 2003).[23] The view that going to war is sometimes the best way to secure the best consequences, in a given set of circumstances, is contingent on there not being international institutions that can operate to resolve conflicts, secure peace, and thereby create better alternatives. If we had such institutions, then the outcomes of the cost–benefit analyses that lead reasonable people to consider that going to war is the best option to pursue, in a given set of circumstances, would look very different, or so this line of argument goes. How convincing one finds this line of argument depends, among other things, on one's belief in the power of such institutions to function effectively, as well as one's belief in the propensity of other disputants to abide by internationally regulated dispute resolution processes. Many deaths might well have been averted if the separation of colonial India into the Republic of India and the Republic of Pakistan had been supervised by an effective international agency. However, it is hard to accept that such an international agency could have effectively prevented World War II, or even ameliorated its effects. There may simply have been no compromise that would have been acceptable to both the Axis powers and the Allied powers, regardless of the international institutional arrangements that were in place at the time.[24]

A lot of arguments for pacifism are grounded in theological considerations. There are significant pacifist schools of thought amongst Buddhists, Hindus, and Jains. The value of *ahimsa* ("non-/without harm") is endorsed in all of these religious traditions (Eller 2010, p. 344). When one deliberately harms another person, one fails to express this value; and what transpires is believed by Buddhists, Hindus, and Jains to be bad for the person committing harm, as well as for the person harmed. The person committing harm accrues bad karma, and this affects the quality of his or her afterlife. We will have more to say about violence and the cycle of karma in the next chapter.

Buddhist, Hindu, and Jain leaders have regularly advocated refraining from responding to most instances of violence with violence. But while Jain theology has generally led to the endorsement of absolute pacifism (Eller 2010, pp. 346–8), the same is not true of Buddhism and Hinduism. Buddhist and Hindu leaders have often advocated violence under conditions where they have considered that the alternatives to violence can be expected to lead to significantly worse consequences than violence. This generalization is even true of Buddhist and Hindu leaders who have been widely portrayed as advocates of absolute pacifism in the West, such as Gandhi. Gandhi held that there are courses of action that are worse than violence; and in situations where these are the only viable alternatives to violent action, violent action ought to be undertaken. In particular, Gandhi considered cowardice to be worse than violence. As he memorably put it: "Where there is only a choice between cowardice and violence, I would advise violence" (Gandhi 1920). One of his examples of a situation in which cowardice is worse than violence is when one has caught a rapist in the act. In such a situation, a refusal to act violently, to stop the rapist, would make one a "partner in violence," according to Gandhi, something he judged to be worse than violent intervention (Juergensmeyer 2007, p. 34).[25] As we will see in the next chapter, the Dalai Lama, who like Gandhi is often portrayed as an absolute pacifist in the West, has also endorsed violent action in specific circumstances.

We saw in Chapter 1 that the Bible offers considerable scriptural support for violent action in particular circumstances. However, it also offers significant scriptural support for peace. Christians are urged to "turn the other cheek" in response to violence (Matthew 5:39), to forgo vengeance (Romans 12:19), and to be non-judgmental and forgiving (Luke 6:37). Also, we are told that peacemakers are blessed (Matthew 5:9). Christian pacifists, including Stanley Hauerwas (1984) and John Howard Yoder (1994), see these texts as representative of the central message of Christianity, which they hold to be a pacifist religious tradition properly understood. Yoder (1994) argues that the rejection of pacifism by other Christian theologians, such as Rienhold Niebuhr (1940), results from their failure to give due weight to the words of Jesus when considering how to understand the overall body of Christian scripture.[26] Even though pacifism is highly influential in contemporary Christian theology, no major Christian churches are pacifist. Pacifist churches include the Mennonite church (which Yoder was a member of), the Quakers, the Amish, and the Church of the Brethren, all of which are minor churches.

Religious War and Cosmic War

Despite the plausibility of pacifist readings of some holy texts, most religious scripture is rich with descriptions of violence and war, much of which is presented in an approving manner. The Old Testament contains many accounts of military conquests that are endorsed by God. As we saw in Chapter 1, in the Book of Deuteronomy, God commands that the Israelites undertake a series of genocidal wars against several neighboring tribes. The Book of Joshua recounts a series of successful battles, undertaken by Joshua and his Israelite followers, as commanded by God; and there are also approving accounts of war in Exodus, Numbers, and 1 Samuel. In case anyone might fail to understand the character of the Old Testament God, the Book of Exodus specifically informs us that "The Lord is a man of war" (Exodus 15:3). The Hindu epics, the *Ramayana* and the *Mahabharata*, contain many descriptions of battles. One component of the *Mahabharata* is the Bhagavad Gita. In this classic Hindu text, Prince Arjuna begins to worry about the pointlessness of war. Perhaps fearing that Arjuna is about to become a pacifist, Lord Krishna berates him and then persuades him of the importance of continuing to wage war. The Koran contains many passages that concern proper conduct in war[27] and the history of Islam is rich with accounts of battles. This should not be surprising as in its early years Islam was chiefly spread by military conquest, initially by Muhammad and his followers, and then by their successors (Juergensmeyer 2003, p. 81).

Islam is far from the only religion to have had its own military forces. Christianity had its Crusaders and orders of holy warriors, such as the Knights Templar. Hinduism has been represented by armed sects that fought against Muslim invaders, including the *Dasnami Nagas* and the *Dadu Panthi Nagas*; the Sikh *Khalsa*, or "company of the pure," fought against both Hindus and Muslims in the eighteenth century; and Buddhist warrior priests have played significant roles in a series of domestic wars in Japan (Eller 2010, pp. 279–83). The many minor religions of the world have, for the most part, been as enthusiastic about violence and war as the major world religions. Most religions specifically connect full participation in that religion with a willingness to fight in wars on its behalf, or to provide support for religious warriors; and many religions recognize specific gods that guide believers when they go to war (Johnson and Reeve 2013).

Although most modern wars are prosecuted by the armies of secular states, it is striking how religious formally secular armies often seem to be. As the saying goes, "there are no atheists in foxholes." This may be because individuals who put their lives on the line in war feel a particular need for divine support, but it may also be because military culture is usually very religious and is often hostile to atheists. Dominic Johnson and Zoey Reeve (2013) recount the story of Specialist Jeremy Hall, a modern

American atheist who wanted to serve his country, in a foxhole if necessary. When stationed in Iraq, Hall was subject to persistent discrimination and abuse by his fellow American military personnel, because he was an atheist. He eventually had to be sent home to America as a consequence. According to Hall, the underlying reason for this discrimination and abuse was a lack of trust. Not believing in God, he was perceived by religious military personnel as someone who was unreliable and "might break" (Banerjee 2008). This perception may have a basis in fact. An ideal soldier, from the point of view of his superior officers, is someone who has no doubt that the cause that he is fighting for is just and who is willing to risk his life for its sake. While it is possible that, after much deliberation, an atheist might come to the conclusion that a particular war is worth dying for, a devout soldier who is fighting for God barely has to think about the subject at all. Once he has established that that war is endorsed by God – and often this is established simply by accepting the pronouncements of respected religious authorities – he can be confident that in participating in that war he is doing what is right. Moreover, he can be much more confident of success than an atheist soldier because he knows that a supremely powerful supernatural being is on his side; and confidence is a crucial asset in war (Johnson and Reeve 2013).

As we saw in Chapter 2, it is plausible to think that religion is an evolutionary adaptation, enabling human groups to cooperate more effectively than they would otherwise. It has been further suggested that there is a particular context in which religion may have been especially important in enhancing cooperation, and that is war. Human groups that were effective at coordinating their activities, so as to attack other groups successfully, take their resources, and occupy their land, as well as groups that were effective in protecting themselves from attack, were groups that flourished. Groups that were ineffective at attacking others, groups that were unmotivated to attack others, and groups that were ineffective at protecting themselves from attack, or unmotivated to do so, all failed to flourish. The strong associations between warfare and religion may be anything but coincidental. Religion may be an evolutionary adaptation for effectiveness in war (MacNeill 2004; Johnson and Reeve 2013).[28]

According to many religions, particular wars are chapters in a grand cosmic struggle that takes place across (and sometimes also beyond) the sweep of history. In the Christian tradition this is the struggle between God and Satan, which is understood to be taking place both on earth and elsewhere. Christians are far from unique in construing history as part of a grand cosmic struggle. The Manicheans also construed history as a component of a grand struggle between God and Satan.[29] Islamic theologians recognize Satan as an opponent of God, but do not usually accord him the same importance as do their Christian counterparts. Nevertheless, Islam construes human history through the lens of a grand narrative of cosmic struggle. For Muslims, history is standardly understood as an ongoing struggle between the *dar al-Islam* – the territory of God, in which Muslim authority holds sway – and the *dar al-harb* – the territory of war. The *dar al-harb* is understood to be perpetually at war, both internally and also with the *dar al-Islam*; and war will not end until the entire world has been subsumed into the *dar al-Islam* (Johnson 1999, pp. 169–72). Zoroastrianism, which pre-dates Islam, Manicheanism, and Christianity, is another religion that construes human history as part of a grand struggle, in this case between light (good) forces led by the god Ahura Mazda, and dark (evil or chaotic) forces led by the god Angra Mainyu (Rose 2011).

Many of the cosmic struggles that the religious postulate are predicted to end with an almighty apocalyptic battle in which God, or the forces of good, defeats Satan, or the forces of evil – but not without vast amounts of damage being caused first. For many evangelical Christians this is the battle of Armageddon. This apocalyptic battle is described in the Bible (Revelation 16:16) in highly metaphorical but obviously also violent terminology, which is liable to be interpreted in a variety of ways. Many evangelical Christians foresee a coming world war between Christian forces and evil forces led by the Antichrist. White supremacist Christian groups are inclined to postulate a coming world war between the races (Selengut 2003, p. 106). The "UFO cult" Heaven's Gate offered an imaginative account of Armageddon, construing it as a coming war between two different species of aliens that inhabit this universe (Urban 2000, pp. 280–1).[30] Heaven's Gate will be discussed further in Chapter 7. Another recent religious group that has postulated (a series of different) apocalyptic scenarios, again inspired by the Book of Revelation, is the syncretist Japanese group Aum Shinrikyo, also to be discussed in Chapter 7. Judaism is yet another religion with an apocalyptic tradition. An apocalyptic battle is prophesized in Ezekiel (38) between the Jewish people and "Gog, of the land of Magog," a very powerful (possibly supernatural) ruler of a nation hostile to the Jewish people. A contemporary apocalyptic Jewish group, the Temple Mount Faithful, have tried to incite conflict with Muslims, in the hope of hastening the time of the prophesized apocalyptic battle (Selengut 2003, p. 108). Curiously, some evangelical

Christians have sought to aid the Temple Mount Faithful's attempt to hasten the onset of the apocalypse, also taking the view that it is better to have the inevitable apocalyptic battle sooner rather than later (Selengut 2003, pp. 109–10). However, they hope and expect that the Temple Mount Faithful will trigger an apocalyptic war with the Antichrist, rather than with Gog of the land of Magog.

Those religious believers who hold that the apocalypse is approaching often take the view that hidden evil forces are especially active in the world in the lead up to it. Their reasoning is liable to follow a pattern of development that is commonly observed amongst conspiracy theorists. Over the course of time conspiracy theorists tend to construe their favored conspiracy in ever more totalizing terms. When evidence comes in that is consistent with the favored theory, they typically take this as proof of the activity of suspected conspirers. When the evidence that they expect to see revealed fails to come to light, they tend to interpret this failure as an indication of a "cover-up"; and they often postulate additional conspirators involved in creating and maintaining the cover-up (Keeley 1999). Timothy McVeigh bombed the Murrah Building in Oklahoma City in 1995, killing 168 people. He did so because he was angry about the 1993 US government siege of the Branch Davidian compound in Waco, Texas, which led to 82 deaths. He blamed these deaths squarely on the US government and he wanted to send a message to the government about the consequences of abusing its power (BBC 2011). McVeigh and other like-minded conspiracy theorists appeared to believe that an apparently bungled raid on the compound, at the conclusion of the siege, which led to a fire that resulted in the majority of the 82 deaths, was, in fact, a deliberate act: the outcome of a conspiracy. This alleged conspiracy involved the Bureau of Alcohol, Tobacco and Firearms (ATF) and the Federal Bureau of Investigation (FBI), the two government agencies involved in the siege. When the media failed to report the events that took place at Waco in the way that McVeigh and his fellow conspiracy theorists construed them, they began to suspect that the conspiracy involved the connivance of yet more government agencies. Later on they began to suspect that parts of the American media were also in on the conspiracy and were deliberately covering up what had really happened (Keeley 1999).[31]

People who are convinced that they need to oppose Satan, or some other supremely powerful evil being, are highly susceptible to belief in a totalizing theory. Satan is generally thought to have the ability to manipulate ordinary humans to do his bidding, so anyone and everyone might be work-ing for Satan, either by directly advancing Satan's schemes, or by covering up evidence of those schemes. Religious groups that believe that the apocalypse is approaching are particularly likely to see evidence of the hidden hand of Satan in apparently natural events. David Koresh, the head of the Branch Davidian movement, repeatedly preached about the coming apocalypse and the fulfillment of prophecies made in the Book of Revelation (Eller 2010, p. 132; Hall 2002, p. 150). A belief amongst members of the Branch Davidian movement that the FBI and the ATF were under the influence of Satan, and that by opposing these agencies they were participating in a final battle against Satan and the Antichrist, may well have been a contributing cause of the many deaths at the Waco compound at the conclusion of the 1993 siege.[32] Koresh and his followers had repeatedly asserted that they were ready to die in a final battle (Palmer 1994, pp. 106–8). There are also reports that they were intent on " ... taking as many of 'the beast' with us as we could," in the event of such an attack (Reavis 1995, p. 216).[33]

Jim Jones and his followers, the members of the People's Temple, began to emigrate from the USA in 1977 and relocate to Guyana, where they had established a commune in a place they named Jonestown (Moore 2011, p. 97). The members of the People's Temple had a strong sense of persecution and had become convinced that they had enemies in the US government who regularly spied on them (Moore 2011, pp. 104–5). They had also begun to identify America with the Antichrist, and had come to believe that America would soon be involved in an apocalyptic war against God (Selengut 2003, p. 126). When the Californian Congressman Leo Ryan announced that he was planning to visit Jonestown to investigate allegations of child abuse and kidnapping, made by apostates who had left the People's Temple, Jones told his followers that an American invasion of Jonestown was imminent (Moore 2011, p. 104). Ryan visited Jonestown briefly in late 1978, and it seems that he formed a mostly favorable impression of the commune (Smith 1999, p. 376). However, at the conclusion of the trip, he and four others were assassinated by members of the People's Temple as their plane was taxiing on the runway of an airstrip near Jonestown in preparation for departure. For the most part, Ryan's visit had gone well, but Jones and his followers remained convinced that there was no escape from a coming confrontation with the American Antichrist. Shortly after assassinating Ryan, Jones and over 900 of his followers killed themselves. Their actions were guided by the doctrine of "revolutionary suicide," which will be discussed in the next chapter.

Cosmic War

The characterization of cosmic war as a struggle between the forces of good and the enemies of the good makes it to very easy to justify participation in cosmic war. What could be more closely aligned with the demands of morality than opposition to evil forces that seek to kill, maim, enslave, or oppress the good and the innocent? The need to defend the innocent from unjust attack is usually accepted as a just cause in just war theory. The forces of Satan, and other supernatural evil beings, are invariably understood to be very powerful, and every tactical advantage that can be found may be required in the struggle against them. As we have already seen, the need for defense against unjust attack can be invoked in just war theory to justify pre-emptive strikes against powerful, threatening opponents. So, the need for defense against unjust attack can be invoked to justify pre-emptive strikes against powerful evil forces serving Satan, or serving any other malign supernatural being or beings.

As well as making it easy to justify pre-emptive strikes, belief in cosmic war makes it easy to justify several other forms of behavior that are diffi-cult to justify in conventional war situations by the lights of the *jus in bello* standards of just war theory. Belief in cosmic war makes it particularly easy to: (1) invoke the "supreme emergency exception," (2) employ the "superior orders plea" in defense of behavior that would not otherwise be considered acceptable during war, and (3) blur the combatant–non-combatant distinc-tion and effectively erase non-combatant immunity.

Cosmic War and the Supreme Emergency Exception

As we saw earlier in the chapter, the supreme emergency exception to just war rules has been invoked when there is an imminent threat to a people's "deepest values" and their "collective survival." The presuppositions that Satan is extremely powerful and liable to attack the innocent at any moment make it easy to appeal to the supreme emergency exception to justify behavior that would ordinarily be regarded as immoral, when that behavior is understood in the context of a fight against Satan (*mutatis mutandis* for other powerful evil supernatural opponents of the good). Satan's *raison d'être* is to attack God and the true religion, and Satan has supernatural powers. So, a situation of imminent threat to the deepest values and collective survival of a religious community can arise very rapidly, when that community is at war with Satan.

Muslim, Christian, Hindu, and Buddhist leaders have all appealed to the existence of emergency situations to justify ignoring moral norms, which they would ordinarily describe as guiding their own behavior, as well as that of their followers (Appleby 2000, p. 82). Some religious traditions have developed specific supreme emergency doctrines, making it all the easier for their followers to justify disregarding the moral norms that they would ordinarily endorse, when they believe that they are in situations of supreme emergency. Judaism has a supreme emergency doctrine, which is invoked by Jewish extremists to justify the temporary disregarding of Jewish laws in situations when the existence of the Jewish people is threatened. This is the doctrine of *pikuach nefesh* (Appleby 2000, p. 82.).[34] Shiite Islam has also developed a doctrine of supreme emergency. In the final year of his life Ayatollah Khomeini decreed that, in situations where the survival of the Islamic Republic of Iran is at stake, parts of Islamic law could be temporarily suspended and replaced by the dictates of the supreme jurist (Khomeini himself) (Appleby 2000, p. 89).

Cosmic War and the Superior Orders Plea

The belief that one is fighting on behalf of God, or some other good supernatural being, in a divinely ordained struggle, leads the religious to be very confident of the rightness of the orders given to them by their superiors in the context of that struggle. "I was only following orders" – the "superior orders plea" – was a line of defense against charges of war crimes that was commonly heard in the Nuremberg Trials following World War II. It was routinely rejected by the Nuremberg judges, when those orders were orders to perform immoral acts that were inconsistent with international law. Principle IV of the Nuremberg Principles states that:

> The fact that a person acted pursuant to order of his Government or of a superior does not relieve him from responsibility under international law, provided a moral choice was in fact possible to him.[35]

Many religions instruct their followers to obey God (or some other supreme good supernatural being) unquestioningly, in all contexts, including war. For example, according to the Koran:

> Fighting has been enjoined upon you while it is hateful to you. But perhaps you hate a thing and it is good for you; and perhaps you love a thing and it is bad for you. And Allah Knows, while you know not. (2:216)

If one's orders are believed to have come from God, then the superior orders plea starts to seem very plausible. As we saw in Chapter 1, some believe that God's commands are what make morality what it is. On this view, if God commanded you to do anything, God would also be making it the case that it was morally obligatory for you to attempt to perform the instructed action, so it would not be possible to obey God's commands and also act immorally. Christians, Muslims, and Jews do not have to accept the divine command theory of the origins of morality to be warranted in following God's orders. Merely contemplating the difference between the perfectly good, infallible deity common to Christianity, Islam, and Judaism and imperfect, fallible humans should be sufficient. If God orders me to commit what I and other humans think of as a war crime, I should ask myself whether it is more likely that I and others are mistaken about the nature of war crimes, or that the perfectly good, infallible God is mistaken in presuming that the ordered action is consistent with the requirements of morality. And, if I believe that God is infallible, then the answer is obvious. God cannot be, and therefore is not, mistaken, but I can be, and therefore am.

I can, of course, be mistaken in thinking that I have received a command from God to perform an apparently immoral act. If I think I have received such a command then I ought to consider the possibility that I have misunderstood the content of the command before obeying it. I should also consider the possibility that the command was actually issued by a being other than God, such as Satan, who is trying to trick me into acting immorally. However, if the instruction from God is transmitted to me by a revered religious authority, who assures me that it is genuine, then I will be unlikely to doubt that it is an authentic divine command. If I am a devout, respectful follower of that religion, I will trust that revered religious authority to be able to identify and transmit a genuine command from God. So, I will be very likely to obey that command, even if it leads to me acting in ways which I would otherwise consider to be immoral.

Cosmic War and Non-Combatant Immunity

The belief that one is fighting a cosmic war and not a merely conventional war can lead to the blurring of the combatant–non-combatant distinction and to the effective erasing of non-combatant immunity. The combatant–non-combatant distinction is not an easy distinction to draw, even for purely secular just war theorists (May 2005). Is a factory worker who produces munitions protected by non-combatant immunity? What about a factory worker who manufactures military uniforms? Or what about an accountant who happens to work for the military? Difficulties are compounded when one starts to believe that apparently innocent people are actually assisting an evil supernatural being, such as Satan (perhaps unknowingly), in prosecuting a cosmic war. Evil supernatural beings can orchestrate a near-infinite variety of fiendish plans, including covering up evidence of fiendish plans, so pretty much any activity can be construed as furthering the cause of evil, from the point of view of those who believe they are fighting a cosmic war, potentially depriving any and every apparently ordinary, innocent civilian of all claims to non-combatant immunity. From the point of view of pretty much everyone other than the members of the People's Temple, Congressman Leo Ryan was an innocent American civilian who had flown to Guyana to visit Jonestown and conduct a fact finding mission. But from the point of view of the members of the People's Temple, he was a dangerous enemy agent in the employ of the Antichrist, and a legitimate target in a war situation.

I have shown that it is easy for those religious believers who hold that they are participating in a cosmic war to endorse the ordinary standards of just war theory, and use these to justify a wide range of violent behavior that would otherwise be unjustifiable, even in conventional war contexts. In Chapter 7, I will examine several case studies in which considerations of cosmic war play a role in religious justifications offered for violence. Before then, though, I will consider the role that afterlife beliefs can play in religious justifications of violence in the next chapter. Chapter 6 then examines the role that sacred values can play in religious justifications for violence.

Notes

1. A very few religions that assert that there is a cosmic war taking place do not urge their followers to contribute to the war effort. As we will see in Chapter 7, Heaven's Gate is one such religion and at one stage Aum Shinrikyo was another.
2. These included Philip Francis Berrigan, Daniel Berrigan, SJ, and Thomas Merton, OCSO.
3. For further discussion of the wrongness of violence, see Bufacchi (2004) and Norman (1995, pp. 36–72).
4. For classic criticism of rule-utilitarianism along these lines, see Smart (1956).
5. A philosopher who advocates a position like the one Greene (2008a) attributes to ordinary people is Richard Norman. He rejects straightforward consequentialist justifications for killing, but allows that these could

be acceptable in catastrophe situations, where there is an overwhelming consequentialist case for killing (1995, pp. 207–8).

6. For further discussion of the (alleged) right to self-defence, see Norman (1995, pp. 120–32) and Ryan (1983). For general consideration of the conflict between the moral demands of equality and the pull of partiality, see Nagel (1991) and Keller (2013).

7. For a philosophical defense of the violent punishment of children, see Benatar (1998).

8. For a history of dueling, see Holland (2004).

9. In many jurisdictions ordinary citizens are permitted to make a "citizen's arrest," but only if they directly observe a crime being committed, or have observed one that has very recently taken place. Ordinary citizens are not entitled to arrest others on the basis of a suspicion that a crime has been committed at some time in the past.

10. A recent exception is provided by the Islamic Emirate of Afghanistan (1996–2001). At the time of Osama bin Laden's declaration of war on America, in 1996, al-Qaeda was based in Afghanistan and the Taliban-controlled government of the Islamic Emirate of Afghanistan decided to allow al-Qaeda to prosecute a war on the USA from within its territory.

11. For further criticism of realist opposition to morality in international relations, see Coady (2008, pp. 52–8) and Walzer (2000, pp. 3–20).

12. Realists need not be opposed to the drawing up of rules of war. Rather, they will oppose the unconditional adherence to such rules.

13. Some just war theories are further elaborated and involve a set of conditions guiding the proper conduct of an occupying power, after a war has been won, and a vanquished land is occupied (*jus post bellum*).

14. Johnson includes a seventh criterion: that the war must be conducted with the aim of promoting peace (1999, pp. 28–9).

15. World War I was triggered when the Austrian Archduke Franz Ferdinand was assassinated by a Serbian nationalist in 1914.

16. This broad line of justification was employed both by Catholic theologians, such as the English Catholic prelate William (Cardinal) Allen, to justify war on Protestants, and by Protestant theologians, such as the Swiss Reformed theologian Heinrich Bullinger, to justify war on Catholics (Johnson 1997, pp. 57–9).

17. Some German bombing campaigns, notably those undertaken in Poland and the Netherlands, were also highly indiscriminate.

18. Walzer conceives of the supreme emergency exception as only being available to communities (2004, pp. 41–5).

19. Samples of scathing comments about pacifism, made by philosophers, can be found in Ryan (1983, p. 509). Some of pacifism's most dismissive opponents are Anscombe (1971) and Narveson (1965).

20. Recently Johnson and Tierney (2011) have argued that in situations where we begin to see a war as inevitable, a cluster of cognitive biases push us to construe that war as significantly more likely to be won than we would have believed before we began to see it as inevitable. If they are right, then, at least under an important class of circumstances, we may indeed be too ready to go to war.

21. For example, Cady (2010).

22. One such death was that of Gandhi, who was assassinated in 1948, by a Hindu nationalist, for consenting to the partitioning of India.

23. Norman distinguishes pacifism from "pacificism," which involves trying to promote peace rather than refusing to act violently (1995, pp. 237–41). Perhaps defenders of this way of construing pacifism, such as Alexandra (2003), are better described as defenders of pacificism? For further discussion of this distinction, see Alexandra (2006).

24. After World War I, the League of Nations was set up, principally to maintain world peace. It proved incapable of preventing aggression by the Axis countries in the 1930s and the onset of World War II is generally regarded as a clear indication of its failure (Scott 1974). It was replaced by the United Nations in 1946.

25. Also, Gandhi took the view that minor acts of violence could be acceptable if these prevented more significant acts of violence from occurring (Juergensmeyer 2003, p. 96).

26. Avalos is critical of the scriptural basis for Yoder's Christian pacifism (2005, pp. 215–20).

27. For example, 2:191, 4:74, 4:76, 8:15–17, 8:65.

28. Is religion an individual-level or group-level adaptation for war? Is it a result of genetic or cultural selection? Johnson and Reeve (2013) are open-minded about the answers to these questions and caution us against assuming that the answers need to be mutually exclusive. Religion may be the result of both individual-level and group level selection, and both genetic and cultural selection.

29. The Manicheans were the followers of the Prophet Mani (AD 216–276). Manicheanism was a very significant religion across Asia between the third and seventh centuries, but lost influence thereafter. Unlike Christians and Muslims, Manicheans deny that God is omnipotent (Coyle 2009).

30. In 1996, six months before all but one of its members committed suicide, Heaven's Gate placed a complicated message about Armageddon on its website, entitled "Time to Die for God? Or Armageddon – Which Side are You On?" See http://www.mt.net/~watcher/cultrep.html (accessed March 11, 2013).

31. For further philosophical discussion of conspiracy theories, see the papers collected in Coady (2006).

32. There are several competing accounts of the events at Waco. For a recent review, see Wright (2011).

33. There are two "beasts" mentioned in the Book of Revelation, both of whom are thrown into a lake of fire by God. See Revelation 13:1–18 and 19:18–20.
34. There are moderate interpretations of *pikuach nefesh*, according to which it amounts to something less than a doctrine of "supreme emergency" (Appleby 2000, pp. 82–3).
35. See http://www.icrc.org/ihl.nsf/FULL/390?OpenDocument (accessed November 12, 2012).

5

The Afterlife

Afterlife Beliefs

The first chapter of this book began with a discussion of the massacre of the Fancher–Baker party at Mountain Meadows. Many nineteenth-century Mormons considered this act to be justified, by an appeal to the afterlife. The adults who were killed were alleged, by those nineteenth-century Mormons, to be eligible for a superior afterlife to the one that they would otherwise have been eligible for had they not been "blood atoned." If the (now abandoned) doctrine of blood atonement is accepted, then John D. Lee and his followers were doing the adult members of the Fancher–Baker party a huge favor by killing them. In this chapter, I look at the role afterlife beliefs can play in justifying killing undertaken in the name of religion. My main focus will be on the use of afterlife beliefs as premises in arguments for the conclusion that the killing of others is justified, and I will concentrate on examples from the Christian and Buddhist traditions. I will also consider the use of afterlife beliefs to justify suicide. But first, the general phenomenon of afterlife beliefs is considered. These are extremely common in many societies. Survey evidence suggests that 82 percent of Americans believe in life after death (Greeley and Hout 1999), as do 58 percent of people living in Britain, 78 percent of people in Iceland, and 80 percent of those living in Poland (Haraldsson 2006).

The natural world does not provide us with evidence in favor of the view that humans will experience an afterlife. We have no evidence of any human, or any member of any other species, actually having an afterlife. There are no known facts about human biology that seem to support the

The Justification of Religious Violence, First Edition. Steve Clarke.
© 2014 John Wiley & Sons, Inc. Published 2014 by John Wiley & Sons, Inc.

hypothesis that humans have an afterlife; and the possibility that humans could somehow live on, after their bodies have ceased to function, seems difficult to reconcile with what we know about biology and physics. So why do so many people believe in an afterlife? It might seem that afterlife beliefs could only be acquired as a result of social conditioning sufficiently thorough to enable people to overcome an underlying natural tendency to form beliefs on the basis of evidence, such as the thorough social conditioning that is often involved in a strict religious upbringing. However, many psychologists and cognitive scientists have recently come to the exact opposite conclusion. They suggest that our normal psychological make-up actually disposes us to hold afterlife beliefs. We are "natural dualists," according to Paul Bloom (2004), naturally thinking of the brain and the mind (or soul) as conceptually distinct from one another.[1] On Bloom's view, the human mind has evolved two distinct cognitive systems, one devoted to understanding the behavior of physical objects, and one that specializes in understanding the social world. We are able to engage one of these systems without engaging the other; and just as thoughts of rocks and trees without minds come naturally to us, so do thoughts of minds or souls that exist in the absence of physical bodies.[2]

Bloom's conjecture gains support from research due to Jesse Bering (2002), which suggests that when people represent dead agents, they typically conceive of them as having emotional states, as well as psychobiological states, such as hunger and thirst, and epistemic states – beliefs, knowledge, memories, and so on. This way of conceiving of the dead appears to begin at an early age. Bering and Bjorklund (2004) conducted a series of experiments, which involved them presenting a puppet show to 200 children between the ages of three and twelve.[3] In the grand tradition of Punch and Judy, this was a violent puppet show. In it a mouse called Baby Mouse is eaten by an alligator while innocently strolling through the woods.[4] To rule out the possibility that the children might suppose that Baby Mouse could remain alive in the alligator's stomach, the children were explicitly told that he is no longer alive. They were then asked a series of questions about Baby Mouse. In these experiments, Bering and Bjorklund found that the clear majority of children in each of three age cohorts had no trouble understanding that Baby Mouse was dead and would not be coming back to life. They also understood many of the consequences of Baby Mouse's death. For example, they understood that Baby Mouse would no longer need food or water. However, many continued to attribute emotional, psychobiological, and epistemic states to the dead Baby Mouse.

There are various suggestions in the academic literature that try to explain why it is apparently natural for us to think that our minds or souls survive death. One is that we experience a failure of imagination when we try to contemplate our own deaths. It is easy enough to understand what it is like for bodies, including our own, not to exist. But it is simply beyond our imaginative capacities to grasp what it could be like for our minds not to exist (Nichols 2007). Another is provided by terror management theory. According to terror management theorists (e.g., Goldenberg 2005), we humans are the only animals that are aware of our own mortality, and the sense of terror that this awareness gives rise to is psychologically debilitating for us. The effort required to reduce, and thereby manage this sense of terror, is said to lead to a number of psychological side effects. Key amongst these is an ongoing feeling of hatred for our own bodies, which are a constant reminder of our mortality. One way to manage this sense of terror is to deny to ourselves – perhaps at an unconscious level – that our existence is limited by our physical bodies, or so say terror management theorists (Hodge 2011, pp. 401 – 2). These and other suggestions in the literature are, of course, somewhat speculative and a compelling overall account of the apparent naturalness and pervasiveness of afterlife beliefs has yet to be provided.[5]

Afterlife beliefs are incorporated into religious doctrines in various different ways. Human minds, or souls, are sometimes understood to continue to exist after death, here on earth, without ordinary bodies, as ghosts or ancestor spirits. They are also sometimes said to be reincarnated, perhaps here on earth, perhaps in other worlds, sometimes as humans and sometimes as members of different species. According to some religions, human souls leave this world at the time of physical death and are transferred to another world and then resurrected. The other world may be heaven or hell, or another universe. It may also be another planet within this universe. Those who are resurrected may then have their souls reattached to replicas of their old bodies, or they may be given new, possibly non-human, bodies. And on some religious views, life after death does not involve any form of embodiment at all. Two very different sorts of afterlife beliefs are particularly influential, with both predominating in more than one major world religious tradition. Both of these sorts of afterlife beliefs have important consequences for us, because both offer a ready justification for violent action. The first is a view that mainstream Christianity and Islam both share, which is that, after people die, God makes a choice between sending them either to heaven or to hell, where they spend eternity, either blissfully happy or in a state of continual torment, depending on which of the two places they are sent.[6]

There are, of course, variations on this basic view. For example, many Catholics, as well as members of various other Christian denominations, allow that God can send some people to purgatory, where they are prepared for subsequent entry into heaven, often by being given punishments to expiate their sins. Mormons hold a still more complicated version of the basic view, with various different subcategories of heaven and hell (Ridges 2007). In the twentieth century, some Christians abandoned the view that there is a hell – despite abundant textual evidence in the Bible suggesting that hell exists.[7] Other Christians have disputed the claim that people are sent to hell for eternity, or have disputed the claim that anyone is actually sent to hell, even if it does exist.[8] The principal objection of these various twentieth-century Christian opponents of the traditional conception of hell is that it seems very difficult to accept that a perfectly good God would condemn sinners to eternal damnation (Walter 1996). As we will see, the existence, or nonexistence, of hell is not crucial to traditional Christian justifications of violence. The possibility of eternal happiness in heaven is sufficient to justify a range of violent acts.

The second sort of influential afterlife belief that can be used to justify violence is the view that we are reincarnated after death. Mainstream Hinduism and Buddhism both share the idea that we are reincarnated after death, sometimes as humans, sometimes as animals, and sometimes as other sorts of beings. The form in which we are reincarnated is a consequence of our karma, a kind of moralized causal property (Wadia 1965). Someone who leads a good life accumulates positive karma and is reincarnated as a higher status human, or as superior sort of being, or in a better situation, or in a better place. Someone who leads a sinful life accumulates bad karma and is reincarnated as a lesser status human, or as an inferior being, or in a worse situation, or in a worse place. Some of the better and worse places that one can be reincarnated in are referred to as heavens and hells by Buddhists and Hindus. However, it is important to be aware that these are quite unlike Western conceptions of heaven and hell. They are usually understood, by Buddhists and Hindus, as other universes, or other aspects of this universe, that are better or worse places to reside in than this world. Also, they are not places that people are sent to for eternity. Someone who is reincarnated in a hell as a result of accumulating negative karma can redeem themselves by accumulating positive karma and can subsequently be reborn in a better place.

The quality of a reincarnation is not usually understood by Buddhists and Hindus to result from the determination of a supreme being. Instead it is understood to result from the operation of natural causal laws governing the universe. The various types of beings that exist are arranged in a hierarchy, and every living person is believed to have been reincarnated many, many times, sometimes rising in the hierarchy as a result of accumulated good karma, and sometimes falling as a result of accumulated bad karma. The cycle of reincarnation does not have to be endless, however. A very good person can escape from it. There is a lack of agreement among different Buddhist and Hindu schools of thought about exactly what happens to such a person: whether they cease to exist, or become merged into a greater being, or continue to exist as individuals, but in a radically different way than the one that is familiar to us. It is generally agreed, though, that escape from the cycle of reincarnation is a highly desirable state of affairs.

Christianity, Violence, and Salvation

For much of its history the Catholic Church has considered it to be justifiable to act violently towards heretics – those who develop revisions of officially prescribed religious dogma – as well as apostates – those who abandon their religion. Officially sanctioned violent actions have included torture and killing. Most of the various Catholic inquisitions, which began in the early thirteenth century and continued until the mid-nineteenth century,[9] including the notorious Spanish Inquisition, were primarily directed at suppressing heresy and apostasy (Vacandard 2010). As we will see, the main line of justification offered for such violent action is explicitly tied to considerations of salvation. For a very long time the mainstream Catholic view was that, while it is morally acceptable to employ coercive means to suppress heresy and apostasy, it is not morally acceptable to use coercive means to convert non-Christians to Christianity. Nevertheless, there have been numerous instances when coercive means were used to compel conversion to Christianity, and arguments in favor of such action were provided by theologian Duns Scotus. We will go on to consider his arguments, which also turn on considerations of salvation.

Salvation is a precondition for entry into heaven and on most Christian (and Muslim) views, entry into heaven enables one to experience persistent happiness for eternity. On many Christian (and Muslim) views, a failure to receive salvation leads to persistent suffering in hell, again for eternity. It seems clear enough that salvation is of great, if not overriding, moral importance. However much happiness one can experience in a lifetime, the sum total provided by a series of ephemeral experiences is going to be completely inconsequential in comparison with persistent eternal happiness. It follows that a thoroughgoing consequentialist, who also believes in salvation, should do everything in his or her power to maximize the number of people who will receive salvation. That is the surest way to promote the best consequences for the most people (Clarke 2012). Non-consequentialists will want to resist the claim that the salvation of others is of overwhelming moral importance, but non-consequentialists generally recognize that the consequences of one's actions are of moral importance. If they believe in salvation then they should recognize that the possibility of salvation is a matter of great moral importance and will often trump many other moral concerns, even if it does not always trump all other moral concerns (Clarke 2012).

The traditional Catholic view about salvation is one that is sometimes referred to as "salvific exclusivist" (e.g., Duncan 2007) and is encapsulated in the slogan *Extra Ecclessiam nulla salas* (outside the church there is no salvation). The 1442 Council of Florence is very clear:

> outside the Catholic Church no one, neither heathen nor Jew nor unbeliever nor schismatic will have a share in eternal life, but will, rather, be subject to everlasting fire.[10]

If the Council of Florence is to be believed, one can only have an opportunity to attain salvation if one is a member of the Catholic Church. The Catholic position on salvation was relaxed by the Second Vatican Council (1962–1965) and has now shifted to what I call a "salvific preferentialist" position (Clarke 2012). On this view, it is possible for followers of other religions, as well as agnostics and atheists, to receive salvation, but membership of the Catholic Church makes salvation significantly easier to attain (Jones 1967). Other Christian groups remain salvific exclusivist to this day. Southern Baptists are not as exclusivist as Catholics once were, allowing that all Christians can attain salvation. But they do insist that non-Christians are excluded from the possibility of salvation.[11]

If (pre-Second Vatican Council) salvation is only possible through the Catholic Church, then anyone who deviates from, or renounces, Catholic dogma is forgoing any chance of salvation. For that matter, according to the Council of Florence, such people are effectively guaranteeing themselves an eternity of suffering in hell. Their salvation is a serious matter, but the concern which was invoked by mainstream medieval Catholic theologians, to justify the torturing and killing of heretics and apostates, was not a concern about what they were doing to their own chances of salvation. Rather, it was a concern about the threat that the malign influence of the doctrines, which they were disposed to promulgate, posed to the salvation of devout Catholics (Avalos 2005, p. 203). As Aquinas writes:

> With regard to heretics ... there is the sin, whereby they deserve not only to be separated from the Church by excommunication, but also to be severed from the world by death. For it is a much graver matter to corrupt the faith which quickens the soul, than to forge money, which supports temporal life. Wherefore if forgers of money and other evil-doers are forthwith condemned to death by the secular authority, much more reason is there for heretics, as soon as they are convicted of heresy, to be not only excommunicated but even put to death. (*Summa Theologiae*, 2nd part of the 2nd part, Question 11, Article 3 (Aquinas 1265–1274))

Those who considered the killing of heretics to be unnecessarily cruel were admonished by Calvin in the mid-sixteenth century in his discussion and defense of the execution of Michael Servetus, a controversial theologian and scholar of the day, who denied the doctrine of the Trinity, and who was consequently burnt at the stake for heresy (Bainton 2005). According to Calvin:

> That humanity, advocated by those who are in favour of a pardon for heretics, is greater cruelty because in order to save the wolves they expose the poor sheep. I ask you, is it reasonable that heretics should be allowed to murder souls and to poison them with their false doctrine, and that we should prevent the sword, contrary to God's commandment, from touching their bodies, and that the whole Body of Jesus Christ be lacerated that the stench of one rotten member may remain undisturbed?[12]

Of course, from the Catholic point of view, Calvin, although a Trinitarian, was a reviser of official doctrine and therefore a heretic; he could have been liable to much the same treatment that he was instrumental in securing for Servetus.

The line of justification that Aquinas and Calvin and many other Christian theologians offered for using violent means to suppress heresy and apostasy is one that appeals to considerations of consequence. Heretics and apostates are disposed to promote doctrines that, if accepted, would lead many people to be denied eternal happiness. Aquinas and Calvin and other prominent theologians generally considered ordinary people to be highly susceptible to the influence of such doctrines. In an age when the majority of people had very little education – most could neither read nor write – this was not an unreasonable attitude to take. Heretics were a particular threat to orthodoxy. Because heresies are revisions of the doctrines of established religions, they retain many of the attractive features of established religious doctrines. Also, they may not require much in the way of doctrinal revision. If all Servetus needed to do, in order to cause his otherwise devout Christian followers to become heretics (and thereby become ineligible for salvation), was to persuade them to abandon the doctrine of the Trinity, then it is easy to see why Calvin and others considered him to be a particularly dangerous person.[13]

It might be wondered why the traditional Catholic justification for suppressing heresy and apostasy does not straightforwardly extend to an argument justifying the forced conversion of any and all non-Catholics to Catholicism. After all, on the traditional view, all non-Catholics are ineligible for salvation and are doomed to spend the rest of their lives in hell.[14] If violent torture for a relatively short period of time were sufficient to cause them to accept Catholicism, and thereby become eligible for salvation, then that would be a small price to pay for an opportunity to obtain eternal happiness, and well justified, at least in terms of considerations of consequence. One can well imagine that if those who had been tortured by religious authorities during their lifetime ended up in heaven as a result, and came to understand that their torture was instrumental in enabling them to gain entry into heaven (and avoid hell), then they would be extremely grateful to their torturers.

One objection to forced conversion is that it may well be unsuccessful. Locke famously argued that, although it is possible to coerce expressions of religious belief, it is not possible to coerce genuine religious belief (1689). But this is an empirical matter and it doesn't seem implausible to think that the use of coercive means might lead to the adoption of genuine religious belief, at least some of the time (Waldron 1991). The forced conversion of many American Indians to Christianity by the Spanish conquistadors seems to have been extremely successful (McKennie Goodpasture 1989). The mainstream Catholic view, which was endorsed by Aquinas and many other Christian theologians, was that faith which was not freely chosen would not be acceptable to God, and so would not be sufficient to enable salvation.[15] In the case of heretics and apostates, however, we are considering people who have previously made a voluntary choice to accept Christianity, which is acceptable to God, and which Aquinas and others understood to be an irrevocable form of commitment (Avalos 2005, p. 202).

The use of coercive means is considered to be justified in these cases, both because such use may be effective in enabling heretics and apostates to regain the appropriate beliefs to become eligible to attain salvation, and because, having freely consented to commit themselves to God, they are considered to have acquired an enforceable, irrevocable commitment to continue to obey God.

Those Catholic theologians who favored using coercive means to secure conversions tended to try to weaken the conditions that would ordinarily be used to judge whether consent was freely given or not.[16] In the context of a discussion of the practice of forced baptism, in 1201, Pope Innocent III pronounced that, if someone who was being compelled to undergo a baptism ceremony ceased objecting, at any point during the ceremony, then the Church was entitled to interpret the cessation of their objections as evidence that they had consented to the baptism (Turner 2006, p. 195).[17] This pronouncement was provided with a justification by Duns Scotus, who reasoned that God understands the weaknesses of humans and understands that it is very difficult for us to fully consent to follow His will. Understanding all of this, God is content to accept any level of assent that we are capable of giving. So, the failure of someone to persistently object to being forced to undergo a baptism is enough of an indication of consent for God, or so Duns Scotus argues (Turner 2006, pp. 195–6). Once a baptism that has been deemed legitimate by the church has taken place, the person who has been baptized is not free to leave the church, and would be treated like any other apostate, or heretic, should he or she attempt to do so. The underlying justification for this entire line of argument appeals, of course, to the moral importance of salvation. The baptized are eligible for salvation and the unbaptized are not. It may seem cruel to use coercive means to baptize people, but if we genuinely believe that this is the only effective way to enable them to become eligible for salvation, then surely such rough treatment is well justified by appeal to considerations of (eternal) consequence.

Duns Scotus also introduced two arguments in favor of fully coerced baptism. Both of these were presented as arguments for the forced conversion of Jews to Christianity. However, no component of either argument depends on any particular details of Judaism, and so both are straightforwardly applicable to any non-Christian. Jews are the subject of these arguments, it seems, because they were the only numerically significant religious minority present in Britain during Duns Scotus's lifetime (1265–1308). The first is an argument for the forced baptism of Jewish children. Aquinas and other mainstream Christian theologians argued against the baptism of non-Christian children, on the grounds that this would be a violation of the natural rights of their non-Christian parents, who exercised legitimate authority over their children. However, Duns Scotus rejected this line of argument, on the grounds that God's rights overrode parental rights. Furthermore, he held that intermediary powers, such as the rulers of Christian states, who stand between ordinary parents and God, have a duty to ensure that God's rights are upheld. Therefore, they have a duty to ensure that infant baptism takes place, regardless of the wishes of parents (Krop 1989, pp. 164–5).

Duns Scotus's other argument for fully coerced baptism is an argument for the fully coerced baptism of Jewish parents. Duns Scotus is not naïve enough to suppose that this is likely to make true believers of them. Nevertheless, he writes:

> it is religiously just for those parents themselves to receive baptism forcibly with threats and fear, because although they will not be real believers at heart, the evil for them to be stopped from serving their law with impunity is less than serving that law freely. What is more, if their children are well educated, they will be real believers in the third and fourth generation.[18]

Even if it is too late to prevent Jewish parents from going to hell, this should not stop us from using coercive means on them to enable their children, and their children's children (and so on), to enter the Kingdom of Heaven, or so Duns Scotus argues. And, of course, the same line of argument can be applied to any non-Christian parent.

Buddhism, Violence, and Reincarnation

Buddhism is often perceived in Western countries as a pacifist religion. So, many Westerners were very surprised when the Dalai Lama effectively endorsed the killing of Osama bin Laden, by American special forces, in a 2011 speech delivered at the University of Southern California (Landsberg 2011). In the speech, the Dalai Lama drew a distinction between Osama bin Laden the person, who deserves compassion, and his destructive actions, leading to the events of September 11, 2001, which "must be brought to justice" (Office of His Holiness the Dalai Lama 2011). The Dalai Lama's words were consistent with previous statements he has made about violence and compassion. Although he is a proponent of

124 *The Afterlife*

"non-violence," the Dalai Lama does not understand violence motivated by compassion to be inconsistent with non-violence. According to him, when "wrathful forceful action" is motivated by compassion it is actually a form of non-violence, even though it is "violence on a physical level" (Jenkins 2011).

To understand how the killing of bin Laden could be construed as an act of compassion towards him, we need to appreciate Buddhist beliefs about the afterlife.[19] As an organizer of violence on a massive scale, bin Laden is someone who would have accumulated a large amount of negative karma throughout his life. If he were to have carried on behaving as he had been – and his public statements and known behavior gave us good reasons to think that this was exactly what he was intending to do – then he would have accumulated even more negative karma. Given the way bin Laden lived, it seems reasonable, if we accept Buddhist beliefs about karma and the cycle of reincarnation, to conclude that he has now been reincarnated as a lesser being, or in a lesser place, such as a Buddhist hell. But if he were to have died later than he actually did, then, all things being equal, he would have gone on to accumulate even more negative karma, and would eventually have been reincarnated as an even lesser being, or in an even worse place – perhaps an even nastier hell. So, it can be act of compassion to kill bin Laden sooner, rather than allow him to die later.

The view that one may commit violent acts, even though these are ordinarily forbidden, if one remains compassionate to one's victims, is endorsed in key texts in the scripture of the Mahayana tradition, the larger of the two main Buddhist traditions existing today (Jenkins 2010, p. 70). Some Buddhist scholars are careful to distinguish compassion from sentimentality, and are willing to endorse violent punishments, killing, and even torture, provided that an outcome of such acts is better karmic consequences for the person who is punished, killed, or tortured (Jenkins 2010, pp. 67–70). The Buddhist justification for compassionate killing, to prevent worse consequences in the afterlife, has sometimes been applied on a large scale. Aum Shinrikyo (now known as Aleph) is a syncretist religious group, but its main intellectual roots are in Tibetan and Japanese Buddhism (Jones 2008, p. 71). It was responsible for the 1995 sarin gas attack on the Tokyo subway system, which resulted in twelve deaths and many thousands of injuries. As we will see in Chapter 7, the leader of Aum Shinrikyo, Shoko Asahara, held that the killing of twelve Japanese commuters was a justified and merciful act, which could reasonably be expected to improve the quality of their afterlives (Juergensmeyer 2003, p. 115).

The "compassionate killing" line of justification is not the only line of justification for violence that Buddhists have sometimes endorsed. In Theravāda Buddhism there is a tradition of arguing that violent state punishments of criminals (including torture and execution) are a "fruition of the victim's own karma" (Jenkins 2010, pp. 64–5). The state has no need to justify violent actions against criminals, because criminals are ultimately responsible for state violence directed against them. Another line of justification for violence, which has been endorsed by some Theravāda Buddhists, involves holding that some classes of non-Buddhist victims of violence lack ordinary human moral status and are "not more to be esteemed than beasts" (Keyes 2007, p 154). So, violent action taken against them is not a matter of moral significance. This line of justification for violence seems to have been influential, at times, in Sri Lanka, Cambodia, and Thailand (Keyes 2007, pp. 154–9). A few Japanese Mahayana Buddhists have appealed to the cycle of reincarnation to justify violence against non-Buddhists. If those who are killed are reborn, then there is no genuine destruction of life to be concerned about (Jerryson 2010, p. 9). Buddhists have also justified violence by citing the need to defend Buddhism from its enemies and by appealing to the consequentialist line of argument that it is justifiable to kill the one to save the many (Demiéville 2010, p. 41).

Buddhism, like Christianity and Islam, is a religious tradition with an expansive body of scripture, which is subject to a variety of interpretations. Some of these interpretations are pacifist ones, but many are not. While Buddhist religious doctrines have exerted a strong influence on majority Buddhist nations, these influences have not resulted in the creation of pacifist states. Predominantly Buddhist nations, such as Thailand, Burma, and Sri Lanka, retain standing armies and have engaged in military action on a not infrequent basis. The predominantly Buddhist Sri Lankan army has recently been engaged in a particularly bloody civil war against the predominantly Hindu Liberation Tigers of Tamil Eelam, which lasted from 1983 to 2009; and the army's campaign was supported by many (but, of course, not all) Buddhist monks (Kent 2010, p. 162). In 1959, the then Sri Lankan prime minister, Solomon Bandaranaike, was assassinated by a Buddhist monk for failing to pursue pro-Sinhalese Buddhist policies aggressively enough.[20] Mongolian Buddhist Khans of the sixteenth century forcibly converted followers of shamanistic religions to Buddhism (Wallace 2010, p. 91); Japanese Zen Buddhists were very prominent in promoting Japanese participation in World War II (Victoria 2006); and Chinese Buddhists were enthusiastic advocates of China's involvement in the Korean war of 1951–1953 (Yu 2010). Very recently, a Buddhist monk has spearheaded efforts to stir up anti-Muslim sentiments in Burma, which have led to the deaths of over 200 people (Kyaw 2013). Buddhism has also been associated with violence in some quite specific ways. Ch'an Buddhist masters in China incorporated physical blows with fists and staffs into their training methods (Victoria 2006, p. 207); Zen Buddhist masters have written fencing manuals (Demiéville 2010, p. 38);, and leading Chinese and Tibetan Buddhists, including the Panchen Lama,[21] raised money to buy a "Buddhist fighter plane" for China when it was involved in the Korean war (Wallace 2010, pp. 146–8).

Killing has karmic repercussions for those killed and it also has karmic repercussions for the killer. The possibility of killing someone, to provide them with long-term benefits in the afterlife, places Buddhist theologians on the horns of a dilemma. On the one hand, it seems that killing is necessarily a violent act and should result in negative karma for the killer. On the other hand, it seems that helping someone to achieve better karmic consequences is a virtuous thing to do, and ought to result in positive karma for the killer.[22] The most common way to try to resolve this dilemma, in Buddhist thinking, is to appeal to the equivalent of the Western intention/foresight distinction (Jenkins 2010, p. 68; Kent 2010, pp. 164–6).[23] If improving bin Laden's karmic future is your intended aim then, even if realizing your intended aim involves bin Laden's death, and even if you correctly foresee that it involves bin Laden's death, you do not accumulate negative karma as a result of killing bin Laden, provided that killing him is not also an intended aim of yours. Furthermore, because your intended aim is the improvement of bin Laden's karmic situation, you accumulate positive karma through your compassionate actions. On some Buddhist views, you can accrue great merit if you are willing to risk your own karmic future by killing others for their own sake (Jenkins 2010, p. 69).[24] Indeed, Shoko Asahara assured his Aum Shinrikyo followers that by killing people who were behaving badly, and who were certain to go to hell, they themselves would progress significantly closer to escaping from the cycle of reincarnation (Kaplan and Marshall 1996, p. 50).

Suicide, Suicide Cults, and the Afterlife

So far we have considered the role that influential afterlife beliefs have played in justifying the killing of other people. It is also worth considering whether and when afterlife beliefs can play a role in justifying suicide. It might be thought that people who commit suicide do not need to justify their actions, provided that these are successful. Once they are dead, they will not have to face the worldly consequences of their actions, or face demands that they justify those actions. However, the act of killing oneself, being an act of killing, raises a serious moral issue, and to the extent that people are concerned by this issue, they will feel the need to justify their contemplated action, at least to themselves. If they adhere to a religion that endorses belief in an afterlife then this adherence can further complicate their thinking. Here we consider whether and how Buddhist beliefs about reincarnation and Christian beliefs about salvation might be used to justify suicide. Then we consider the role that afterlife beliefs have played in the justification of self-killing in some recent "suicide cults."

Buddhist theologians have generally taken a dim view of suicide and if we think about the karmic consequences of suicide it is easy to see why. Suicide is a form of killing so, on mainstream Buddhist (and Hindu) views, it will cause negative karma and, all things being equal, it will result in a worse afterlife for the person committing suicide than they would otherwise experience (Keown 1998). It is also generally thought to be ineffective if used in the hope of escaping from the cycle of reincarnation (Harvey 2000, pp. 286–7).[25] But could there be a Buddhist argument for compassionate suicide that parallels the Buddhist argument for compassionate killing discussed earlier? The argument for compassionate killing depended on the claim that the person to be compassionately killed was very likely to make their karmic situation worse by leading a bad life in the future. It would seem difficult to apply this line of reasoning to justify suicide. If a person realized that they were leading a bad life, and thereby accruing negative karma, then the most obvious way for them to cease accruing negative karma would be to cease leading a bad life, to start to behave virtuously, and so start to accrue positive karma. Bin Laden appeared a worthy target for compassionate killing because he (apparently) did not accept that he was leading a bad life, and so lacked motivation to change his ways. But Buddhists who realize that they are leading bad lives should be motivated to change their ways. It seems that an act of suicide can only be justified, via the argument for compassionate killing, if there is some good reason why the person seeking to justify suicide is no longer capable of leading a virtuous life. If a case can be made for this conclusion, then an argument for compassionate suicide can get off the ground. But it would seem that the range of possible circumstances in which people might find themselves such that they are actually incapable of leading a virtuous life is going to be narrow.[26]

The Christian argument for killing heretics and apostates, to prevent them from promulgating views that would lead people who accepted these views to miss out on a chance of salvation, seems even more difficult to use to justify suicide than the Buddhist argument for compassionate killing. If I come to realize that my own religious views are misguided, and are going to lead to me being denied a chance of salvation, then not only will I be highly motivated to cease promulgating those harmful views, I will also be highly motivated to change those views and adopt ones that actually will give me a chance of attaining salvation. But once I change my religious views, and adopt what I now take to be the correct ones, I can no longer apply the Christian argument for killing heretics and apostates to my own case.

The possibility of salvation and eternal happiness in heaven could provide a prima facie justification for suicide under some circumstances, if we accept the following argument. Suppose that I am a devout Christian and I sincerely believe that I have led a virtuous life until now and have scrupulously observed the various requirements of my religion. I have every reason to expect that, if I were to die now, I would go on to attain salvation and experience eternal happiness in heaven. However, I have often found myself tempted to commit sinful acts that could lead to my being denied a chance of salvation, and I am worried that I may eventually give in to temptation. I conclude, therefore, that I should "quit while I am ahead" and kill myself now, so as to ensure that I attain salvation, rather than risking the possibility of giving into temptation in the future and thereby making it less likely that I will attain salvation after I eventually die of natural causes.

The above line of reasoning would be a non-starter for a Muslim because the Koran prohibits suicide.[27] However, things are less clear for Christians, as the Bible does not contain any specific rulings about suicide. Nevertheless, since the fifth century, mainstream Christians have taken the view that suicide is absolutely prohibited. In the early fifth century, Augustine influentially argued that the Commandment "You shall not murder"[28] is properly interpreted as applying to one's own person as much as it applies to others (Augustine 1871, Book 1, Chapter 20). Aquinas spelt out three further arguments against suicide: that it is contrary to our nature, that it harms our community, and that it constitutes a failure to observe a duty to God who, according to Aquinas, has a right to determine the length of our earthly existence (Aquinas 1265–1274, 2nd part, Question 64, Article 5).

On mainstream Christian views, suicide is far more likely to send one to hell than help one to attain salvation.

Before Augustine's views on suicide became Christian orthodoxy, there were a few church fathers who not only thought that suicide was sometimes permissible, but actually advocated it in specific circumstances. Augustine's contemporary Justin (345–419) advocated suicide as an appropriate response for women whose chastity was seriously threatened (Amundsen 1989, p. 121).[29] The Donatists, a schismatic group inspired by Donatus, the Bishop of Carthage from 313–355, were advocates of "heroic suicide." In practice this involved killing themselves – often in dramatic ways, such as jumping into a fire or down a ravine – rather than allowing others, who were threatening to kill them, to act on those threats (Amundsen 1989, pp. 130–4). A sub-group of the Donatists, known as the Circumcellions, was reported to have approached travelers and pagan worshippers and demanded that they kill them, threatening to attack the travelers and pagan worshippers if they did not (Robertson 1854, p. 182). The Donatists and the Circumcellions acted in these ways in the hope and expectation that they would be killed and would attain salvation. The behavior of the Donatists and the Circumcellions, which is condemned by mainstream Christians, is perhaps as close as any Christians have come to acting on the salvific argument for suicide described earlier.

In recent decades there has been a series of spectacularly violent events in which followers of religious groups have either been involved in complicated mixes of mass suicide and murder, or pure instances of mass suicide. Perhaps the most notorious of these is the 1978 Jonestown massacre, in Guyana, which involved the deaths of over 900 members of the People's Temple. A total of seventy-seven members of the Order of the Solar Temple died in a series of murder-suicides, staged between 1994 and 1997, in Switzerland, France, and Canada. Also in 1997, thirty-nine of the forty members of Heaven's Gate committed suicide in California. In two other recent mass killings of followers of religious groups, it is unclear whether or not suicide was a cause of death. Eighty-two members of the Branch Davidian died in Waco, Texas, in 1993, as a result of a fire in their compound, which started during a US government siege. It is unclear whether this was deliberately set by suicidal members of the Branch Davidian, or was started accidentally, perhaps by them, or perhaps by US government agents (Hall 2002; Wright 2011). It is also unclear whether some of the deaths of almost 800 members of the Movement for the Restoration of the Ten Commandments of God, in Uganda in 2000, were the result of suicide or not (Mayer 2011).

Although all of these groups appear to have endorsed some or other afterlife beliefs, it is surprising how insignificant a part a desire for the afterlife played in motivating many of the mass killings that their members engaged in.[30]

The Jonestown massacre appears to have been triggered by a growing sense, amongst the residents of the People's Temple commune in Jonestown, Guyana, that their community was being persecuted, and by a conviction that the world was a terrible place and about to get worse. The leader of the People's Temple, Jim Jones, was an advocate of "revolutionary suicide," a confusing doctrine, according to which the mass deaths of members of the People's Temple would both free them from impending miseries in this world and somehow advance the cause of international socialism (Chidester 1988, pp. 129–59).[31] As far as we can tell, members of the People's Temple killed themselves because of their adherence to the doctrine of revolutionary suicide rather than because they hoped to attain immediate salvation (Hall 2003; Moore 2011).[32] The Old Believers appeared to have committed mass suicide primarily because they were concerned to leave this earth before the coming of the Antichrist, rather than because they were particularly concerned to go to heaven sooner than they would otherwise (Robbins 1986, p. 4). If members of the Branch Davidian committed suicide during the Waco siege of 1993, then this is probably for similar reasons to the mass suicide of the Old Believers. The leader of the Branch Davidian, David Koresh, preached about the coming apocalypse and the fulfillment of prophecies made in the Book of Revelation (Eller 2010, p. 132; Hall 2002, p. 150). Apostates from the Branch Davidian had been warning that the Branch Davidian's compound was likely to turn into "another Jonestown" well before the Waco siege took place in 1993 (Hall 2002, p. 149). And if members of the Movement for the Restoration of the Ten Commandments of God committed suicide, then this action is likely to have been prompted by the apocalyptic and millennial rhetoric of leading members of that movement (Mayer 2011, pp. 206–8).

Afterlife beliefs do seem to have played a significant role in the reasoning that led to the deaths of members of two recent "suicide cults." One of these was the "UFO cult," Heaven's Gate. We will defer discussion of Heaven's Gate and their afterlife beliefs until Chapter 7. The other is the Order of the Solar Temple. Members of the Order of the Solar Temple endorsed a complicated mélange of esoteric religious doctrines (Chryssides 2006). One of their key beliefs was that they (but not any other people) were not originally from earth, but were superior alien beings from another world, temporarily taking human form, and in transit here on their way back to their world of

origin (Mayer 2003, p. 214).[33] Their world of origin was sometimes identified as Jupiter (Mayer 2003, pp. 215 – 16). The belief that members of the
Order of the Solar Temple were aliens to this world, and would only be here
for a relatively short time before returning to their world of origin, transformed the moral significance of their suicide. From their point of view, the
act of killing themselves merely amounted to casting aside their temporary
human bodies and returning from a visit to a relatively backward place to
resume their lives in their original alien bodies; hardly a matter of any great
moral importance.

Notes

1. Bloom (2004) appears to be thinking of Cartesian substance dualism, as
   opposed to various other forms of dualism discussed by philosophers of mind.
2. Similarly, we are easily able to conceive of zombies: beings with bodies, as well
   as brains directing the activities of those bodies, but no minds or souls.
3. Also discussed in Bering (2011, pp. 120 – 5).
4. Baby Mouse is renamed "Brown Mouse" and "White Mouse" in some of Bering
   and Bjorklund's (2004) experiments.
5. For recent criticism of these and other explanations of the naturalness of afterlife beliefs, see Hodge (2011).
6. The Bible is vague about exactly what goes on in hell, only explicitly men-
   tioning ongoing torment by fire (e.g., Mark 9:42 – 8). Traditionally Christians
   have followed Aquinas in holding that, in the context of biblical discussions of
   hell, the term "fire" is used generically, to refer to a range of different punishments (Aquinas 1265 – 1274, Suppl. Question 97, Articles 1 and 5). The Koran
   is much more explicit about what happens in hell. There is scalding water to
   be drunk (6:70); foreheads, flanks, and backs to be branded (9:35); garments
   of fire to be worn (22:19); and food like "murky oil" that "boils within bellies"
   to be eaten (44:43 – 7).
7. For example, see Luke (12:15); Mark (9:42 – 8); Matthew (10:28) and 2 Peter
   (2:4). For further discussion of biblical textual evidence for the existence of
   hell, see Marshall (2003).
8. For philosophical discussion of the various possible ways of construing the
   Christian hell, see Kvanvig (1993).
9. In 1858 Italian officials of the inquisition abducted a six-year-old Jewish boy
   in Bologna upon learning that he had been secretly baptised by a Christian
   servant of his family. In their eyes this made the child a Christian and someone who needed to be protected from attempts by his Jewish family to turn
   him into an apostate. The resulting scandal dramatically weakened the political power of the Vatican and effectively ended the inquisition (Kertzer 1998).

10. Cited in Avalos (2005, p. 197).
11. According to the current Southern Baptist faith and message statement: "There is no salvation apart from personal faith in Jesus Christ as Lord." See http://www.sbc.net/bfm/bfmcomparison.asp (accessed February 7, 2013).
12. Cited by Duncan (2007, p. 2).
13. The denial of Trinitarianism was sufficient to make Servetus's views heretical. Servetus also opposed infant baptism and this opposition was widely considered to be heretical as well (Bainton 2005).
14. However, the church has usually allowed that morally upstanding people who lived before the time of Christ, and so never had an opportunity to hear Christ's message, could attain salvation.
15. See *Summa Theologiae*, 2nd part of the 2nd part, Question 10, Article 8 (Aquinas 1265–1274).
16. Another argumentative strategy that has occasionally been used is to assert that particular groups of people are not capable of free choice. This strategy was adopted by Sepúlveda in his debate with Las Casas in the "Vallodolid controversy" (1550–1551). Sepúlveda argued that the American Indians had debased themselves by a lack of temperance and by the commission of abominable acts, such as cannibalism. Because of their failure to follow "natural law," they had regressed to the level of Aristotelian "natural slaves" and could no longer exercise free choice. The forced conversion of these natural slaves to Christianity was understood by Sepúlveda as a way of restoring their full humanity and their concomitant ability to exercise free choice (Andújar 1997).
17. Baptism is widely considered to be sufficient to enable admission into a Christian Church.
18. Cited in Krop (1989, p. 165).
19. The Dalai Lama's endorsement of the mission to kill bin Laden is consistent with the Buddhist reasoning about violence, non-violence, and the afterlife outlined here. However, he does not explicitly justify that endorsement by appealing to this reasoning.
20. Curiously, the Buddhist monk in question converted to Christianity two days before he was executed for the assassination (Heatherington 2005, pp. 537–8).
21. The Panchen Lama is the second ranking figure in Tibetan Buddhism, after the Dalai Lama.
22. Kent (2010, pp. 163–6) reports that uncertainty about the karmic consequences of their harmful actions are a major concern of Sri Lankan Buddhist soldiers.
23. The intention/foresight distinction is at the heart of the Catholic "Doctrine of Double Effect" (Aulisio 1995).
24. As Jenkins puts things, "the more willing bodhisattvas are to go to hell, the more certain it is that they will not" (2010, p. 69).

25. However, if a person has achieved "enlightenment" whilst alive and is spiritually ready to escape from the cycle of reincarnation then, on some Buddhist views, suicide may result in their immediate escape from the cycle of reincarnation (Keown 1998, pp. 392–3).

26. There is a long tradition of self-immolation by Buddhist monks, as a form of political protest (Jerryson 2010, p. 7). When monks who plan to commit suicide via self-immolation seek to justify their intended behaviour, they typically argue that they are not currently able to lead virtuous lives because of political oppression. The death by self-immolation of at least 100 Tibetan Buddhists has taken place since 2009. Of these a significant number have been Buddhist monks. All deaths appear to be a form of protest against the oppressive nature of Chinese rule in Tibet (International Campaign for Tibet 2013).

27. Koran 4:29.

28. Exodus 20:13

29. Ambrose (AD 339–397) argued similarly (Amundsen 1989, pp. 120–1).

30. There is nothing new about religiously inspired mass suicides. In the late seventeenth and early eighteenth centuries, in Russia, tens of thousands of "Old Believers" – dissenters from reforms that had taken place within the Russian Orthodox Church – killed themselves in a series of collective suicide events, most of which involved self-immolation (Robbins 1986).

31. Jones's doctrine of revolutionary suicide was a variation on the more coherent doctrine of revolutionary suicide advocated by Huey Newton, the leader of the Black Panthers. In Newton's view, a revolutionary might expect to have to give up his or her life in the course of the fight for justice. Newton did not advocate killing oneself as a direct means of advancing a just cause. Indeed, he would have castigated such action as an instance of "reactionary suicide" (Newton 2009, p. 2).

32. At one point Jones entertained the idea that the members of the People's Temple might be reborn and reunited after death on another planet. However, this idea was soon dropped (Chidester 1988, pp. 130–1).

33. Sometimes members of the Order of the Solar Temple described themselves as gods rather than superior aliens (Mayer 2003, p. 219).

6

The Sacred

The Sacred and the Holy

In this chapter, I examine the concept "sacred." I consider various ways in which it is used, in both religious and non-religious contexts. I then look at its role in Durkheim's thinking about religion. The sacred is central to Durkheim's account of religion, an account that has been extremely influential in anthropology, sociology, and religious studies. I also consider recent work on sacred values, in psychology and negotiation studies, before looking at some contemporary work on sacralization in cognitive science and neuroscience. In the final section of the chapter, I discuss the role sacred values can play in religious justifications of violence.

The vast majority of religions make use of the terms (which I will use interchangeably) "sacred" and/or "holy." To Jews, Israel is the "Holy Land," given to the descendants of Abraham by God as part of a sacred covenant.[1] In the early nineteenth century, Mormons considered "the Land of Missouri" to be another holy land. According to Joseph Smith, the founder of the (Mormon) Church of Jesus Christ of Latter-Day Saints, Missouri was the original site of the Garden of Eden. It was consecrated by God, and then given by Him to His people, the Mormons (Bagley 2002, pp. 8–9). The Jewish Torah, the Christian Bible, and the Muslim Koran are considered to be sacred texts by followers of Judaism, Christianity, and Islam, respectively. Abbeys, chapels, churches, mosques, shrines, synagogues, tabernacles, temples, and wats are generally considered to be sacred places, at least by the religious believers who worship in them. Particular religions also consider some rituals to be sacred, certain relics to be holy, and particular people to be holy men and

The Justification of Religious Violence, First Edition. Steve Clarke.
© 2014 John Wiley & Sons, Inc. Published 2014 by John Wiley & Sons, Inc.

women. For many religions human life itself is sacred and people ought not to be killed without invoking the authority of an appropriate supernatural being. In the Judeo-Christian tradition, human life is considered to be sacred because humans are said to be created in the image of God. Genesis 1:27 tells us that "God created man in His *own* image; in the image of God He created him; male and female He created them."

Any demonstration of disrespect towards, or any mistreatment of, sacred lands, scripture, buildings, relics or people can be expected to provoke outrage amongst those who hold these to be sacred, and is liable to incite violence. The threat of such violence was manifested very recently in the case of Rimsha Masih, a young Christian Pakistani girl, who is said to suffer from Down syndrome, and who was arrested in mid-August 2012 on suspicion of violating Pakistan's blasphemy laws. Pakistan's blasphemy laws regulate considerably more than just blasphemy, and Masih was not accused of blasphemy as such, but of burning parts of a sacred text: verses from the Koran. Had she been convicted of this charge she could have received the death penalty.[2] This accusation led to a severe heightening of tensions between the Christian minority and the Muslim majority in the area on the outskirts of Islamabad where Masih lived. A senior member of the local Muslim community ordered all Christians to take their belongings and vacate the area by the end of August. Fearing for their lives, most of the 900 members of the local Christian community promptly left the area (Boone 2012). The case against Masih was dropped in November 2012, due to a lack of reliable evidence (Edwards 2012).[3]

The Masih case is far from unique and violence often results when conflicts about sacred people, places, objects, and rituals arise. In 1984, the then prime minister of India Indira Gandhi was assassinated by her Sikh bodyguards. The assassination was widely thought to be a response to Gandhi's decision to allow Indian special forces to storm the Golden Temple, the holiest of Sikh temples. The Golden Temple complex had been occupied by armed followers of the radical Sikh separatist preacher Sant Jarnail Bhindranwale since 1980, and by 1984 it was heavily fortified. The Indian army's assault on the temple complex was badly mishandled and resulted in over 2,000 deaths, including the deaths of innocent worshippers who had nothing to do with the occupation (Juergensmeyer 2003, p. 99). It also resulted in the destruction of many revered ancient structures located in the temple complex, along with the burning of religiously significant manuscripts stored within these structures (Hassner 2006). The killing of a Hindu prime minister by Sikhs triggered widespread rioting in Delhi, and other places in

India, as well as the slaughter of nearly 3,000 Sikhs by angry Hindu mobs (Bedi 2009).

In November 2002, violent riots broke out in the city of Kaduna in north-central Nigeria, a city with substantial populations of both Christians and Muslims, resulting in more than 220 deaths (Astill and Bowcott 2002). The trigger for these riots was an irreverent article, published in *ThisDay*, a Nigerian national newspaper. The article discussed the Miss World beauty pageant, which was scheduled to take place in Nigeria in December that year. Isioma Daniel, the journalist who wrote the article, implied that the Prophet Muhammad would have wanted to marry one of the contestants, had he met them. Conservative Muslims were already opposed to the pageant, which in their eyes promoted both promiscuity and immodesty. The suggestion that the Prophet Muhammad might wish to marry a promiscuous, immodest, beauty pageant contestant was taken by them to be an outrageous insult to the most revered and sacred person in the history of Islam (Cowell 2002). Following the riots the pageant was relocated to London. Isioma Daniel resigned from her job shortly after the article appeared, and left Nigeria soon afterwards, fearing for her safety. She now lives in Europe. Soon after the riots the deputy governor of the conservative, predominantly Muslim state of Zamfara in Northern Nigeria, which follows shariah law, issued a fatwa calling on Muslims to kill Isioma Daniel. The next day the Zamfara state information minister confirmed that this was indeed state policy. According to the minister: "It's a fact that Islam prescribes the death penalty on anybody, no matter his faith, who insults the Prophet" (Astill and Bowcott 2002).[4]

It might be thought that it would be a simple matter to avoid mistreating, or showing disrespect, to the sacred people, places, objects, rituals, and values of other religious groups, and thereby avoid provoking violence. But matters can become complicated when differing conceptions of the sacred come into conflict with one another. Jerusalem is considered a holy city by Jews and also by Muslims (who refer to it as Al-Quds) and, unsurprisingly, both Jewish and Muslim communities wish to control Jerusalem. But it is not possible for both communities to have exclusive control of the same city. A more indirect conflict between differing conceptions of the sacred prompted the destruction of two giant sixth-century Buddhist statues in the Bamiyan valley in Afghanistan in March 2001. The statues were dynamited on the orders of the Taliban leader Mullah Omar; and members of al-Qaeda assisted the Taliban in completing their destruction. At that time most of Afghanistan was governed by the Taliban. The Bamiyan statues might have been holy relics for Buddhists, but both the Taliban and al-Qaeda considered them to be sacrilegious idols. They took the view that the statues were attempts to visually represent God, something which is strictly forbidden in Islam. The Taliban and al-Qaeda felt that they had a religious duty, therefore, to destroy the Bamiyan statues (Berger 2006, pp. 247–9).

Although the concept of the sacred is strongly associated with religion it is not an exclusively religious concept. Nation states sometimes treat places, people, objects, rituals, and values as sacred. Buildings of national significance, such as war memorials commemorating the struggles that led to the founding of a particular nation, are often considered to be sacred and demonstrations of disrespect towards these are usually taken very seriously. In 2011, Charlie Gilmour, the son of Pink Floyd guitarist Dave Gilmour, was sentenced to sixteen months in prison for violent disorder during a protest. The length of the sentence took into account the fact that he demonstrated disrespect for the Cenotaph, a war memorial located in London, by swinging from a Union Jack flag that was attached to its side (Odone 2011).[5] The sites of significant battles are often also treated as sacred, as are national flags. Secular governments sometimes use coercive means to prevent the desecration of their country's national flag, at least on their own territory.[6] In Turkey secular sacralization has gone further and it has become illegal for anyone to name themselves "Atatürk" – Mustafa Kemal Atatürk being the founder of the secular state of Turkey. It is also illegal in Turkey for anyone to insult Atatürk, or to destroy objects that represent him. In many countries it is common to hear talk of the core values of that country, such as liberty, justice, and equality, being sacred (Atran 2010, p. 344).[7] In Iran many people appear to believe that their nation has a sacred right to a nuclear energy program. This view is not grounded in religion, but is based on a sense of national destiny that has been strongly promoted by the Iranian government and is related, by them, to Iran's history of resistance to foreign oppression (Dehghani et al. 2009).

Durkheim

As we saw in Chapter 2, the sacred is a key term in Durkheim's (1912) account of religion. We also saw that Durkheim held that religious thinking is organized around a central distinction between the sacred and the profane. He came to this view via a process of inference that would be considered unscientific nowadays. Rather than try to gather information about all of the religions of the world, and then generalize on the basis of information gathered, Durkheim chose to conduct "one well-made experiment," on what he took to be the simplest of all known forms of religion: Australian Aboriginal religion. He then used this "experiment" as a model on which to base his interpretations of all other religions (Cladis 2001, p. xvi). Durkheim did not actually visit Australia to conduct the well-made experiment. Instead he relied on the reports of other anthropologists who had visited Australia and who had studied Australian Aboriginal religion (Durkheim 1912, pp. 77–8).

In Durkheim's (1912) view, the religious believe that sacred places, people, practices, and objects are locations where supernatural beings, entities and/or processes make contact with the natural, profane world. There is thought to be an inherent danger in dealing with the sacred, both because the supernatural is mysterious and sometimes harmful to natural beings, and because supernaturally generated sacred powers and properties are widely believed to be liable to spread through the natural, profane world via simple association. Durkheim writes of the "extraordinary contagiousness of the sacred" (1912, p. 237). He gives the example of the "nanja tree, where the spirit of an ancestor lives" (1912, p. 237). A particular nanja tree is sacred for an individual who is considered to be a reincarnation of an ancestor resident in that tree. If a flying bird lands on the tree, the bird shares in its sacred powers, and it becomes forbidden for the individual in question to touch that bird (1912, p. 237). There is surely something right about Durkheim's view that the sacred is contagious, as sacredness is believed to be spread by association in many cultures and in many religious traditions. The Shroud of Turin is widely believed by Christians to be a sacred object because it is also widely believed that it had the body of Christ wrapped inside it. Similarly, the bones, teeth, hair, and other remains of long dead saints, prophets, and gurus are often also believed to be sacred, by virtue of these once having been parts of living sacred individuals.[8]

The sacred comes in two forms, according to Durkheim: the pure and the impure. These " … are not two separate genera but two varieties of the same genus that includes all sacred things" (1912, p. 306). Some religious forces are " … benevolent, guardians of the physical and moral order, dispensers of life, health, all the qualities that men value," but, "On the other hand, there are negative and impure powers that produce disorder, cause death and illnesses, and instigate sacrilege. Man's only feeling for them is fear usually tinged with horror" (1912, p. 304). Just as the religious set up prohibitions to control interactions between the pure sacred and the profane world, they also set up prohibitions to control interactions between the impure sacred and the profane world. Cursed people, such as untouchables in India, cursed animals, such as snakes (which are cursed by God in the Bible[9]), cursed relics, and so on, are often shunned by the religious and interaction with these is usually carefully regulated. Because the outcome of construing a person, place, process, or object as an instance of either a pure form of the sacred, or an impure one, can be much the same, it is not always necessary for the religious to be clear about whether a particular instance of the sacred is pure or impure. To illustrate this point Durkheim tells us that there are particular Semitic peoples for whom " ... pork was forbidden, but it was not always certain if it was forbidden as an impure thing or as something holy" (1912, p. 305).[10]

The genuinely religious adopt quite specific attitudes to the sacred, according to Durkheim. They revere the pure sacred and fear the impure sacred. They demonstrate both reverence and fear by setting up and observing rules regulating contact between the sacred and ordinary profane beings and objects (Durkheim 1912, p. 40). These are not the only possible attitudes that might be taken towards the sacred. Another possibility is to seek to control sacred powers, and try to use these for one's own direct benefit, or try to benefit from them indirectly, by providing others with controlled access to them, in return for payment. This opportunistic attitude to the sacred is characteristic of magicians, in Durkheim's view:

> The religious prohibition necessarily implies the notion of the sacred; it comes from the respect that the sacred object inspires, and its aim is to prevent any lack of that respect. By contrast, magical prohibitions presuppose only the utterly secular notion of property. The things the magician recommends keeping separate are those that, because of their characteristic properties, cannot be mixed or brought into contact safely. Although he may ask his clients to keep their distance from certain sacred things, it is not out of respect for them and fear that they might be profaned – for magic, as we know, thrives on profanations – but only for reasons of secular utility. (1912, p. 223)

Magicians differ from the religious in another way as well, according to Durkheim (1912). Communities who share attitudes of reverence for the same sacred items are able to experience "collective effervescence" when they conduct rituals that celebrate their shared reverence for the (pure) sacred. They are often prompted to do so when they face some kind of a crisis, such as the death of a community member. The shared experience of ritual participation is transformative and can have the effect of bonding members of a community together very effectively (Bellah 2011, pp. 17–18).[11] This may be, in part, because the members of the community in question express reverence for the same sacred beings, places, entities, and processes as Durkheim supposed. It may also be because, as we saw in Chapter 2, the conducting of strenuous ritual activities prompts the body to release endorphins, facilitating social bonding (Dupue and Morrone-Strupinsky 2005; Machin and Dunbar 2011). Durkheim tells us that magicians do not form the close knit communities that are characteristic of the religious. According to him, " … magic does not bind its followers to one another and unite them in a single group living the same life. *A church of magic does not exist*" (1912, p. 43, italics in text). Magicians, those who are learning to practice magic, and those who pay magicians for their services are all typically motivated by self-interest, rather than the interests of a community united by a shared interest in magic. So, associations that might develop between any, or all, of these types of people are typically short-lived and are inherently unstable.

Durkheim's work on the sacred has been differently received in different academic disciplines. Although Durkheim is regarded as a seminal figure in anthropology, the consensus view in that field is that he was mistaken in thinking of the sacred, along with the contrast between the sacred and the profane, as universal. It seems that there are cultures, such as the LoDagaa in Ghana, that do not employ the concept of the sacred, and that make no distinction equivalent to the distinction between the sacred and the profane (Goody 1961, p. 151).[12] Marcel Mauss and Claude Levi-Strauss were key figures in mid-twentieth-century anthropology. They both thought of themselves as following in Durkheim's footsteps, and each championed the Durkheimian view of religion as a means by which strongly bonded social groups are formed. But they both persistently downplayed the importance of the notion of the sacred in their own work on religion (Masuzawa 1993, p. 56).

In stark contrast to anthropology, in sociology it has often simply been taken for granted that Durkheim was right about the fundamental importance to religion of the notion of the sacred, and also about the fundamental importance of the distinction between the sacred and the profane (Guthrie 1996, pp. 124–5). In theology and religious studies there has also been much enthusiasm for "the sacred." Rudolph Otto (1923) is a prominent theologian who was particularly enthusiastic. For him, "the holy" is a category of interpretation which is peculiar to religion and essential to understanding religious experience. The prominent historian of religion Mircea Eliade (1959) made many of the same claims about "the sacred" that Otto had made earlier about "the holy."[13] Eliade (1959) also defended many of the claims about the distinction between the sacred and the profane that had been made by Durkheim (1912).[14]

Sacred Values

Sacred values – sometimes also referred to as "protected values" (e.g., Baron and Spranca 1997) – have become a subject of increasing interest in psychology and negotiation studies over the past two decades. Sacred values have typically been understood, in psychology and negotiation studies, as those values that people endorse that they are not prepared to compromise under any circumstances. Tetlock, Peterson, and Lerner (1996) offer the following definition of sacred values: " ... those values that a moral community treats as possessing transcendental significance that precludes comparisons, trade-offs, or indeed any mingling with secular values."[15] This definition seems consistent with the way the term sacred is most often used, especially by the religious. For religious Zionists the Land of Israel is sacred territory. To many of them, the idea that control over any of this sacred territory might be given up is completely unacceptable, regardless of the potential benefits to Israel that could result. In 1995, the Israeli prime minister Yitzhak Rabin was assassinated by Yigal Amir, a religious Zionist. Rabin was close to agreeing to a deal which would have provided numerous benefits to Israel, in return for ceding control of parts of the Gaza Strip and the West Bank to an interim Palestinian government. Amir and other religious Zionists considered that the Israeli government had no moral authority to relinquish control of these areas. The Gaza Strip and the West Bank were part of the territory granted to the Jews, by God, in the Abrahamic covenant. According to religious Zionists, the first duty of God's chosen people is to obey God and uphold His covenant. Rabin's attempt to cede control of some of this sacred territory constituted a clear breach of God's covenant, justifying his assassination in their eyes (Stern 2003, pp. 90–2).

The religious strongly resist compromises of their sacred values and the same appears to be true of secular people who hold particular values to be sacred. The National Rifle Association (NRA) is a powerful American lobby group that promotes the right to bear arms, for self-defense as well as for hunting and for sporting contests. The NRA's notorious slogan, "from my cold dead hands," sends a clear message: a message that is consistent with the view that the right to bear arms is a sacred right. The NRA is announcing that it will not give up that right under any circumstances, regardless of the incentives that might be offered to them to do so. The only way to deprive their members of their guns is to kill them. Not only do many NRA members hold that the right to bear arms is a sacred right, some also think of their guns as sacred objects. In the words of Charlton Heston, the former president of the NRA, " ... we know that there is sacred stuff in that wooden stock and blued steel."[16]

The rational actor model of human behavior, which has been extremely influential in psychology and economics, suggests that people should not have sacred values. It is not in anyone's self-interest to refuse to be open to compromise. No matter how important your most important value might seem to you, it is always possible that a deal could be struck which would allow you to acquire sufficient quantities of something else that you also value to make it worth your while to compromise on that most important value.[17] So, if people are understood as acting to further their own interests, then they should never refuse to consider compromises or trade-offs of even their most important values. Perhaps guided by this thought, it is has sometimes been suggested that claims of sacred values, which can never be compromised, are for the most part insincere; and that when someone claims that they will not compromise on a value, regardless of the incentives offered to them to do so, they may well be deploying a clever negotiating tactic intended to drive up the price on offer for a compromise. If this is so, then objections to negotiation will dissolve once a sufficiently strong offer is made (Tenbrunsel et al. 2009, p. 264). Perhaps, despite what they say, the NRA members are willing to compromise on their right to bear arms, but are holding out for the right offer; and their talk of a sacred right is cynical bluster, designed to increase the value of such an offer.

Another suggestion is that many apparently sacred values are actually "pseudo-sacred." They are values that are treated as sacred by a group when that group is in a strong negotiating position, and can afford to stand on principle, but which are considered to be subject to compromise when that group finds itself in a weak bargaining position (Bazerman, Tenbrunsel, and Wade-Benzoni 2008; Tenbrunsel et al. 2009). The Lacandon Mayans in Mexico appear to regard trees as sacred. They believe that whenever a tree is cut down a star falls from the sky. The Lacandons would prefer not to have to negotiate over the future of their forests. Nevertheless, the Mexican government has successfully negotiated a deal with the Lacandons, allowing selective harvesting of trees in those forests. When asked why they had agreed to such a deal, the Lacandons' tribal leader explained that this was the best way to keep as many stars in the sky as possible (Bazerman et al. 2008, p. 116). The Lacandons do not appear to have been acting out of self-interest when they struck this deal. However, they realized that they were not in a strong bargaining position, and that if they did not compromise, the outcome would have been even worse for their forests, and for the stars, than it would have been if they had stood on principle and refused to compromise. While the Lacandons' willingness to compromise seems eminently sensible, it marks them out from others who also appear to possess sacred values and who are unwilling to compromise on these under any circumstances. The distinction between the sacred and the pseudo-sacred does seem to capture the difference between the Lacandon attitude and the attitude of those who attest to holding (uncompromisable) sacred values, even if the term "pseudo-sacred" is somewhat insulting to the Lacandons.

A reason for thinking that many attestations of sacred values are genuine, and are not the manifestation of clever negotiating strategies, or instances of the merely "pseudo-sacred," is the range of strong emotional reactions that challenges to sacred values seem to provoke (regardless of the negotiating position of those who uphold the sacred values in question). As we saw in the cases of Rimsha Masih and Isioma Daniel, discussed earlier in this chapter, apparent evidence that others have violated sacred values tends to provoke outrage amongst those who sincerely hold such values to be sacred (Tetlock 2003, pp. 320–1). Also, the mere suggestion that those who hold sacred values might be willing to compromise these values is liable to incite them to anger (Baron and Spranca 1997). Another way to provoke anger amongst those who hold sacred values is to suggest "heretical counterfactuals," or propositions about how the world could possibly be, which would violate or undermine sacred values if these were actually true. Tetlock et al. (2000) conducted a study which involved asking participants to consider a series of counterfactual claims that would be considered heretical by most Christians. For example, Tetlock and his colleagues asked their research subjects to consider the counterfactual claim that, "If Jesus had given in to one of the devil's temptations during his fast of 40 days and nights in the wilderness, Jesus's mission on earth would have been hopelessly compromised" (2000, p. 864). The research subjects were not asked to accept that this had actually happened. They were only asked to contemplate what consequences would follow if it had happened. But even an invitation to contemplate this possibility, which would issue a challenge to sacred values, if it were true, was enough to provoke outrage amongst research subjects who scored highly on a measure of (Christian) religious fundamentalism.

The emotional responses that typically accompany expressions of sacred values appear to have a pronounced effect on decision making. People who are invited to trade-off a sacred value against a non-sacred value are apt to become emotionally outraged. Their outrage makes their decision emotionally demanding, but otherwise extremely easy to make (Hanselmann and Tanner 2008).[18] Because of the strong emotions associated with sacred values, attempts to negotiate with those who hold them are liable to backfire if these values are treated as if they are non-sacred values. Ginges et al. (2007) conducted a field study involving research subjects drawn from three groups who are interested parties in the Israel–Palestine dispute, and who were living in the West Bank or in Gaza: Palestinian refugees, Palestinian students, and Jewish Israeli "settlers." One sub-group of each of these groups of research subjects was asked to contemplate a proposed peace deal that violated sacred values. A second sub-group was asked to contemplate a "sweetened" version of the same deal, involving an additional incentive to motivate compromise.

For example, a sub-group of the Palestinian students was asked to contemplate a 'two state solution,' which would involve a Jewish State of Israel and a Palestinian state in the West Bank and Gaza. It also involved Palestinians giving up claims to sovereignty over East Jerusalem. A second sub-group was asked to consider a sweetened version of the same deal, under which Israel also paid each Palestinian family US$1,000 a year for ten years (Ginges et al. 2007, p. 7360). Given the assumptions about instrumental decision making that inform the rational actor model of human behavior, it would be expected that the Palestinian students who were offered the sweetened deal would be more likely to accept that deal, and more welcoming of it than those who were offered the unsweetened deal. And indeed, this was what was found amongst those students who did not regard Muslim control of East Jerusalem as a sacred right. However, for those students who did regard Muslim control of East Jerusalem as a sacred right, the opposite reaction was observed. The offer of a sweetener backfired, making the research subjects who were offered it even angrier than those who were offered the (sacred values violating) unsweetened deal, and more likely to support violence. It seems that the use of material incentives to try to overcome the role of sacred values in preventing compromise backfired in the study. Subjects who regarded Muslim control of East Jerusalem as a sacred right, and who were offered the incentive, appear to have taken this as an insult – a suggestion that their sacred values were not genuinely sacred to them, but were on sale if the price was right.

Given the refusal of those who hold sacred values to compromise those values, it might seem reasonable to assume that that violent conflict is almost inevitable when different religions adhere to sacred values which are incompatible with one another. However, there are a few strategies that negotiators can use to reduce the likelihood of conflict between competing religious groups with incompatible sacred values. These strategies will be discussed in Chapter 9.

Sacralization

How do particular cultures and religious traditions come to treat certain values (but not others) as sacred? It might be supposed that sacralization occurs slowly, over many generations, as the traditions of particular cultures gradually develop. But it appears that at least some sacred values can be acquired relatively rapidly. The popular Iranian conviction that Iran has a sacred right to a nuclear energy program seems to have emerged in only a few years (Dehghani et al. 2009, p. 931). One way in which the Iranian government may have been effective in convincing many of its citizens that they have a sacred right to a nuclear energy program is by the frequent use of sacred rhetoric. Sacred rhetoric appears to cause at least some people to treat the subject of that rhetoric as beyond the domain of legitimate consequentialist calculation.

Western countries have been concerned, for some time, that Iran is seeking to develop nuclear weapons along with the ability to generate nuclear energy; and Western negotiators have frequently attempted to persuade Iran to compromise on its nuclear ambitions. Western discourse about the Iranian nuclear program has usually been couched in terms of risks and benefits. In Iran this language has mostly fallen on deaf ears. Iranian government representatives have repeatedly and loudly talked about their nuclear program as non-negotiable. They will "never ever" compromise; they have an "inalienable right" to a nuclear energy program; they "will not retreat one iota"; and so on (Dehghani et. al 2009, p. 931). Plainly, a nuclear energy program is something that could be compromised on, as Western negotiators have often pointed out. However, the use of sacred rhetoric seems to be effective in encouraging Iranians, including Iranian government negotiators and other Iranian government representatives, to dismiss the possibility of compromising Iran's "inalienable right" to a nuclear energy capability out of hand.

Very recently a limited deal has been reached between Iran and "six world powers" regarding Iran's nuclear ambitions (Karimi 2013). The deal itself is rather complicated and involves the lifting of some sanctions in return for Iran curtailing certain aspects of its nuclear program, so as to provide assurances to other countries that Iran will only develop nuclear power and not nuclear weapons. This should not be understood as a compromise of Iran's assertions of a sacred right to a nuclear energy program. In fact, Iran's President Hassan Rouhani has hailed the deal as the "recognition of Tehran's right to enrich uranium by the world powers" (Soltani 2013). A key plank of the deal is that Iran will cease enriching uranium above 5%, which is all that is necessary for the generation of nuclear energy, and a long way below the 80% necessary for making nuclear bombs. Iranians do not see this (or any other) aspect of the deal as a compromise of their sacred right to a nuclear energy program (Soltani 2013). Indeed, Iranian negotiators offered to make this concession in 2007 (CNN 2007).

Another way in which particular values can become sacralized is by relating these values to people's sense of identity (Atran and Axelrod 2008, p. 228). If you conceive of yourself as the sort of person who possesses particular values, as a core part of your being, then your identity will be threatened if these values are compromised. The American revolutionary Patrick Henry is famous for the slogan "Give me liberty, or give me death." The slogan is usually understood as a declaration that his liberty is not something that Henry will give up, regardless of what threats are made or what inducements are on offer. However, the slogan can also be understood as a claim about Henry's sense of identity. Henry is an individual who understands himself as possessing the essential quality of liberty. Liberty is sacred to him because he believes that he cannot be deprived of it and still go on being Henry.[19] Perhaps, similarly, Iranian nationalists conceive of Iranians as a people who possess the essential trait of being motivated to resist foreign oppression. If they ceased trying to resist foreign oppression, then, on this view, they would cease to be true Iranians. Resistance to foreign oppression is sacred to Iranian nationalists and, building on this starting point, the Iranian government has managed to convince many nationalistic Iranians that, therefore, they have a sacred right to a nuclear energy program.

It is known that sacred rhetoric can be effective in encouraging people to treat the subjects of that rhetoric as sacred, and that the values that people identify with are more likely to be treated as sacred than other values that people hold, which they do not regard as essential to their identity. However, there is much that is not known about the processes of sacralization. A recent study by Sheikh et al. (2012) suggests, as Durkheim would have predicted, that rituals can be effective in encouraging groups of people to think of the values incorporated into those rituals as sacred, as is being reminded of rituals that have been conducted previously and which incorporated those values. That same study also suggests that the efficacy of rituals at sacralizing values is amplified when members of an in-group, conducting sacralizing rituals, perceive their group to be under threat from out-groups who do not accept the values incorporated into those rituals (Sheikh et al. 2012). However, there is much that we do not yet know about the processes by which people come to treat previously non-sacred values as sacred. Also, we know very little about de-sacralization – the process by which people cease to treat as sacred some or all of the values, objects, places, rituals, and persons that they had hitherto treated as sacred.

Justification and the Sacred

The responses that people typically have to displays of disrespect towards – or mistreatment of – the subjects of their sacred values are, almost invariably, responses that they understand in moral terms. Conservative Muslims in Nigeria generally consider that Isioma Daniel acted immorally by making disrespectful comments about the Prophet Muhammad. The fact that she was not a Muslim does not seem to be relevant to them. How are we to understand their way of thinking? A cosmopolitan would probably agree that Daniel acted immorally. The cosmopolitan would focus on the lack of sensitivity she displayed to the values of people from other backgrounds, and argue that it was wrong for her to display such insensitivity.[20] But this line of criticism of Daniel seems very different from, and much milder than, the ferocious conservative Muslim response to her newspaper article. Daniel's lack of cultural sensitivity might motivate calls for a firm reprimand, but it hardly seems sufficient to warrant calls for her death. You don't provoke a fatwa, calling for your killing, by showing cultural insensitivity. However, you can provoke a fatwa, calling for your killing, by breaking a sacred rule that ought never to be broken by anyone.

In any case, a cosmopolitan interpretation of the moral complaints of those whose sacred values have been disrespected, or mistreated, would fail to account for cases where the upholding of sacred values leads to displays of insensitivity towards other cultures. As we saw earlier, the Taliban and al-Qaeda destroyed the Bamiyan statues because they believed that these violated Islamic sacred values. The Taliban and al-Qaeda were fully aware that they were demonstrating cultural insensitivity by destroying the Bamiyan statues. The Taliban had been lobbied by a number of foreign agencies, who attempted to persuade them not to destroy the statues, and who suggested various alternatives to destruction. A Japanese parliamentary delegation even offered to provide humanitarian aid, in exchange for the Taliban allowing the statues to be moved out of Afghanistan (Rathje 2001). But the Taliban could not accept this offer while also fulfilling their sacred duty to destroy what they took to be sacrilegious representations of God; so it would not have been an acceptable alternative for them, even if it would have allowed them to display a measure of sensitivity towards another culture.

People generally seem to treat sacred values in the way that thoroughgoing deontologists hold that we should treat all moral values. Sacred values are typically expressed through the formulation and application of strict rules of behavior. Exceptions to these rules are usually considered to be morally unacceptable, even when the allowing of particular exceptions might serve to promote the greater good (Baron and Ritov 2009). Some (but probably not all) people who uphold sacred values will allow that exceptions to these can be made when more important sacred values are at stake. Sacred items are often thought of as possessing a rough hierarchy of importance. Chapels are more important than churches, archbishops are more important than bishops, Mecca is more important than Al-Quds, and so on. The genuinely religious will not sell sacred items, such as sacred land, regardless of the price on offer. To do so would be to fail to treat such items as sacred. But suppose that more important sacred land, which has fallen out of their possession, is offered as a trade for less important sacred land. In such a case, some religious people will be willing to allow a trade, on the grounds that it enables them to respect the hierarchy of the sacred. If they do take this attitude, then they will be doing the equivalent of what W.D. Ross (1930) suggested that we do in the face of conflicts between competing moral duties, which is to allow exceptions to prima facie duties when these are outweighed by more important moral duties.

In a recent paper, Berns et al. (2012) present evidence from an fMRI study that appears to demonstrate that sacred values are processed in the brain in much the same ways, and in much the same places, as are deontological moral judgments. It would be very difficult to violate people's sacred values while they are participating in an fMRI study, and, even if this could be done, it would be almost impossible to do so in a way that would satisfy most research ethics committees. Berns et al. (2012) got around these problems by using a clever proxy for the violation of sacred values. They identified the sacred values of research subjects and then offered the subjects money to sign a document disavowing those values. For example, subjects who held that their belief in God was sacred were offered money to sign a statement declaring the God does not exist. The study rested upon the assumption that subjects who genuinely held sacred values would be loath to compromise their integrity by signing such a document, even if they were paid to do so.[21] The decision making of those whose sacred values were tested in this manner engaged areas of the brain associated with deontological processing. Study participants would have been tempted by the opportunity to make easy money by signing a piece of paper which has no legal standing. However, when they contemplated the money they might make this way, they would have experienced a sudden jolt of emotion, as their "inner deontologist" – whom we met in Chapter 3 when we discussed the neuroscience of moral cognition – was suddenly engaged in cognition. The inner deontologist would have immediately announced that it would be wrong for them to make money by disavowing sacred values. For those whose values are genuinely sacred, there can be no consequentialist overriding of the objections of the inner deontologist, no matter how much money is at stake.

Claims of sacred rules and rights can seem arbitrary from the point of view of those who do not accept the beliefs and values underpinning these. The Iranian government has been successful in convincing many of its citizens that they have a sacred right to a nuclear energy program, but no other society seems to claim such a sacred right. And while Muslims forbid attempts to visually represent God, the followers of most other religions do not forbid depictions of their own god or gods. But although sacred rules and rights can look arbitrary to outsiders, they tend to cohere with other beliefs, values, rules, and rights in ways that make sense to members of in-groups. Once outsiders understand how sacred rules and rights cohere with other beliefs, values, rules, and rights, they begin to look a lot less arbitrary to those outsiders too. As we saw, the Iranian government relates its assertion of a sacred right to a nuclear energy program to a long-standing history of resistance to foreign oppression. The underlying value here is the value of national autonomy, a value which many non-Iranians share, or can at least understand. The Islamic prohibition on depicting God is grounded in the underlying belief that it is impossible for flawed humans to successfully represent the perfect God.[22] Many other religions emphasize the inadequacies of humans when compared with God (or other supernatural beings), so there are many who will share the view that humans are incapable of accurately depicting God. Even if they do not share the belief that the most appropriate response to this state of affairs is to prohibit depictions of God, they can begin to appreciate the Islamic rationale for prohibiting depictions of God.

It is common for people to associate the sacred exclusively with religion, and there appear to be many more claims of sacred values in religious contexts than in secular ones. Why is this? As was argued in Chapter 1, religion enables justificatory appeals to the existence of a deeper reality than the one that is apparent to us. It is easier to tell a coherent story about the importance of respecting sacred values when one has access to the natural/supernatural distinction and other aspects of religious metaphysics than it is to do so without the aid of religious metaphysics. If particular people, places, objects, and rituals are imbued with supernatural powers, then it can seem appropriate to treat these with respect. It is especially appropriate to do so when powerful supernatural agents command us to treat particular people, places, objects, and rituals with respect. It is more difficult, although not impossible, to persuade others to accept that natural items, lacking in supernatural powers, such as guns and nuclear energy programs, should be treated with respect.

The behavior of people seeking to uphold sacred values conforms to patterns consistent with deontological reasoning (Baron and Ritov 2009) and the neural activity of people seeking to uphold sacred values seems to conform to patterns consistent with deontological reasoning (Berns et al. 2012). The best explanation for these observed patterns is that reasoning about sacred values simply is a form of ordinary deontological reasoning. Therefore, it justifies particular forms of behavior, including violent behavior, in the same way as do other forms of deontological moral reasoning. The deputy governor of Zamfara State's justification for ordering the killing of a person who was held to have insulted the Prophet Muhammad follows much the same pattern as Kant's deontological justification for killing those who have violated the moral rule against murder.[23] In both cases it is held that if a binding moral rule has been broken then there is a moral duty, incumbent upon governing authorities, to mete out deserved punishment. The appropriate punishment for the violation of a sacred rule will not always be death, but it will almost always be a severe form of punishment, as those who uphold sacred values would be failing to treat these values with due respect if they did not punish violators harshly.

Notes

1. Genesis 15:18–21.
2. No one has been sentenced to death under Pakistan's blasphemy laws yet. However, long prison sentences for those convicted of blasphemy in Pakistan are not uncommon. In 2010, a Christian couple was sentenced to twenty-five years in prison after being convicted of touching the Koran with unwashed hands (Boone 2012).
3. A related court case against a local Mullah, who is accused of planting evidence on Masih and desecrating the Koran in the process, is reported to still be pending (Edwards 2012).
4. The validity of this fatwa has been disputed (Somerville 2002).
5. "The Cenotaph" is the popular name for a cenotaph in London. Cenotaphs are monuments to the dead whose remains are elsewhere. There is only one such monument in London.
6. Flag desecration is currently illegal in a number of countries, including Austria, China, Croatia, Germany, Israel, Japan, Mexico, the Philippines, and Turkey.
7. New atheist Daniel Dennett reports that his own sacred values are "democracy, justice, life, love and truth" (2006, p. 23).
8. There seem to be limits to the contagiousness of the sacred. For example, the Shroud of Turin may be sacred, by virtue of contact with the body of Christ, but people who touch the Shroud, such as the various scientists who have tried to establish its authenticity, are not thought to have acquired sacred powers.
9. Genesis 3:14.
10. Durkheim cites Robertson Smith (1894, p. 153) in support of this claim.
11. According to Durkheim, such ceremonies, "… raise the vital tone of the group. Now, when people feel the life within them – whether in the form of painful irritation or joyous enthusiasm – they do not think of death; thus they are reassured, they take heart, and subjectively it is as though the rite really had repelled the dreaded danger" (1912, p. 303).
12. There also seem to be various cultures (including the LoDagaa and also the Azande) that make no clear distinction between the natural and the supernatural (Goody 1961, pp. 150–1). Without this distinction in place, it would

not be possible for them to use the term sacred in the way that Durkheim analyses it.

13. Eliade acknowledged his intellectual indebtedness to Otto (Eliade 1959, pp. 8–10).

14. For discussion of differences and similarities between Durkheim and Eliade's distinctions between the sacred and the profane, see Stirrat (1984).

15. This definition is reproduced in Tetlock (2003, p. 320).

16. Cited in Marietta (2008, p. 767, note 1).

17. Unless your most important value is of infinite value, or there is only one thing that you value.

18. If they are asked to decide whether or not to make a trade-off between one sacred value and another sacred value – a "tragic trade-off" – they typically also find decision making emotionally demanding, but find such decisions very difficult to make (Hanselmann and Tanner 2008).

19. Not all properties that one sees as essential are bound up with one's identity. Patrick Henry is widely believed to have been born on May 29, 1736, and, arguably, it is an essential property of his that he was born on this date. Suppose that someone had managed to convince Henry that he was actually born on May 30, 1736. It is hard to believe that, under such circumstances, he would have suffered from a loss of a sense of identity.

20. For a discussion of philosophical cosmopolitanism, see Appiah (2006).

21. For a succinct summary of the study, see Berns and Atran (2012, p. 635).

22. Koran 112:4: "Nor is there to Him any equivalent." The Koran also contains a separate condemnation of idolatry (21:52–8).

23. For further discussion of Kantian deontology, see Rauscher (2012).

7

Recent Justifications of Religious Violence

Introduction

In this chapter I consider recent instances where violent action has been carried out in the name of religion along with attempted justifications for it. I could have chosen less recent instances to examine but I have decided to focus on recent ones to make a point. It is sometimes suggested to me that while religion has been used to justify violence in the past, religion has changed, and these days it is very rare to find instances of violence justified by religion. By showing that a range of different contemporary religions have been appealed to, in recent times, to justify violence, I demonstrate, in passing, the implausibility of this suggestion. As was mentioned earlier, I will follow a common, abbreviated way of writing (and speaking) and will simply refer to such attempted justifications as justifications. I will look at six case studies. Although these cases are a diverse assortment, underlying similarities can be discerned. In each case, the proffered justifications for violence appeal to one or more of the three forms of justification of violent action that have been examined in the three chapters preceding this one: appeals to cosmic war, the afterlife, and to sacred values.

All of the six cases studied have attracted widespread media interest. All are studies of instances, or series of instances, of deliberate violent action undertaken by a religious group or, in one case, by a religiously inspired individual. Each involves the killing of one or more people. Each of the case studies is concerned with violence that has taken place in the past twenty

The Justification of Religious Violence, First Edition. Steve Clarke.
© 2014 John Wiley & Sons, Inc. Published 2014 by John Wiley & Sons, Inc.

years and in each case a moral defense of the violence that has taken place has been offered, either by the killers, or by sympathetic co-religionists.[1] In all of the cases examined, the moral defense of violent action offered relies crucially on religious premises. Two of the religious groups examined are from the United States, as is the religiously inspired individual whom we will consider. One of the groups originated in Japan, another was based in Israel and another, al-Qaeda, is an international organization, which was initially established in Afghanistan.

In the first case study, "The Gatekeepers and Deific Decree," violent action is justified by appealing to cosmic war. In the second, "Aum Shinrikyo," cosmic war is offered as a defense of violence, and an appeal is also made to the afterlife to provide a second, separate justification for violence. Considerations of cosmic war and the afterlife are joined together to provide a unified justification for religious violence in the third case study, "Heaven's Gate." In the fourth, "The Killing of George Tiller," sacred values are invoked to justify a killing. In the fifth, "Meir Kahane and the Kach Party," considerations of cosmic war and of sacred values are offered as separate lines of justification for religious violence. The final case study, "Al-Qaeda," describes how appeals are made to cosmic war, and to sacred values, to provide logically separate justifications of religious violence. Considerations of the afterlife are also invoked, to justify the use of a particular type of violent action, but these are not used to provide a distinct justification for undertaking violent action.

The Gatekeepers and Deific Decree

In 1990, Christopher Turgeon formed a Christian ministry in Washington state that he called "Ahabah Asah Prophetic Ministries," and which he later renamed "The Gatekeepers." He moved his ministry to California in 1997. Turgeon believed that he was a prophet. He had believed this for the best part of a decade, ever since he was a 19 year-old-student in Bible college, when he first heard God speak to him (Koch 1992).[2] In 1996, God apparently told Turgeon that it was time to go to war against the US government (Leong 2008, p. 101). This message made sense to Turgeon, who had become convinced that the US government had come under the control of a Satanic secret society. Turgeon had also become convinced that God would allow him and The Gatekeepers to "plunder" unjust and wicked people, such as those working in the adult entertainment industry, in order to raise funds to pursue the divinely ordained war.[3] The Gatekeepers proceeded to conduct a series of armed robberies targeting "evildoers" (Leong 2008, pp. 101–2).

A member of The Gatekeepers, Dan Jess, had left the group before they moved to California in 1997, and was alleged to have called Turgeon a "false prophet" (Leong 2008, p. 101). In March 1998, Turgeon advised a meeting of the active male members of The Gatekeepers that God had told him that Jess must be killed.[4] Turgeon later described Jess as " … a government informer who was actively pursuing the destruction of our families and our organization"; he also stated that Jess " … had formerly been a soldier in our organization and had betrayed us" (North 2001a). Blaine Applin, a member of the Gatekeepers, volunteered to help Turgeon kill Jess, asserting that "God told me that I must be the one who does it."[5] Turgeon and Applin drove to Jess's home in Washington state on March 28, 1998. As they were driving Turgeon asked God to cause them to make an unscheduled stop if it was not His will that they kill Jess. No unexpected stop was required, and instead Turgeon and Applin saw seven rainbows, which they took to be a sign that God had blessed their mission. In the early morning of March 29, Applin knocked on Jess's door and shot him several times when he answered, leading to Jess's death. Turgeon served as a lookout and driver. The two returned to California and continued to rob "evildoers" and raise money for the war against the US government and Satan, but were caught by the police two months later (Leong 2008, p. 101). They were each given lengthy prison sentences in California for their crime spree. They were also tried and convicted in Washington state for killing Jess. Turgeon received a fifty-year sentence and Applin thirty-nine years.[6]

When they were tried for the murder of Jess, both Turgeon and Applin pleaded not guilty. Their lawyers appealed to "deific decree," an unusual and controversial legal doctrine, to try to demonstrate that they were not guilty.[7] Under deific decree, defendants who can convince a court that they sincerely believed that God had communicated with them, and commanded the performance of a criminal act, can be judged not guilty of that criminal act, by reason of insanity (Hawthorne 2000, p. 1755). Deific decree is one of several bases for finding a defendant not guilty by reason of insanity. The jury in question was instructed, among other things, that deific decree could only be applied if the command of God "destroyed the defendant's free will and his ability to distinguish right from wrong" (Leong 2008, p. 102). The jury was not persuaded by the defense lawyers that this was the case and the two men were held to be responsible for their actions.[8] Turgeon was not happy that his lawyers had attempted to demonstrate that he was insane. He insisted that his actions were those of a sane man and that to argue otherwise is to play into Satan's hands (North 2001b).

The doctrine of deific decree is a somewhat confusing doctrine. Why would we take a sincere belief that God had commanded someone to commit murder to be evidence of insanity? It cannot be because we take all sincere beliefs in deific command as evidence of insanity, as we would not ordinarily take a sincere belief that God has commanded someone do a good deed, or to obey the law, as evidence of insanity. Morris and Haroun suggest that the doctrine is grounded in the widely held belief that God is good and, therefore, would not order someone to commit murder; so, anyone who sincerely believed that God has ordered them to commit murder must have experienced a delusion (2001, p. 1004). In nineteenth-century America, when the doctrine of deific decree was first being formulated, it was often assumed that a genuinely religious person would also be a Christian and would, therefore, conceive of God as a perfectly good being.[9] However, the Christian who is convinced that God definitely would not order someone to commit murder has some explaining to do to account for the biblical story of Abraham and Isaac, in which God puts Abraham's faith to the test by commanding him to sacrifice his son Isaac, and in which Abraham attempts to obey God's command.[10] Christians do not usually regard Abraham as delusional.

While Turgeon and Applin may have lacked a legal justification, or a satisfactory legal excuse for their actions, their moral justification seems clear enough. It involves an appeal to cosmic war. They viewed themselves as loyal soldiers, serving God in a just war against the American government, which, they believed, had come to be controlled by Satan. As we saw in Chapter 4, defense of one's religion has often been thought of as a just cause for war in traditional Christian just war theory. So the mere fact that The Gatekeepers were serving God, in defense of Christianity, would be sufficient grounds for their participation in this war to be just, by the lights of traditional Christian just war theory. Modern secular just war theory does not recognize such grounds for going to war. Nevertheless, Turgeon and Applin could still make a case for the conclusion that their participation in this particular war meets the standards of modern just war theory. Modern just war theory recognizes defense from unjust attack as a just cause for war and The Gatekeepers were acting to defend their country from further unjust attack by Satan and his followers, who had already unjustly taken control of the government of the USA. As we also saw in Chapter 4, one of the restrictions on participation in a war, in modern secular just war theory, is that one must have a reasonable prospect of success. It might be wondered, therefore, how The Gatekeepers could have thought that they would have a reasonable prospect of success if Satan and his followers had already taken over the United States government. Presumably, The Gatekeepers' estimate was that they did have a reasonable prospect of success. They believed that they had God on their side and this belief would have significantly increased their estimate of the chances of them winning the war against Satan.

It might be thought that, even if Turgeon and Applin were morally justified in participating in a war against Satan, they we not justified in killing Dan Jess. Their line of defense in court involved a version of the "superior orders plea," which, as we saw in Chapter 4, was a line of defense that was routinely rejected by the judges at the Nuremberg trials after World War II. However, as was also discussed in Chapter 4, the superior orders of a perfectly good and infallible being seem relevantly different from those of an ordinary military officer. While it is possible that an ordinary military officer might issue an immoral order, it does not seem possible that a supremely good and infallible being, such as the Christian God, might do so. As was argued above, the legal doctrine of deific decree seems implicitly to rest on the assumption that God is good and would not issue an immoral decree. A deific decree is experienced as compelling precisely because, from the point of view of the sincere believer who receives the decree, it seems that it cannot be wrong to obey such a decree. Turgeon and Applin received a clear, direct order from God to kill Jess. From their point of view, there was no possibility of misunderstanding the order; and furthermore there was a good reason for God's issuing of the order, which was that Jess was a dangerous enemy agent. Just to be absolutely sure that they had understood His orders correctly, and that there was no last minute change of heart, they checked with God shortly before the killing, and received what they took to be a clear sign (the seven rainbows) that they had understood the orders correctly and that these were unchanged.

Aum Shinrikyo

On the morning of March 20, 1995, five members of the religious group Aum Shinrikyo boarded five different subway trains, all of which converged on Kasumigaseki station, immediately below the main government district in Tokyo, Japan. Each of the Aum Shinrikyo members carried a sealed vinyl bag containing sarin gas. As the trains they were traveling on neared Kasumigaseki station they pierced their respective vinyl bags with sharp-ended umbrellas and vacated the trains. Deadly poisonous gas leaked from the abandoned vinyl bags, killing twelve people and injuring thousands (Kaplan and Marshall 1996, p. 251). Aum Shinrikyo was under police investigation at the time, following a series of violent incidents which had resulted in the deaths of several renunciates as well as the death of an attorney who had been investigating the group's activities. The leader of Aum Shinrikyo, Shoko Asahara, apparently believed that the subway attack, which he attempted to blame on "US troops" (Kaplan and Marshall 1996, p. 259), would distract police from their investigations (Reader 2002, p. 178). Asahara and his followers apparently also believed that the battle of Armageddon was imminent and they expected that the Japanese government, along with most Japanese people, would soon cease to exist. A temporary respite from the police investigation might allow sufficient time to complete preparations needed to enable them to survive the coming apocalyptic struggle. Asahara was tried for orchestrating the sarin gas attack, as well as orchestrating a series of murders, and on the February 27, 2004, he was sentenced to death by hanging. Although most of the approximately 40,000 followers that Aum Shinrikyo had in 1995 have now left the group, following revelations about the violent and criminal behavior of their leadership, Aum Shinrikyo continues to exist. It has been renamed Aleph, and still retains about 1,000 followers in Japan, who live under strict government surveillance (Hongo 2011).[11]

Aum Shinrikyo is a syncretist religious group. Its main intellectual roots are in Tibetan and Japanese Buddhism (Jones 2008, p. 71). These were supplemented with apocalyptic biblical material as well as sayings of the sixteenth-century French mystic Nostradamus (Juergensmeyer 2003, p. 110). Its charismatic founder and leader Shoko Asahara was born in 1955. As a result of infantile glaucoma he was completely blind in one eye and only partially sighted in the other. He began his adult life as a yoga instructor, acupuncturist, fortune teller, and seller of herbal medicine.[12] In 1984, Asahara founded a yoga school known as the "Aum Association of Mountain Wizards" (Kaplan and Marshall 1996, p. 11).[13] Following a trip to India in 1987, and after meeting and befriending the Dalai Lama,[14] Asahara decided that he had acquired enlightenment, as well as various supernatural powers; and he transformed his yoga school into a religious organization, which he renamed Aum Shinrikyo, or "Aum Supreme Truth." Henceforth his students were expected to address him as *sonshi*, a Japanese form of address for a revered guru (Kaplan and Marshall 1996, pp. 7–15).

Aum Shinrikyo proved to be attractive to many, especially in Japan, but it is not immediately apparent why. Asahara demanded that his followers display absolute devotion towards him (Reader 2002, p. 164).[15] He also demanded large amounts of money from them. Monks and nuns were required to entrust all their assets to Aum Shinrikyo (Kaplan and Marshall 1996, p. 22). Other followers were encouraged to pay for expensive meditation courses, as well as a variety of procedures and remedies that were alleged to have magical properties by virtue of their association with the guru. A potion made with DNA drawn from Asahara's blood cost US\$7,000 (Kaplan and Marshall 1996, p. 33), and a quart of his dirty bath water ("miracle pond") sold for almost US\$800 (Kaplan and Marshall 1996, p. 18).

Asahara taught that the battle of Armageddon was imminent and that his enlightened followers would be best placed to survive this catastrophic event (Kaplan and Marshall 1996, p. 17). He predicted various different dates and formats for Armageddon. In 1986 he predicted that a world war between the USA and Russia would take place in 1999. In 1993 he predicted that a war between the USA and Japan would occur in 1997. And in January 1995 he predicted that a cataclysmic confrontation between Aum Shinrikyo itself and "evil" would take place that calendar year (Reader 2002, p. 176). It seems that evil was to be abetted by a number of conspirators, whom a cynic might describe as the usual suspects of popular conspiratorial literature. These included Satan, the Freemasons, and the Jews (Kaplan and Marshall 1996, p. 219). With large amounts of money provided by its many followers, supplemented with profits from various business ventures,[16] Aum Shinrikyo attempted to create or acquire a range of weapons of mass destruction. They ran a biological weapons program, attempting to acquire or create, and then weaponize, several deadly diseases including anthrax, botulinum toxin, and Q fever.[17] They also attempted to acquire nuclear weapons and investigated the possibility of acquiring or creating laser weapons, railguns,[18] and an earthquake generating device (Muir 1999, p. 88). And, as we now know, they succeeded in creating sarin gas. Aum Shinrikyo also created its own commando unit which was trained to help them take control of any parts of the Japanese government that might remain after Armageddon had taken place. The commando unit was given the somewhat Orwellian name "the Soldiers of White Love" (Kaplan and Marshall 1996, pp. 154–6).

One line of justification for Aum Shinrikyo's violent actions was cosmic war. Early on, Asahara and his followers understood themselves to be planning to live through an apocalyptic war, in which they would be a neutral party, seeking to survive, and feeling justified in employing extreme and violent measures to do so. They also aimed, after the apocalyptic war was over, to create the Kingdom of Shambhala, an ideal society – which would be ruled by Asahara – inhabited by people who will have realized their potential psychic powers (Watanabe 1998, p. 83). By 1995, they had come to believe that they would soon be attacked by an alliance of evil forces that would try to destroy them. The attack by the alliance of evil forces would trigger Armageddon, thereby causing the deaths of most of humanity. In such circumstances, they felt justified in taking violent pre-emptive action to defeat those evil forces.

A second line of justification for Aum Shinrikyo's violent actions involved an appeal to the afterlife. It is a variant of the Buddhist line of justification for killing that underpinned the Dalai Lama's endorsement of the killing of Osama bin Laden by American special forces, which was discussed in Chapter 5. Under the right circumstances, killing people who are likely to go on leading bad lives is, according to Asahara's interpretation of Tibetan Buddhist principles, a merciful act that would reasonably be expected to improve the quality of their afterlives (Juergensmeyer 2003, p. 115). A true guru will know when such circumstances obtain. According to Asahara:

> The teachings of esoteric Buddhism of Tibet were pretty savage. For instance, when a guru ordered a disciple to kill a thief, the disciple went ahead and did it as an act of virtue. In my previous existence, I myself have killed someone at my guru's order. When your guru orders you to take someone's life, it's an indication that that person's time is already up. In other words, you are killing that person exactly at the right time ... ' (Watanabe 1998, pp. 84–5)

Asahara believed that the Japanese people were in a state of ongoing moral and spiritual decline (Jones 2008, p. 75). The killing of any or all Japanese – in the course of an operation ordered by him – would be a justifiable, compassionate act that would improve the quality of the afterlives of those killed. Asahara was convinced that those who were killed in the sarin gas attack would experience positive karmic consequences, for which they should be grateful (Kaplan and Marshall 1996, p. 251).

Heaven's Gate

On March 26, 1997, the dead bodies of thirty-nine members of the small American religious group Heaven's Gate were found in a mansion twenty miles north of San Diego, California. All of the deaths appear to have been suicides, and these had taken place over three days, from March 23 to March 25, 1997.[19] Each dead body was clothed in a matching uniform of black shirt, black pants and black Nike trainers, and most were covered in purple shrouds (Urban 2000, p. 279).[20] Each shirt had a cloth patch sewed onto it, on which the words "Heaven's Gate Away Team" had been stitched (Cowan and Bromley 2008, p. 170). The dead members of Heaven's Gate left behind a number of video tapes and Internet resources explaining that, despite appearances, they were not committing suicide, but were "leaving their vehicles" and would soon be acquiring "next level vehicles," in which they would live "among the stars" as happy immortal aliens (Zeller 2011, pp. 176, 181). The timing of their deaths appears to have been driven by a concern to leave the earth before it is "recycled" and all life forms on the planet "spaded under" – an event which they believed to be imminent – along with a belief that the perigee of the Hale-Bopp comet, on March 22, 1997, indicated an opportunity for them to leave the earth and ascend to the "next level" (Zeller 2011, pp. 181–7).[21] Although it is sometimes reported that all of the members of Heaven's Gate committed suicide, this is not the case. There was at least one survivor: Rio DiAngelo. According to DiAngelo, he wanted to ascend to the next level with the rest of the group, but was instructed to stay behind by the group's leader, Marshall Applewhite. Ten years after the event, DiAngelo reported that he remained convinced that the thirty-nine apparently dead members of Heaven's Gate are now living elsewhere in the universe, at the "level above human" (DiAngelo 2007a).[22]

Heaven's Gate was founded and led by Marshall Applewhite, a former Presbyterian theology student and music teacher, and Bonnie Lu Nettles, a registered nurse, in 1972. Shortly after meeting one another they formed a new religion, which was loosely related to Christianity, and they started to refer to themselves as "The Two."[23] They also adopted a series of whimsical paired names including, Bo and Peep, and Guinea and Pig, before settling on Ti (Nettles) and Do (Applewhite) (Zeller 2006, p. 78).[24] Nettles died of cancer in 1985 leaving Applewhite as sole leader. Soon after her death Applewhite asserted that while Nettles' earthly "vehicle" had broken down, she had not ceased to exist, but had acquired a "next level vehicle," and is an immortal alien living elsewhere in the universe (Zeller 2011, p. 181).

The followers of Heaven's Gate believed in an unusual form of salvation. According to them there is a "Kingdom of Heaven." It is here in this universe and it is inhabited by technologically advanced, happy, immortal, good next level beings. The good next level beings have planted "gardens" of civilization throughout the universe, and periodically send messengers to these civilizations, to help prepare "good seeds" for "harvesting" (ascension to the next level).[25] Jesus Christ was a messenger from the next level, and so were Applewhite and Nettles.[26] Successful preparation for harvesting required one to become a "useful soul," which involved living a spartan life of devotion to spiritual ends. Next level beings were believed, by followers of Heaven's Gate, to be androgynous and sexless and one crucial form of preparation was the overcoming of sexual desire. To help overcome their sexual desires Applewhite and some (but not all) of his male followers had had themselves castrated (Urban 2000, p. 286).

According to Applewhite, ordinary Christianity is based on a misunderstanding of Christ's teachings. Christ was a messenger from a superior alien civilization whose mission was to enable those who were suitably prepared to ascend to the "next level" in this universe. However, Christ's teachings have been systematically misinterpreted. This is no accident, if Heaven's Gate theology is to be believed. In addition to the good next level aliens, who wish to help us, the universe contains a race of evil aliens known by the followers of Heaven's Gate as "Luciferians" (Davis 2000, p. 248). Not only have the Luciferians succeeded in corrupting Christ's message (and thereby creating mainstream Christianity), but they have also taken control of almost all world governments, major corporations, and religious institutions, and have turned most ordinary people into their unwitting docile servants (Urban 2000, pp. 280–1; Davis 2000, pp. 249–51).

To try to combat the Luciferian near-takeover of the earth, following the failure of Christ's mission, the good aliens of the next level decided to send another "away team" comprised of Applewhite and Nettles (Urban 2000, p. 281). Judging by the small number of people who may possibly have ascended to the next level, alongside Applewhite, this mission does not seem to have been any more successful than the earlier one. The view that the earth is soon to be recycled by the next level and harvested of its useful souls, with the remainder to be spaded under, did not appear in Heaven's Gate literature until 1991 (Zeller 2006, pp. 85–6). The late adoption of this apocalyptic view may have been prompted by Applewhite's recognition of the very modest successes of the second away team in combating the influence of the Luciferians. Applewhite would have been painfully aware that, after twenty-five years of trying, he had only managed to attract and retain thirty-nine followers.[27]

Regardless of whether the killing of the thirty-nine members of Heaven's Gate is understood as a group suicide, or as the shedding of "human vehicles" in the expectation of acquiring next level vehicles, it was a violent act. The followers of Heaven's Gate appear to have believed that they were undertaking a justified form of violent action. Their justification was salvific and consequentialist in form. They were motivated by the promise of the science fiction equivalent of heaven – eternal lives of happiness as superior alien beings in this universe. Whatever the wrongness of taking their own lives, it is surely outweighed by the benefits of eternal happiness for thirty-nine individuals, or so they would have reasoned. A thoroughgoing consequentialist might try to find fault with this thinking, criticizing the followers of Heaven's Gate for only being concerned to secure their own eternal happiness and for disregarding the welfare of others. However, they can respond to this line of criticism by pointing to the many efforts they had made over the years to try to persuade others to join Heaven's Gate, and so obtain the possibility of eternal happiness. They could also point out that, by the point in time at which they needed to "shed their vehicles," there was no longer sufficient time for any other people to undertake the preparations needed to make them eligible to acquire a next level vehicle before the earth was scheduled to be recycled.

The timing of the deaths of the thirty-nine followers of Heaven's Gate cannot be properly understood without also appreciating the broader theological views of those followers, including their belief in an ongoing cosmic war. It is in the context of believing that a cosmic war was taking place, between the good next level beings and the evil Luciferians, that the followers of Heaven's Gate came to believe that the earth was about to be "recycled" and that they must, therefore, ascend to the next level before the opportunity to do so was lost. The followers of Heaven's Gate had become convinced that the Luciferians had gained such a hold over the population of the earth that the next level beings had abandoned faith in the efficacy of missions to harvest useful human souls and had decided to destroy the Luciferian-infested earth instead. Their violent action was not designed to promote victory in the ongoing cosmic war. It was designed to ensure their future existence. The followers of Heaven's Gate had come to consider themselves to be refugees, trying to escape from a war zone, as it were. Cosmic war was about to lead to the destruction of the earth, but while the rest of us had now lost the opportunity to escape before our planet was destroyed, they still had such an opportunity, or so they believed.

The Killing of George Tiller

On May 31, 2009, George Tiller, an American physician based in Wichita, Kansas, who provided abortions, was shot and killed. Tiller was the eighth person killed by anti-abortion activists in America since 1991.[28] Because Tiller provided controversial late-term abortions,[29] and because he operated in a very conservative Midwestern American town, his practice became something of a lightning rod for anti-abortion activists. It was firebombed in 1986, and in 1991 the Christian anti-abortion activist group Operation Rescue organized the "Summer of Mercy" protests in Wichita; mass protests which were focused on abortion clinics in the city, including Tiller's clinic. The protests lasted for six weeks and resulted in over two thousand arrests.[30] In 1993, Tiller had been shot five times by anti-abortion activist Rachelle "Shelley" Shannon but survived the ordeal. Shannon was subsequently sentenced to eleven years in jail for attempted murder. Operation Rescue moved its headquarters to Wichita in 2002 and, after this move, Tiller's practice became a consistent focus of their activities (Friedman 2010).

The man who killed Tiller, Scott Roeder, was raised in Kansas and became a born again Christian in the early 1990s after watching an evangelical television program (Friedman 2010). He became an anti-abortion activist soon afterwards. Roeder had been thinking about killing Tiller for at least fifteen years before he acted and he had visited Shelley Shannon in prison twenty-five times or more (Friedman 2010). While not an actual member of Operation Rescue, he was a strong supporter of their activities, and he claims to have made donations to them worth at least US$1,000 (Thomas 2009). Roeder was tried for the murder of George Tiller and appealed to "justifiable homicide" in his defense; but his defense was judged unsuccessful and he was convicted of murder and sentenced to fifty years in prison, the maximum sentence available in Kansas (Sylvester 2010).

Although Operation Rescue has made statements that might well be interpreted as encouraging violence against abortionists in the past,[31] it has not supported Scott Roeder's actions, which its president has described as both immoral and stupid (Newman 2009). In reacting to Roeder's actions this way, Operation Rescue is echoing the views of mainstream Christian "pro-life" organizations and churches, which are firmly committed to non-violent opposition to abortion.[32] One Christian pro-life organization which has supported Roeder's actions is the "Army of God." The Army of God claims to be a real army commanded by God (Jefferis 2011, p. 53).

Their day-to-day operations are overseen by their "Chaplain," Pastor Michael Bray, a seasoned anti-abortion activist who served jail time in the 1980s for arson attacks on abortion clinics (Juergensmeyer 2003, p. 20). Shelley Shannon, who attempted to murder George Tiller, was an associate of the Army of God (Juergensmeyer 2003, p. 21).[33] Other members and associates of the organization have committed acts of murder, arson, and kidnapping (Jefferis 2011, pp. 21–51).

Pastor Michael Bray is the author of *A Time to Kill* (1994), a book in which he outlines the "justifiable homicide" defense of the use of lethal force against abortionists (Jefferis 2011, pp. 54–8). The justifiable homicide defense of the use of lethal force against abortionists is elegantly simple. Roeder, Bray, and others who employ it, argue that violent attacks on abortionists are a means of defending innocent third parties, who abortionists are attempting to kill. If we saw someone attempting to kill another person in the street we would be excused from blame and punishment if we intervened and tried to protect that third party, according to the law in many countries, even if we used (necessary) lethal force when doing so. Many would also say that we are morally obliged to intervene. So we are morally and legally justified in committing acts of homicide in defense of innocent third parties, at least under some circumstances. Roeder, Bray, and others see the unborn as innocent third parties, who are under imminent threat of being killed by abortionists; and they feel morally obliged to intervene, to try to protect the unborn.[34] Although the judge presiding over Roeder's murder trial allowed Roeder to put the "justifiable homicide" defense to the jury in the trial, he refused to allow the jury to consider the lesser charge of manslaughter, both because abortion is legal in Kansas and because Tiller, who was standing in a church at the time of the shooting, did not pose an imminent threat to anyone (Associated Press 2010).

Underpinning the justifiable homicide defense is the view that human life has an inherent value which is not exceeded by any other values. This is a view that is mainstream to Judeo-Christian morality, and which informs Western legal traditions that have been shaped, among other things, by Judeo-Christian morality. In the Judeo-Christian tradition, human life is thought to have inherent value because, as we saw in Chapter 6, it is thought to be sacred. Human life is thought to be sacred because humans (and no other living creatures) are made in God's image. So, indirectly, Roeder's appeal to justifiable homicide is an appeal to sacred values; or, in language that would be more likely to be heard from a devout Christian, it is an appeal to the doctrine of the sanctity of life. The conviction that the doctrine of the sanctity of life is applicable to fetuses is usually based on a religiously inspired metaphysical view which has it that human "ensoulment" occurs at conception (Stern 2003, p. 157). The life of a being that God has endowed with a rational soul (and hence made in His image) is considered sacred, whereas the life of a being which lacks a rational soul is not.[35] Although the view that ensoulment occurs at conception is very widespread amongst contemporary Christians, it lacks a clear scriptural basis. Indeed, while Christian theologians have consistently condemned the killing of "ensouled" embryos, Christian views about when ensoulment occurs have varied widely over time, with many very influential Christian theologians, including Augustine and Aquinas, taking the traditional Aristotelian view that human ensoulment cannot occur until the human embryo is sufficiently formed to house a soul (traditionally four to five months after conception, which is roughly the time of "quickening" (Ford 1988)).[36]

Anti-abortion activists who appeal to the justifiable homicide defense of violent action sometimes supplement this with an appeal to straightforward considerations of consequence. A point that the Army of God is keen to stress is that George Tiller would have killed many thousands of unborn infants had he remained alive and remained able to continue conducting abortions. So his killing has resulted in many lives being saved (Jefferis 2011, pp. 69–72). The moral weight of this consideration depends on one's view of the importance of consequences for morality, one's assessment of the actual consequences of Tiller no longer being alive, and also on one's view of the moral status of fetuses. The Army of God and other Christian anti-abortion activists accept the doctrine of the sanctity of life, so they cannot and do not simply appeal to the beneficial consequences of the death of Tiller, or any-one else, to justify killing. However, because they are convinced that Tiller has taken life, some of these activists, including Roeder, have felt entitled to apply "God's law"[37] and deprive Tiller of his life. Because they believe that further beneficial consequences have derived from Tiller's death, they have been especially keen to see God's law applied.

Although it does not play a role in the justification offered for the killing of abortionists, Michael Bray and other leading figures in the Army of God hold the belief that they are participants in an ongoing cosmic conflict. They are "Christian Reconstructionists" and view their actions as contributions to God's struggle against Satan (Stern 2003, pp. 162–71; Juergensmeyer 2003, pp. 27–30). Christian Reconstructionists hold a "postmillennial" view of the arc of history. They believe that Christ will only return to earth after a thousand years of authentic Christian rule. They therefore believe that they have a religious duty to "recapture" the institutions of secular America, so as to enable Christ's return (Juergensmeyer 2003, p. 28). Attempts to shut down abortion clinics are but one step in this long process. The Army of God also actively opposes (but has not so far sought to violently agitate against) homosexual activity and birth control.[38] The ultimate ambition of Michael Bray and other leading figures in the Army of God is the creation of a theocratic Christian world government (Juergensmeyer 2003, pp. 28–30).

Meir Kahane and the Kach Party

Meir Kahane was an American Rabbi, born in Brooklyn in 1932, who initially came to prominence in 1968 as the founder and first Chairman of the New York based Jewish Defense League. The Jewish Defense League, which is still in existence, is primarily a vigilante organization created, in apparent imitation of the Black Panthers, to protect ordinary American Jews from anti-Semitic hate crimes and other forms of discrimination.[39] Its members also devoted much energy to agitating against the Soviet Union's restrictions on Jewish emigration to Israel. In 1971, Kahane himself emigrated to Israel and founded the Kach ("Thus") Party that same year. Kahane and the Kach Party's main goal was the expulsion of Arabs from Israel, by force if necessary. Kach also lobbied for the prohibition of marital and sexual relations between Jews and Gentiles, and the general imposition of Jewish religious law in Israel (Sprinzak 1985). The Kach Party contested a series of national elections, beginning in 1973, and in 1984 Kahane was elected to the Knesset (the Israeli parliament) as the sole representative of Kach.[40] However, Kach was barred from participating in the next national election, in 1988, due to its racist and undemocratic party positions (Juergensmeyer 2003, p. 55). Despite having run for office several times, Kahane was resolutely opposed to democracy, which he considered to be an alien, Gentile idea, unsuitable for the religious state of Israel that he aimed to create (Ravitzky 1986; Sprinzak 1985). Kahane was assassinated by an Arab-American gunman in 1990 at the conclusion of a public speech that he had given in a New York hotel.

In addition to participating in elections, and otherwise trying to persuade the Israeli public to embrace their political agenda, Kach Party members and sympathizers undertook a variety of actions to further that political agenda, some of which were violent. Notably, they conducted a campaign of harassment and intimidation, aimed at making life unbearable for ordinary Arabs to encourage them to leave Israel. This campaign involved relatively low-level violence – beating up vulnerable Arabs, setting fire to Arab-owned cars, and so on.[41] Kach Party members and sympathizers were also involved in several more spectacular episodes. In the 1980s, Kahane was arrested, and detained for nine months, following the uncovering of a plot by Kach Party members to fire a long-range missile at the Dome of the Rock Mosque in Jerusalem (Pedahzur and Ranstorp 2001, p. 16). A second plot to destroy the Dome of the Rock Mosque, this time by blowing it up, was organized by Kach Party member Yoel Lerner, also in the 1980s. Lerner was a close friend of Kahane and, like Kahane, originally hailed from New York (Pedahzur and Perliger 2009, p. 85). The plot was uncovered before Lerner and his associates were able to act and Lerner ended up spending two and a half years in prison as a result. The most violent act of any follower of Kahane occurred after Kahane's death. This was the 1994 massacre of Palestinian Muslim worshippers at the Cave of the Patriarchs in Hebron by a lone gunman, Baruch Goldstein (Juergensmeyer 2003, pp. 50–1). Goldstein opened fire on a large crowd of Muslim worshippers with an assault rifle, killing twenty-nine worshippers and injuring another 125 to 150, before being overwhelmed by the crowd and pummeled to death. Like Lerner, Goldstein was also originally from New York and had known Kahane since his childhood (Pedahzur and Perliger 2009, p. 70). After issuing statements of support for Goldstein's actions, the Kach Party was banned in Israel, as was Kahane Chai ("Kahane Lives"), an offshoot of Kach that was formed after Kahane's death by his son Binyamin Kahane (Gunitskiy 2002).

The justifications that Kahane offered for violent action, on behalf of Kach and his followers more generally, appealed to considerations of sacred values and cosmic war. In Kahane's view, the Jewish people are a unique and holy people chosen by God, who ought only to be concerned with their own redemption in the eyes of God; and who, therefore, are entitled to disregard the moral claims and interests of Gentiles and act violently towards any Gentiles who stand in the way of Jewish interests. Kahane notoriously claimed that Jewish violence in defense of Jewish interests is never bad (Sprinzak 1991, p. 56).[42] Secular and liberal Jews were routinely dismissed by Kahane as "Gentile Jews," "Hebrew speaking Gentiles," and so on (Ravitzky 1986). So, his line of argument could easily be used by Kahane and his followers to justify violent action against many of their Jewish opponents. Also holy in Kahane's view is the Land of Israel. This is a standard view amongst ordinary Orthodox Jews, but Kahane went far beyond ordinary Orthodoxy in holding that Jews have an obligation to risk their lives, and to die if necessary, to prevent any desecration of the Holy Land whatsoever. No part of the Holy Land should ever be surrendered to Gentiles and Gentiles should be evicted from the Holy Land as soon as possible (Sprinzak 1985).

Kahane had a very idiosyncratic view of the creation of the secular state of Israel in 1948. According to him, the State of Israel was created by God in order to punish the various Gentile nations for their mistreatment of God's chosen people over many centuries (Sprinzak 1991, p. 49). So, Israelis are actually serving God when they harm Gentiles. They are assisting God in meting out deserved punishment to " ... a world that has mocked and despised and degraded the Almighty God of Israel" (Kahane 1982, p. 3). According to Kahane, the creation of Israel was only the first of a series of events that God has orchestrated in advance of a soon-to-arrive moment of full and final redemption for devout Jews. Kahane warned that God's fury might be turned against Israelis if they did not properly prepare for His impending arrival and repent for their sins. Kahane estimated that God would only allow Israel a relatively short period of time following its creation – approximately forty years – and those Jews who had not repented by the time that period had elapsed would be met with God's fury – already being directed at the Gentiles – rather than God's redemption (Sprinzak 1991, pp. 53–4). Because they are, in effect, now in a state of religiously ordained war against all Gentile nations, devout Jews are obliged to fight on God's side against the Gentiles, and those Jews who fail to fight for God are considered by Kahane to be legitimate targets in this cosmic war. As Kahane informs us in his book *The Jewish Idea*:

> We see that G-d has declared war on the wicked and described Himself as Master of war, and that we must emulate Him in war the way we emulate His mercy and kindness, etc. Let death take those pompous individuals who rebel against G-d and against His attributes and principles, who err and mislead others as if they were more righteous than their Creator, pious fools who hypocritically reject the war against evil and evildoers, bleating about peace when we need war, falsifying and distorting G-d's Torah and the laws of compulsory war against the wicked.[43]

As with Kahane's appeal to sacred values, the appeal to cosmic war directly justified violence against Gentiles, and also indirectly justified violence against Kahane's Jewish opponents.

Al-Qaeda

In 1988, Osama bin Laden (1957–2011), an intensely religious Sunni Muslim,[44] who was born in Saudi Arabia and who had been involved in fighting against the Soviet Union's forces in Afghanistan since 1980, founded the Islamic extremist group al-Qaeda. The name "al-Qaeda" translates into English as "the base." Although al-Qaeda was, and is, a military organization, its name is not a military reference. Bin Laden sought to create a "solid base" on which to build what he and his followers considered to be an ideal Islamic society (Berger 2006, p. 75). After the withdrawal of Soviet forces from Afghanistan in 1989, bin Laden and his leadership group moved around the Islamic world, and their activities became increasingly focused on opposition to American influence in the region. In 1996, bin Laden issued a declaration of war (or, more specifically, "defensive jihad") against the USA; in 1998, al-Qaeda helped organize the bombing of US embassies in Tanzania and Kenya, leading to approximately 220 civilian deaths; and in 2000 they orchestrated an attack on the USS Cole, which was harbored in the Yemeni port of Aden at the time, causing the deaths of seventeen US Navy personnel. In 2001, as is well known, al-Qaeda orchestrated the 9/11 attacks on the World Trade Center in New York and the Pentagon in Washington, leading to approximately 3,000 civilian deaths.[45] This provoked the US attack on Afghanistan in late 2001, where the al-Qaeda leadership group was then located and, among other responses, a world-wide manhunt that eventually led to bin Laden being killed by US special forces in 2011.

While al-Qaeda's actions have garnered significant popular support in many, predominantly Islamic, countries (Berger 2006, p. xxvi), they have not received the support of mainstream Islamic authorities and scholars, many of whom have condemned their killing of civilians as un-Islamic (Wiktorowicz and Kaltner 2003, p. 76).[46] Al-Qaeda has issued a large number of declarations and statements to the media over the years[47] and much of what is said in these is intended to justify their war against America and her allies, and to justify the ways in which they have conducted it.[48] Many parts of the various statements and declarations of al-Qaeda read like anti-imperialist critiques of American foreign policy that might be voiced by secular left wing groups anywhere in the world. Al-Qaeda has repeatedly demanded that American and other Western troops be withdrawn from Islamic countries and that America and other Western countries cease interfering in the political affairs of Islamic countries. They have also displayed a concern for more global issues, joining secular left wingers in criticizing America for refusing to ratify the Kyoto protocol and for refusing to ratify the treaty establishing the International Criminal Court (Lawrence 2005, pp. 168–9).

However, the concerns of al-Qaeda only partially overlap with those of secular left wingers. This becomes apparent when the detail of al-Qaeda's justification for a campaign of "defensive jihad" against America is examined. Al-Qaeda not only demand that America and her allies cease interfering in Muslim majority countries, but also that they refrain from all involvement in the affairs of lands that have been under the control of Islamic rulers in the past, but which do not have Muslim majorities, and are no longer subject to Islamic rule, such as South Sudan and East Timor,[49] even if their involvement results in the strengthening of local autonomy (Lawrence 2005, p. 134). Bin Laden was outraged by the roles that the United Nations Secretary-General and Australian troops played in enabling the secession of East Timor from Indonesia in 1999. According to him:

> That criminal Kofi Annan publicly put pressure on the Indonesian govern-
> ment, telling it that it had 24 hours to partition and separate East Timor from
> Indonesia, otherwise he would have to introduce military forces to do it. The
> Crusader armies of Australia were on the shores of Indonesia and they did
> in fact intervene and separate East Timor, which is part of the Islamic world.
> (Lawrence 2005, p. 137)

And elsewhere he has complained about Australia's " … despicable attempts to separate East Timor" (Ibrahim 2007, p. 232). There are not many informed secular left wingers who would construe Western involve-ment in enabling East Timor to acquire independence as a part of an attack on the Islamic world. East Timor was, and is, a heavily Catholic country,[50] which only became part of the Muslim-majority state of Indonesia after being invaded by Indonesian troops in 1976. It gained independence following a UN-supervised referendum in 1999.

A second way in which the concerns of al-Qaeda differs from those of sec-ular left wingers is that, although bin Laden characterizes al-Qaeda's actions against America as a form of defensive jihad, he is also an enthusiastic advo-cate of "offensive jihad." According to him, but not according to the many moderate Muslims whom he frequently criticizes, this is "a religious duty rejected only by the most deluded" (Ibrahim 2007, p. 32). He spells out what actions he thinks are required to fulfill this duty in very explicit language:

> Muslims are obligated to raid the lands of the infidels, occupy them, and exchange their systems of governance for an Islamic system, barring any practice that contradicts the *sharia* from being publicly voiced among the people, as was the case at the dawn of Islam.[51] (Ibrahim 2007, p. 51)

Perhaps in part because bin Laden believed that he and other Muslims have a duty to impose shariah (Islamic) law on America (as well as the rest of the world), he often felt the need to berate America for what he saw as its moral and religious failings. According to him, America is "the worst civilization witnessed in the history of mankind" (Ibrahim 2007, p. 202). Its faults include failing to prevent homosexual activity, gambling, prostitution, and the use of intoxicants, as well as destroying nature, permitting usury, spreading diseases, and separating religion from government (Ibrahim 2007, pp. 202–4).

When offering justifications for violent conduct in their war against America and her allies, and for their threat to go on to conduct "offensive jihad" and forcibly impose shariah law on the entire world, al-Qaeda and bin Laden appeal to all three of the means that we have examined by which religion is used to justify violence. The most important of these, for them, is cosmic war. Bin Laden consistently construes global affairs as a struggle between God and true Muslims on the one side and a unified evil force led by America on the other. According to him there is no choice but to take up arms. He has claimed that America has made "a clear declaration of war on God, His messenger and Muslims" (Juergensmeyer 2003, p. 148). And there is no prospect of striking a lasting peace with America and its allies, because they are dominated by Christians and Jews and, if bin Laden is to be believed, Christians and Jews will not be satisfied until everyone follows their faiths (Lawrence 2005, p. 135).

Bin Laden refers to the American-led unified force that opposes God in a variety of colorful ways. He speaks of "the organization of global unbelief" (Lawrence 2005, p. 261), and "the aggressive Crusader–Jewish alliance" (Lawrence 2005, p. 7); and he has claimed that this organization or alliance has conducted a "neo-Crusader–Jewish campaign led by Bush, the biggest Crusader, under the banner of the cross" (Lawrence 2005, p. 100), and that this is "the strongest, fiercest, most dangerous and violent Crusader campaign against Islam since Muhammad was sent" (Lawrence 2005,

p. 135). He also makes it clear enough that he sees Satan as the ultimate power lurking behind his American-led enemies. He refers to America and her allies as "the allies of Satan" (Lawrence 2005, p. 180); and to the American military as "the Devil's army" (Ibrahim 2007, p. 13) and as "soldiers of Satan" (Lawrence 2005, p. 61).

Sacred values are almost as important as cosmic war in bin Laden's thinking. Bin Laden's original declaration of jihad against America was provoked by the presence of Americans in the Arabian Peninsula (Lawrence 2005, p. 25). Part of his concern was increased American influence in Saudi Arabia, but at least as important to him is the fact that there are non-Muslims in the Arabian Peninsula at all. He regards their presence as a major violation of Islamic sacred values, and easily sufficient to justify coercive action.[52] Bin Laden's thinking is not idiosyncratic on this point. Muslims have a history of regarding the land around the holy cities of Mecca and Medina as sacred and of treating it as territory that is forbidden to non-Muslims. On his deathbed the Prophet Muhammad is said to have uttered the words "let there not be two religions in Arabia." In 641, the Caliph Umar acted to honor these words, evicting long-established Christian and Jewish communities from the area (Lewis 1998, p. 16). There is scope for disagreement about what constitutes the sacred area. On a narrow construal it is the Hijaz, a region in western Saudi Arabia. As might be expected, bin Laden adopts a broad construal, including the whole of Saudi Arabia, as well as Yemen (McAuley 2005, p. 275) and Kuwait (Ibrahim 2007, p. 107), in the area that is forbidden to non-Muslims. Significant numbers of US military personnel were stationed in Saudi Arabia between 1990 and 2003. The Saudi government were not insensitive to the issue of non-Muslims being present in sacred territory, obtaining a decree from Shaikh bin Baz, the foremost Islamic judicial authority in Saudi Arabia at the time (and Grand Mufti of Saudi Arabia from 1993 until his death in 1999) authorizing the presence of US and allied forces on Saudi soil. The granting of this decree outraged many Muslim fundamentalists, including bin Laden (Lawrence 2005, p. 3).

Bin Laden and al-Qaeda have an objection to democratic forms of government which also turns on the importance of sacred values. Legislation, on their view, is the exclusive right of God and the only proper role that governments have is to enforce God's laws. Countries that make their own laws, rather than applying God's laws, are granting themselves a status equal to God, and that is a clear form of blasphemy. Because democracies, such as the United States, allow everyone a say in the formulation of laws, they presume that all of their citizens have a status equal to God; so they turn all of their citizens into blasphemers (Ibrahim 2007, pp. 130–6). Al-Qaeda does not need additional reasons to go to war with the USA, and bin Laden did not particularly present this complaint as a justification for violent action. But if they did need an additional reason to go to war with America, the fact that the USA is a nation that turns all of its citizens into blasphemers would be sufficient reason, from their point of view, to justify such action.

Afterlife beliefs are not as important for bin Laden and al Qaeda's justification of violent action as cosmic war and sacred values, but they do play a role in justifying a particular means of pursing that violent action. The hijackers of the four planes involved in the 9/11 attacks in America, who were expecting to die in the course of the attacks, were assured by al-Qaeda that God would reward them for their act of martyrdom with entry into heaven.[53] They might well have worried that they would end up in hell, rather than heaven, as the Koran specifically prohibits suicide.[54] The writings of Ayman al-Zawahiri, bin Laden's deputy, were intended to allay such fears. He argued that the operation was technically not an act of suicide, because of the motives that lay behind it, and so, despite appearances, it was not prohibited by the Koran (Ibrahim 2007, pp. 137–61).

Concluding Remarks

When the various justifications for violence offered in the six case studies discussed in this chapter are considered, one general point becomes obvious: the recent proponents of religious violence examined here do not lack the ability to articulate arguments justifying their actions. In five of the six case studies, we are presented with well-formed arguments justifying violent action. The exception is "The killing of George Tiller." In this case study, an argument justifying the use of violence against abortion providers, at the time that they are attempting to conduct abortions, is presented; but it is misapplied in an attempt to justify the killing of an abortion provider who was not actually attempting to conduct an abortion at the time that he was killed. One might, of course, reject the religious premises that these five justificatory arguments rely on, but to do so is not to deny that the arguments offered are well-formed. One might also introduce countervailing considerations and argue that, when these countervailing considerations are taken into account, the justificatory arguments offered no longer entail the conclusions generated. But, again, to do so is not to challenge the ability of the religious to offer well-formed arguments justifying violent action. The same response can be made to well-formed secular arguments justifying violence. Indeed, pacifists often provide such a response to well-formed secular arguments justifying violence.

Secular people and (the majority of) religious people, who are familiar with, but who are not members of, the religious groups under examination in our case studies, will be very unlikely to accept the key premises that the religious individuals and groups examined in our case studies do accept. This is because these premises presume the truth of religious metaphysical schemas that they are very unlikely to find credible and not because the various religious metaphysical schemas described in our case studies are hard to comprehend. Most of the reasoning examined in our case studies is not particularly hard to comprehend, even for those secular people who are largely unfamiliar with religious reasoning. Appeals to cosmic war are perhaps the easiest form of religious justification of violent action for secular people to comprehend. Most secular people will be familiar with appeals to the concept of a just war, which is often invoked in public discourse in attempts to persuade them to endorse their country's participation in this or that war. All five of the religious groups examined above appeal to cosmic war;[55] and in all five cases it seems plausible to think that, if they really are at war, then they are fighting a just war. If a religious group is under attack, or in imminent danger of being harmed, by Satan, or evil, or the Luciferians, or God's enemies, or the allies of Satan, then presumably that religious group is entitled to use all reasonable means to defend its members, including violent ones. And, arguably, if innocent third parties are being attacked, by any of the above, then religious groups are also entitled to forcibly intervene to protect those innocent third parties.

Appeals to the afterlife, as a form of justification for violent action, will be unfamiliar to some secular ears, but these are generally not hard to understand, as they typically involve straightforward considerations of consequence. Indeed, in all three of our case studies in which these are invoked, they are used to motivate the incorporation of considerations of consequence into justifications for violent action. If members of Heaven's Gate will not in fact die, if they kill themselves in the right way, at the right time, but will go on to live lives of eternal happiness instead, then the consequences of killing themselves in the right way, at the right time, are surely to be preferred to the consequences of not killing themselves. If Japanese people really will experience significantly better afterlives if they die sooner rather than later, then, all things being equal, considerations of consequence will lead us to prefer their dying sooner rather than later.

And if the 9/11 hijackers will experience an eternity of bliss in heaven, rather than an eternity of suffering in hell, as a result of conducting the 9/11 attacks, then at least one set of consequences, which needs to be considered when we evaluate the morality of the 9/11 attacks, tells in favor of conducting those attacks.

Appeals to sacred values are probably the most difficult, of the forms of religious justification for violence that are examined in this book, for the secular to understand. However, as we saw in Chapter 6, the sacred is not an exclusively religious concept, and some of the appeals to the sacred that are made in our case studies are conceptually close to secular appeals to sacred values. The view that human life is sacred, which is widespread amongst religious believers, is very close to the deontological view that human life may not be taken, even if the beneficial consequences of doing so outweigh the harmful ones. This is a view that underpins much ordinary secular morality, and which is enshrined in common law. The appeal to justifiable homicide, offered in defense of Scott Roeder for his killing of George Tiller, involves an appeal to a variant of this widely accepted view about the moral status of all living humans, with just one minor conceptual shift. Instead of holding that it is always immoral to attempt to kill innocent humans, *after they have been born*, the Army of God and other defenders of Scott Roeder hold that it is always immoral to kill innocent humans, *after they have been conceived*. We may not agree with this view, but it is easy enough to comprehend.

The conviction that particular lands, such as Israel and Arabia, are sacred and that everyone except members of certain religious groups should be forcibly removed from them is challenging for non-religious people to comprehend. But it is not wholly without analogs in the secular world. As we saw in Chapter 6, secular sacralization occurs in many countries, which treat battlefields and memorials to national heroes as sacred sites, although these countries do not usually prevent members of out-groups from entering such sites. Also, national emblems such as flags are often sacralized. Bin Laden's view that all forms of government, other than Islamic theological government, are blasphemous, and Meir Kahane's view that a particular people are holy and therefore entitled to disregard the moral claims and interests of all other peoples, are extreme appeals to sacred values. There do not appear to be any near analogs of these extreme appeals to sacred values in the secular world, but they do not seem particularly difficult to understand.

The religious groups examined in our case studies all appear to appreciate that the justifications for religious violence to which they appeal are not likely to win over non-believers, and for the most part their appeals are directed towards their own followers. All of the religious groups under discussion are interested in making new recruits, but most of them recognize that openly proclaiming justifications for violent action is not a good way to do so. Shoko Asahara was secretive about Aum Shinrikyo's Buddhist line of justification for religious violence, publicly preaching the view that all life is sacred, and only discussing this line of justification for violence with his leading disciples (Kaplan and Marshall 1996, p. 50). Marshall Applewhite talked in vague metaphorical language about ascension to the next level, and those who were not already members of Heaven's Gate would have been unlikely to realize that he was advocating mass suicide. Scott Roeder and his supporters deny that they advocate the initiation of violent action. They present themselves – and no doubt they see themselves – as ordinary decent people who are concerned to intervene and prevent violence that is already taking place. The rhetoric of The Gatekeepers, the Kach Party, and al-Qaeda is more strident, and these groups openly acknowledge that they consider certain forms of violent action to be justified. However, their stated justifications for violence are primarily directed at other participants in the religious traditions that they are operating within. The Gatekeepers made efforts to recruit other Christians to their war on the USA and al-Qaeda has made many efforts to recruit other Muslims to their war on America,[56] while the Kach Party was concerned to recruit other Jews to contribute to their efforts to remove Gentiles from Israel. These three groups have been open about their endorsement of violence. However, none has been particularly concerned to justify themselves to anyone other than people with whom they already share a religious tradition. For the most part they are simply reprising variants of arguments justifying violent action that will already be familiar to – but are often rejected by – others with whom they share a common religious heritage.

Notes

1. In one of our case studies, "Meir Kahane and the Kach Party," the justifications that I will consider are generic ones provided by Meir Kahane, who was killed before the most violent act examined in the case study took place.
2. He has also claimed to be a "modern manifestation" of the biblical prophet Elijah (North 2001b).
3. Turgeon's conception of an unjust and wicked person was extremely broad. For example, he and his followers believed that they were justified in stealing a motorcycle from a US Navy lieutenant. The lieutenant was considered to

be an evildoer because he watched "R-rated" movies and supported the US Navy's practice of commissioning female officers (North 2001b).

4. See Court of Appeals Washington, Division 1 (2003).

5. See Court of Appeals Washington, Division 1 (2003).

6. The discrepancy in sentence lengths was in recognition of the fact that Turgeon was the leader and Applin the follower in the mission to kill Jess.

7. Deific decree has been savagely attacked by Hawthorne who describes it as a "pseudo-doctrine" and as "internally incoherent" (2000, p. 1775). For a history of the application and development of the doctrine, see Morris and Haroun (2001).

8. The jury instructions provided Applin and Turgeon with two opportunities to prove that they were legally insane, either by applying deific decree, or by using the much more commonly applied M'Naghten test of insanity. (Leong 2008, pp. 102–3). The M'Naghten Test:

> To establish a defence on the ground of insanity, it must be clearly proved that, at the time of the committing of the act, the party accused was labouring under such a defect of reason, from disease of the mind, as not to know the nature and quality of the act he was doing; or, if he did know it, that he did not know he was doing what was wrong. (Cited in Morris and Haroun (2001, p. 999))

9. In 1890 the US Supreme Court effectively equated religious belief with Christian religious belief, when it ruled that the Mormon belief in polygamy was not, despite appearances, a religious belief. According to the court, belief in polygamy is not a genuine religious belief because it " … is contrary to the spirit of Christianity and of the civilization which Christianity has produced in the Western world" (Morris and Haroun 2001, p. 982).

10. Genesis 22:1–19.

11. Another hundred or so Aum Shinrikyo followers became members of a breakaway group, Hikari no Wa (the circle of light) in 2007.

12. In 1982, Asahara was convicted of selling fake medicine and fined the equivalent of US$2,000 (Watanabe 1998, p. 82).

13. Also translated as the "Aum Mountain Ascetics Group" (Repp 2011, p. 148).

14. After the subway gas attack, but before Asahara was put on trial, the Dalai Lama was questioned repeatedly about his relationship with Asahara. He continued to describe Asahara as a friend, but conceded that he was "not necessarily a perfect one" (Kaplan and Marshall 1996, p. 260).

15. Sometimes the attempts of Asahara's followers to display their absolute devotion to him bought them into conflict with the broader world. In one notorious incident members of Aum Shinrikyo attempted to hijack a plane after

two flight attendants sat in the first class area that Asahara had claimed for himself alone (Repp 2011, p. 160).

16. Kaplan and Marshall estimate that by the mid-1990s Aum Shinrikyo had accumulated at least US$200 million in assets (1996, p. 92).

17. Despite some reports to the contrary, all of Aum Shinrikyo's efforts to create or acquire biological weapons ended in failure (Leitenberg 1999).

18. A railgun is an electromagnetic projectile launcher. Experimental versions of railguns have been successfully tested by the US military, and by some other military forces, but no railgun has yet been developed that is considered to be a feasible piece of military equipment.

19. The deaths resulted from swallowing " … a lethal concoction of phenobarbitals, vodka, and apple sauce" (Davis 2000, p. 241).

20. Also, each body was found with a sports bag, a five dollar bill, several quarters and a stick of lip balm (Harding 2005, p. 305).

21. They may have believed rumors that a spaceship had been spotted trailing the Hale-Bopp comet, and decided that this spaceship was coming to pick them up and take then to "the next level" (Cowan and Bromley 2008, p. 171).

22. Given that the rest of us are supposed to be "spaded under" very soon, it is hard to see much point in Heaven's Gate leaving DiAngelo behind. DiAngelo attempts to explain further in a self-published book on Heaven's Gate (DiAngelo 2007b).

23. A reference to Revelation 11:3: "And I will give *power* to my two witnesses, and they will prophesy one thousand two hundred and sixty days, clothed in sackcloth."

24. Also Tiddly and Wink, Nincom and Poop (Urban 2000, p. 276), Winnie and Pooh, Admiral and Captain, Chip and Dale, and Him and Her (Harding 2005, p. 311).

25. In keeping with the science fiction themes of Heaven's Gate theology, messengers to earth were said to be ordinary humans who had been implanted with computer chips by the next level beings (Zeller 2006, p. 90).

26. Sometimes Applewhite claimed that Jesus was a previous incarnation of himself (Davis 2000, p. 252).

27. Although, at one point in the 1970s, Applewhite and Nettles had at least 100 followers (Zeller 2011, p. 76) and perhaps as many as 200 (Harding 2005, p. 299).

28. Stern (2003) lists seven such killings and, as far as I can tell, there have been no further killings by anti-abortion activists in America since 2003, apart from the killing of Tiller; hence, the figure eight.

29. Abortions provided after the twenty-first week of pregnancy are known as late-term abortions.

30. For further discussion of the "Summer of Mercy," see Risen and Thomas (1998, pp. 323–33).

31. An early slogan of Operation Rescue was "If you believe abortion is murder, act like it's murder" (Mapes 2009).

32. For example, in 1994, a group of Southern Baptist ethicists and theologians issued a joint statement which became known as the "Nashville Declaration of Conscience." In it they declared that, although abortion is immoral, the killing of abortion providing doctors is " ... not a morally justifiable or permissible Christian response to abortion" (Conclusion 6.1) (The Ethics and Religious Liberty Commission of the Southern Baptist Convention, 1994).

33. The Army of God maintains a tribute page to Shelley Shannon: http://www.armyofgod.com/ShelleyWhois.html (accessed November 22, 2012).

34. For further discussion of use of the justifiable homicide defense by violent anti-abortion activists, and their appeal to scripture to ground this use, see Jefferis (2011, pp. 52–63).

35. For a discussion of philosophical issues raised by the concept of ensoulment, see Haldane and Lee (2003).

36. Quickening occurs when a pregnant woman first feels a fetus moving in her uterus. In the past this sensation was sometimes thought to result from the pregnant woman feeling the fetus being ensouled.

37. As spelled out in Genesis 9:6:

> Whoever sheds man's blood,
> By man his blood shall be shed;
> For in the image of God
> He made man.

38. See, for example, the Army of God's webpages "The Homo News," http://www.armyofgod.com/Leviticus4.html (accessed November 22, 2012), and "Birth Control is Evil," http://www.armyofgod.com/Birthcontrol.html (accessed November 22, 2012).

39. Kahane's account of the creation of the Jewish Defense League was published posthumously. See Kahane (2000).

40. Initially Kach ran for the Knesset under the name "The League List."

41. For a description of such activities by a participant, see Sprinzak (1991, pp. 57–8).

42. There has been a recent controversy in Israel about a book published in 2009 by the West Bank settler and rabbi Yitzhak Shapira, which echoes this view. Shapira (2009) claims that it is permissible for Jews to kill Gentiles when they are a threat to the interests of the Jewish people.

43. This extract from *The Jewish Idea* is reprinted in Juergensmeyer and Kitts (2011, p. 72).

44. On most accounts bin Laden is said to have lived an intensely and devoutly religious life from his very early years (e.g., Berger 2006, pp. 20–3, 390). However, some commentators suggest that there was a period in the early 1970s during which he was not particularly religious and when he lived " ... the lifestyle of a playboy" (Orbach 2001, p. 54).

45. Al-Qaeda did not initially claim responsibility for the 9/11 attacks. In a message broadcast on Al Jazeera in October 2004, bin Laden acknowledged that they were responsible for the attacks, slightly more than three years after the event (Ibrahim 2007, pp. 213–9).

46. Indeed, even most Islamic fundamentalist groups have condemned al-Qaeda's actions (Wiktorowicz and Kaltner 2003, pp. 76–7).

47. The most significant of these are collected in volumes edited by Lawrence (2005) and Ibrahim (2007).

48. Bin Laden's justification for the killing of American civilians, which does not rely on religious premises, is that, as participants in a democracy, American citizens have the opportunity to change their government's policies and so they bear responsibility for those policies (Lawrence 2005, p. 47).

49. Bin Laden also complains about the loss of Andalusia (Spain), which was ruled, at least in part, by Muslims from 711 to 1492 (Ibrahim 2007, p. 145). Under the interpretation of Islamic jurisprudence favored by bin Laden, once a land has been bought under Islamic control, it permanently belongs to Islam, regardless of what went before, or after, a period of Islamic control (Ibrahim 2007, p. 294).

50. According to Nations Online, 96 percent of the population of East Timor are Catholic: http://www.nationsonline.org/oneworld/timor_leste.htm (accessed November 22, 2012).

51. Bin laden comes very close to inadvertently justifying Western hostility to Islam in his discussion of offensive jihad. He does this when he describes the West's behavior towards the Islamic world as a reaction to its realization that Muslims like him believe that they have a religious duty to impose Islamic rule on the entire world. According to bin Laden, " ... the West did not treat Islam in this atrocious manner until after it (first) understood the truth about Islam" (Ibrahim 2007, p. 55).

52. Bin laden was additionally outraged by the presence of non-Muslim women (especially Jewish women) in Arabia (Berger 2006, p. 293).

53. From a set of instructions found to have been in the possession of several of the 9/11 hijackers: " ... it is only a few minutes before the happy, satisfying life and the eternal Paradise begins in the company of the prophets, the upright people, the martyrs and the righteous ... " (Juergensmeyer and Kitts 2011, p. 84).

54. Koran 4:29.

55. Furthermore, in the remaining case study, "The Killing of George Tiller," as we saw, many of the proponents of the "justifiable homicide" defense of the killing of George Tiller believe that they are participants in a long-running cosmic war. However, this belief was not invoked in the justification of the killing discussed in the case study.

56. I do not mean to suggest that The Gatekeepers lack all interest in making converts to Christianity, or that al-Qaeda is uninterested in making converts to Islam.

8

Tolerance

Liberal Democracy and Religious Tolerance

When they are presented with evidence that many religious groups have well-developed arguments justifying religious violence, people sometimes respond by suggesting that these arguments can be countered by arguments in favor of religious tolerance. It is widely believed that there are strong arguments in favor of religious tolerance; and it is sometimes supposed that when people are made aware of these arguments they will see that they ought to refrain from acting violently in the name of their religion. In this chapter I look at religious tolerance. I consider what tolerance is, and I consider how religious tolerance has traditionally been justified. I then examine social psychological research on the relationship between religion, tolerance, and intolerance in order to better understand when and how religion produces tolerance and intolerance. Then I consider the question of whether or not religious groups that hold that violent acts are justified by their religion are liable to be persuaded to tolerate other religions and refrain from acting violently towards them if arguments that they accept, which justify religious violence, are countered by arguments in favor of religious tolerance.

The propensity of members of religious groups to act violently when they believe that violent action is justified by their religion raises a problem for religiously tolerant, liberal democratic societies. Religious freedom is usually upheld as a core value in liberal democratic societies, and so liberals should want members of religious groups to be able to conduct their own freely chosen religious activities without interference (Trigg 2012). However, liberals are also committed to preventing violent actions taking

The Justification of Religious Violence, First Edition. Steve Clarke.
© 2014 John Wiley & Sons, Inc. Published 2014 by John Wiley & Sons, Inc.

place between individuals residing within liberal democratic societies. Some religious groups hold that violence is justified by their religion under particular circumstances, and some believe that other religions should not be tolerated. Members of some of these religious groups, such as al-Qaeda and Aum Shinrikyo, also believe that their religion justifies the overthrowing of liberal states in order to establish theocratic states. So, the activities of some religious groups can constitute a threat to liberal states, as well as a threat to individuals residing within those states.

In liberal societies individuals are free to pick and choose their religion. They can attempt to affiliate themselves with any religion, for whatever reason happens to seem compelling to them, or for no reason at all. They can also renounce their religion at any time, and take up any another religion, or forgo religion altogether. They can practice their religion in secret, or they can do so openly; and they can proselytize on behalf of their religion. They can also amend current religious doctrines, in whatever ways they see fit, to create new versions of existing religions; and they can devise entirely new religions.

The view that individuals ought to be free to pick and choose their religion is now a mainstream one in Western countries, but it only became a mainstream view relatively recently. Its rise is conventionally associated with the Western Age of Enlightenment of the seventeenth and eighteenth centuries. At that time church and state began to be separated in various European countries and principled arguments for religious tolerance were developed (Zagorin 2003).[1] As we saw in Chapter 5, the traditional Catholic view was that people are justified in using violent means to suppress heresy and apostasy, so, traditionally, the Catholic Church was opposed to key forms of religious toleration.[2] Traditionally it has also been opposed to freedom of conscience and to democracy. The Catholic Church did not suddenly change its tune with the onset of the Age of Enlightenment. Indeed, Catholic leaders could be heard denouncing religious tolerance, freedom of conscience, and democracy right up until the early decades of the twentieth century (Coady 2013, p. 191). Fortunately for liberal democracies, mainstream Catholic ideas have shifted considerably over the past century. However, in the twenty-first century there is no shortage of intolerant minor religious groups that are prepared to use violent and overtly coercive means to promote their religion and, if they can, to create political structures that would function to compel acceptance of that religion.[3] The difficulty for liberal democracies, given that members of such groups reside within their territories, is to know whether and when they should try to "tolerate the intolerant."[4]

It is sometimes assumed that religious toleration is unique to the West and is of relatively recent origin. This is not the case. Many of the multinational empires of the ancient world tolerated a wide variety of religions, as did more recent empires, such as the long-lasting Ottoman empire of the late thirteenth to early twentieth centuries (Walzer 1997, pp. 14–36). Under the Ottoman "millet" system, while Islam was the state religion, particular ethnic-religious communities were given official recognition and were allowed to organize their own religious affairs (Kaplan 2007, pp. 240–5). But, while a significant degree of religious toleration was extended to minority ethnic-religious communities, very little religious toleration was extended to individuals. It was extremely difficult for individuals to shift religious allegiances under the millet system (Kymlicka 1996). This system was designed to promote tolerant and harmonious relations between the different ethnic-religious groups that resided within the Ottoman empire, rather than individual religious freedom. In contrast, modern Western liberal legal and administrative arrangements are designed to promote both intergroup tolerance and individual religious freedom.

What Tolerance Is

Acts of toleration involve non-interference, but not all acts of non-interference are acts of toleration. Toleration implies a sense of disapproval that we have overriding reasons not to act on (Williams 1996, p. 20). I do not demonstrate tolerance of Australian Rules football by failing to interfere in games of Australian Rules football, as I approve of Australian Rules football – indeed I wish that the game was more widely played. Nor do I demonstrate tolerance of rugby union, which I am generally indifferent to, by allowing games of rugby union to take place. I do, however, demonstrate a tolerant attitude towards rugby league by allowing games of rugby league to take place. Rugby league strikes me as a tedious game, and one which I (mildly) disapprove of. However, I have an overriding reason not to act on my disapproval of rugby league. I consider that people are entitled to participate in and watch the sports of their choice; and this entitlement extends to sports that I consider to be tedious.

My actual ability to interfere with games of rugby league is quite limited. I can run on to rugby fields and thereby disrupt games as they are being played. Other than this sort of direct intervention, though, there is not much I can do to prevent games of rugby league from taking place. If I believed that I had no power to interfere in rugby league games whatsoever, then I would not, properly speaking, be demonstrating tolerance of rugby league by my inaction. Rather, I would be demonstrating that I was resigned to the fact that games of rugby league were taking place.[5] Also, my non-interference must result from a principled refraining in order to count as a genuine act of toleration. If I disapprove of rugby league, but fail to disrupt games of rugby league because I am lazy, rather than because I have made a principled decision not act on my disapproval of rugby league, then my non-interference does not demonstrate tolerance on my part. Consistent with the above reasoning, Cohen offers what is perhaps the most sophisticated definition of toleration currently available. According to him:

> an act of toleration is an agent's intentional and principled refraining from interfering with an opposed other (or their behaviour, etc.) in situations of diversity, where the agent believes she has the power to interfere. (Cohen 2004, p. 69)[6]

Like Cohen, I hold non-interference to be crucial to toleration; but this claim should not be understood too broadly. To tolerate an act or practice is to forgo opportunities to interfere directly in instances of that act or practice. However, a tolerant person can take a variety of indirect measures to make it less likely that a tolerated act or practice will not be conducted, and can do so without ceasing to be a tolerant person. This combination of direct non-interference and indirect influence is often manifested in situations where religious groups live side-by-side in religiously pluralist societies. A devout Christian may decide that there are principled reasons to tolerate Jewish and Muslim religious practices within her community. However, she may also believe that she has a religious duty to preach to local Jews and Muslims to try to persuade them to convert to Christianity. If she was successful in persuading all members of the local Jewish and Muslim communities to convert, then her actions would have the effect of ending the religious practices that she disapproves of, at least within her community; but her success would not be evidence that she had acted intolerantly towards either Jews or Muslims.

Tolerant attitudes are often not appreciated by those who are tolerated, as the tolerated can be offended by the disapproval implied by a tolerant attitude.[7] Gay activist groups sometimes object when religious leaders announce that we should tolerate homosexuality (Jakobsen and Pellegrini 2003). These groups argue that homosexuals are worthy of a much greater degree of respect and recognition of status than the term "toleration" implies. For similar reasons, minority religious groups in religiously pluralist societies have often found the idea of mere religious toleration to be insulting and unsatisfactory; some have pushed for official recognition of a right to religious freedom. The 1688 Act of Toleration was an act of the Parliament of England which extended freedom of worship to practitioners of some forms of Christianity other than Anglicanism. Notably though, freedom of worship was not extended to Catholics and non-Trinitarians. Dissatisfaction with this arrangement, along with the implication that dissenting religion was a (tolerated) legal concession and not a right, prompted vigorous debate in England's American colonies, and led to the assertion of a right to freedom of religion in the 1776 Virginia Bill of Rights. This, in turn, led to the assertion of a right to freedom of religion in the United States Bill of Rights (Trigg 2012, pp. 72–5).

Tolerance is often held up as a virtue, but there are few people who wish to be tolerant of all acts and practices. I have principled reasons to tolerate *some* of the acts and practices that I disapprove of, but I do not have principled reasons to tolerate *all* of the acts and practices that I disapprove of. A vegetarian parent who decided to tolerate the consumption of meat by her children might not be tolerant if her children told her that they wanted to eat the flesh of an endangered species. Similarly, people who argue that we should tolerate the practices of other religious traditions would be unlikely to extend toleration to the Aztec religious practice of human sacrifice. Those who argue for particular instances of tolerance face a twofold challenge. They need to justify the claim that particular practices that are disapproved of should, nevertheless, be tolerated, and they also need to locate and justify appropriate limits to tolerance (Raphael 1988). In liberal societies, Mill's (1859) "harm principle" is often seen as a guide to the proper limits on tolerance (Raz 1988). Acts and practices that cause unjustified harm to others should not be tolerated, according to Mill (1859). Of course, there is significant room for dispute about what constitutes harm and what forms of justification could legitimately be offered for harming others.

Justifying Religious Tolerance

The most straightforward justification for religious tolerance is pragmatic. The majority may not approve of the religious practices of some or other minority group residing within their country, but if they attempt to suppress the religious practices of this minority group, then this may lead to civil unrest and perhaps civil war. If the minority religion is also prevalent in other counties, then attempts to suppress the practice of that religion can lead to international conflict. Realizing all of this, the majority are liable to conclude that the expected benefits of suppressing the disapproved of religious practices are outweighed by the expected costs of attempting to suppress these practices. The pragmatic line of argument for religious tolerance was championed by David Hume (1778). Many thinkers in the liberal tradition, including Mill and Locke, have found it deeply unsatisfactory. If the basis for tolerating the religious practices of minority groups is only that the expected costs of suppression outweigh the expected benefits, then it seems that we would be entitled to suppress the practices of minority religious groups in circumstances where the expected benefits outweigh expected costs. Also, circumstances change, and as they change so do the outcomes of cost–benefit analyses. Even if we are pragmatically justified in tolerating particular religious practices now, there is no guarantee that we will remain pragmatically justified in tolerating those practices in the future. At most, the pragmatic defense of tolerance can offer us the conclusion that religious majorities should tolerate the practices of some religious minorities, in some places and at some times, but need only do so until such time as the majority is in a position to effectively suppress that minority religion without thereby incurring onerous costs.

Non-pragmatic arguments justifying religious tolerance are associated with the liberal tradition. On classical liberal views there is a clear distinction to be drawn between the public sphere and the private sphere, and the state is understood to have no entitlement to interfere with activities conducted in the private sphere. Religious practice is usually understood, by liberals, to fall within the private sphere and, therefore, ought not to be subject to state interference (De Roover and Balagangadhara 2008). Mill (1859) grounded his defense of classical liberalism, and his associated defense of religious tolerance, on an appeal to the value of individual autonomy. We are better able to express the value of autonomy when we can shape the direction of our own lives, without interference from the state, or from others. One important way in which we can shape the direction of our own lives is by being able to practice our chosen religion. So, we should be able to choose to practice which ever religion we happen to prefer, and others should refrain from interfering in our religious practices.

A very different line of argument in favor of religious tolerance, which was developed by Pierre Bayle, is one that appeals to epistemic humility. According to Bayle (1685), all religious believers should allow that there is some chance that their own religious beliefs are false; and they should also allow that there is some chance that another set of religious beliefs is true. Religious believers ought, Bayle reasons, to be interested in finding the truth, and interested in avoiding falsehoods. Therefore, he argues, they should tolerate and indeed respect other religious beliefs, as these may turn out to be true, just as their own religious convictions may turn out to be false.

Yet another argument in favor of religious tolerance comes from John Locke (1689). Locke argues that religious persecution is ineffective. We can compel people to assert that they don't hold particular religious beliefs, but we cannot actually compel them not to hold particular religious beliefs, or so Locke assures us. Because we cannot effectively persecute dissenting religious belief, we make our own lives easier by not wasting our time trying to do so, and by being tolerant of religious dissenters. In developing this line of argument, Locke is implicitly assuming that when authorities persecute religious dissenters they are trying to change the dissenters' religious beliefs. However, the authorities in question may only really be interested in suppressing dissenting religious practices and may not be overly concerned with actual beliefs. In any case, it is not obvious, as Locke seems to assume, that we cannot effectively change at least some beliefs, including religious beliefs, with the use of coercive means (Waldron 1991).

Religion, Toleration, and Causation

It is often claimed that most religions, or at least mainstream religions, promote tolerance. It is especially common to hear the claim that Christianity promotes tolerance. And indeed there are prima facie reasons to think that Christianity is an overall promoter of tolerance. The Bible urges us to adopt a loving attitude to others, including our enemies, to forgive offences, and to "turn the other cheek" in response to aggression; a cluster of attitudes that seems to be conducive to tolerance.[8] Religious people – and this seems to be a cross-culturally robust generalization – generally perceive themselves as pro-social and helpful, agreeable, and ready to forgive others (Saroglou et al. 2005, pp. 323 – 4). However, the conclusion that is generally accepted in social psychology is that the religious do not reliably exhibit these qualities (Batson, Schoenrade, and Ventis 1993).

The apparently cynical attitude of mainstream social psychologists about religion and its effects on tolerance results from a series of studies dating back to the mid-twentieth century that indicate a positive correlation between the degree of involvement with religion and intolerance and prejudice (Powell and Clarke 2013). Religiosity has been found to correlate with increased racial prejudice (Allport and Kramer 1946), intolerance of non-conformists (Stouffer 1955), and a punitive rather than forgiving attitude (Kirkpatrick 1949). According to Daniel Batson, thirty-four of forty-four findings, from thirty-six studies conducted between 1940 and 1975, suggest a positive relationship between intolerance and involvement in religion, with only two of these forty-four findings bucking this trend (Batson 2013, p. 90).[9] Religion correlates with heightened tolerance of in-group members, but it also correlates with increased intolerance of out-group members; and in religiously pluralist countries, such as the USA, the overall effect of religion is to promote intolerance and prejudice (Powell and Clarke 2013). The relationship between religion and intolerance is nothing if not paradoxical. Increased involvement in religion, which often involves increased exposure to exhortations from religious leaders to be tolerant and to avoid prejudice, tends to result in heightened intolerance and increased prejudice.

Before we consider social psychological research on the relationship between religion and intolerance in more detail, a few notes of caution are in order. The first is that it should not be assumed that religion itself causes tolerance of in-group members and intolerance of out-group members. Group dynamics may do most, or even all, of the work of causing such attitudes.[10] People are generally more tolerant of, and less prejudiced against, others whom they perceive as members of the same groups as themselves (and with whom they share values, norms, traditions, and ways of conceiving the world); they are generally less tolerant of, and more prejudiced against, those whom they perceive as members of out-groups (Hewstone, Rubin, and Willis 2002). There is no logical reason why having a favorable attitude towards members of one's in-group should lead to an unfavorable attitude towards members of out-groups. However, strong positive identification with an in-group has been shown to correlate, under a broad range of circumstances, with derogation of those who are perceived as members of out-groups (e.g., Levin and Sidanius 1999; Mummendey, Klink, and Brown 2001).

Another complication is that many religious groups overlap with ethnic groups and social classes. It may be that identification with ethnic groups, or social classes, rather than religion, is what actually drives many of the instances of in-group tolerance and out-group intolerance and prejudice that are associated with particular religions. In some cases it will be very difficult to distinguish intolerance and prejudice based on religion from intolerance and prejudice based on ethnicity and/or class difference. An Orthodox Christian Serb, who is overtly intolerant of and prejudiced against Bosnian Muslims, may not single out either Bosnian ethnicity or Islam as the chief motivator of this intolerance and prejudice, but may simply have a hostile reaction to a group of people who are both ethnically and religiously distinct from her own group, and with whom her own group has a history of enmity.

A further reason why it is difficult to determine whether religion is a cause of tolerance or intolerance is a methodological one. It is not easy to conduct experiments that identify clear instances of tolerance of out-groups. To tolerate a group, one must disapprove of that group and also think that one has a principled reason not to act on that disapproval. This is a complicated state of affairs and not one that is easily and reliably identifiable in social science studies and experiments. In practice, the term "intolerant" is often conflated with the term "prejudiced" in the social sciences, where prejudice is usually understood to involve a set of negative stereotyping beliefs about an out-group, along with feelings of dislike for that group and a disposition to behave negatively towards them; and tolerance is understood as the absence of prejudice (Jackman 1977). It is plausible to think that many of those who are intolerant of a particular group are also significantly prejudiced against that group and that many of those who are tolerant of that group, although they may mildly disapprove of that group, are not discernibly prejudiced against them. So, although the common conflation of prejudice with intolerance in the social sciences is unfortunate, it is probably not a debilitating methodological problem in most actual social scientific studies of tolerance and intolerance.[11]

A second methodological concern is that studies of intolerance and prejudice are studies of intolerance and prejudice directed against particular groups. From data showing that research subjects are intolerant of and prejudiced against certain groups, it is often assumed by social psychologists that we can draw the conclusion that these research subjects are generally intolerant and prejudiced. But this seems like overreaching. Someone who is prejudiced against and intolerant of some groups may well be tolerant of other groups. A prejudice against Jews, Italians, and Japanese is entirely compatible with tolerant attitudes towards Arabs, Greeks, and Koreans. So, it looks like our choice of groups to be considered as potential subjects of prejudice and intolerance will make a substantial difference to our final conclusion (Gibson 2005). The unevenness of actual patterns of tolerance and intolerance is especially problematic when our subject is religious tolerance and intolerance, as particular religions may proscribe some instances of intolerance, but prescribe others. Many evangelical Christian churches proscribe racism, but prescribe intolerance of homosexuality, for example.

In practice, studies of prejudice and intolerance often tend to be studies of majority group attitudes towards minority groups, which are now widely regarded as unjustified. We are liable to infer, from evidence, say, that white middle-class Protestants living in rural areas of America tend to be prejudiced against and intolerant of Blacks, Jews, and Catholics, that white middle-class Protestants living in rural areas of America are generally prejudiced and intolerant. But, if we had studied the same research subjects' attitudes towards pedophiles, drug-dealers, and fascists, and found that they were generally prejudiced against and intolerant of these groups, then we would be unlikely to infer that they are generally prejudiced and intolerant. Strong disapproval of this latter assortment of groups is widely regarded as justified by the mainstream and is not usually taken as evidence of a prejudiced and intolerant mind-set.[12]

Gordon Allport made an influential attempt to explain how it could be that religiosity correlates with intolerance of out-groups, despite the many exhortations of religious leaders to be tolerant of others. Allport (1966) distinguished between two different orientations towards religion: an extrinsic orientation and an intrinsic orientation. For those with an extrinsic orientation to religion, religion is construed instrumentally, as a means to other ends. These ends are various and include increased social status and increased opportunities for networking, as well as psychological benefits, such as increased self-esteem and a reduction in feelings of subjective uncertainty. For those with an intrinsic orientation to religion, however, the key tenets of their religion are internalized and become the "master motives" guiding their lives. Allport (1966) claimed that an extrinsic orientation towards religion was entirely compatible with prejudice and intolerance, whereas an intrinsic orientation was not; and he held that the fact that significant numbers of people have an extrinsic relationship to religion explained the correlation between religiosity and intolerance and prejudice. In studies of reported attitudes, research subjects with an extrinsic religious orientation have consistently been found to be more prejudiced and intolerant than those with an intrinsic religious orientation (Batson 2013).

Allport's use of the distinction between intrinsic and extrinsic attitudes to religion was well received by those who were concerned to respond to the charge that religion promoted intolerance and prejudice. On Allport's account, it was not the genuinely religious who were understood to be intolerant and prejudiced, but only those with a shallow and superficial attitude towards religion. However, there are two reasons to be dissatisfied with this line of reasoning. The first is that, although intrinsic religion does not correlate with intolerance and prejudice, it does not correlate with tolerance either (Donahue 1985). A second problem is that a reliance on self-reporting makes the case for the conclusion that an intrinsic religious orientation does not promote intolerance suspect. Those who have an intrinsic attitude to religion are highly motivated to provide answers on questionnaires (and in other places) that are in accord with the religious teachings that they accept. However, their typical self-assessments, as being tolerant and unprejudiced, are not borne out by their observed behavior. The observed behavior of those who have an intrinsic orientation to religion is generally less tolerant than the observed behavior of the non-religious, except in regard to forms of intolerance and prejudice that are specifically proscribed by their religious communities (Batson et al. 1993; Batson 2013).

Daniel Batson (1976) suggested that, in addition to intrinsic and extrinsic religion, there is a third dimension of religion, orthogonal to the other two, which he referred to as "Religion as Quest." Batson was trying to identify a style of religiosity that was prominently characterized by Gandhi (1948), among others. In stark contrast to religious fundamentalists, who hold that key religious doctrines are firmly established truths that are not open to doubt, "questers" embrace religious doubt, which they consider to be healthy; and they are open to far-reaching changes in the direction of their religious life. They regard their religious life as an ongoing journey of discovery. For them, the primary purpose of religion is to try to find answers to deep questions, such as the question of the "meaning of life"; and they typically accept that answers to such questions may only be gradually and perhaps only partially revealed during the course of their lifetimes.

Someone who has an open-minded questing orientation towards religion is likely to be receptive to other points of view; and it seems plausible to think that they will be more tolerant of other ways of living than those who do not treat key religious doctrines as open to doubt. Indeed, a questing attitude towards religion would seem to make it easier for someone to accept Bayle's (1685) argument for tolerance grounded on epistemic humility, which was discussed earlier in this chapter. Whereas a religious fundamentalist will be unlikely to concede that there is any chance that their religious beliefs are false, a quester will happily concede this possibility. There is evidence that religion as quest correlates strongly with tolerance and an absence of prejudice (McFarland 1989; Batson et al. 1993). And unlike intrinsic religiosity, a quest orientation towards religion correlates with tolerance, regardless of whether particular forms of intolerance and prejudice are proscribed by one's religious community or not (Batson 2013). However, as a strong questing orientation towards religion is comparatively rare, at least amongst followers of mainstream religions (Batson et al. 1993; Greer et al. 2005), it seems safe to say that, currently at least, religion correlates strongly with intolerance towards, and prejudice against, out-groups. Despite what may be preached in churches and other places of worship, mainstream religious organizations are not effective promoters of tolerance.

Violent Religious Groups, Tolerance, and the Liberal State

The governments of liberal states can – and in many cases already do – actively promote attitudes of tolerance amongst their citizens and other residents; and this may lead some of the religious, who would otherwise be inclined to act violently in the name of their religion, to refrain from such action.[13] However, it is unrealistic to suppose that the mere promotion of the value of tolerance will persuade many of those who have well-developed arguments justifying religious violence to refrain from acting violently. As we have seen in Chapters 4, 5, and 6, from the point of view of many of those who believe that they are justified in acting violently in the name of their religion, the stakes that may be determined by undertaking violent action are very high. Violations of sacred values can be prevented, cosmic wars can be won, and more people can end up in heaven rather than hell, or experience better reincarnations than they would otherwise experience.

Those who believe that sacred values are in danger of being violated, and who believe that they have a duty to prevent violations of sacred values, typically also believe that there should be no compromising on sacred values; so, they will be very unlikely to start tolerating violations of sacred values simply because they have been told that they should try to be tolerant. Those who believe that they are participating in a cosmic war against Satan, or against some other evil supernatural being, or group of evil supernatural beings, are unlikely to be persuaded, by simple appeals to the value of tolerance, to refrain from participating in the cosmic war that they believe is taking place. They may concede that tolerance is a worthy virtue, which they would ordinarily seek to exemplify, but also argue that in a war situation we need to set aside the concerns of peacetime, and do whatever is necessary to ensure that war is won; and this may include acting intolerantly and violently towards those who do not follow the correct religion. It is also possible that they may interpret calls for tolerance as a ruse – orchestrated by those working for the evil supernatural being, or beings, that they are fighting against – to try to trick them into not doing their religious duty. If they do think this way, then calls by a state's government for religious tolerance may lead them to suspect that the state's government is under the influence, or control, of the evil supernatural being, or beings, that they are fighting against, and this suspicion may further increase their propensity to act violently against the state and against other people residing within it.

There is not much chance of persuading those who hold that considerations of the salvation of others justify violent action, to start tolerating behavior that, they believe, will prevent others from attaining salvation. From the point of view of those who believe that adherence to the correct religion is a necessary condition for salvation – such as Aquinas and Duns Scotus – it is hard to see why concerns about religious tolerance should stand in the way of the all-important business of ensuring that others are able to enter heaven (and avoid being sent to hell). Intolerance of another person's religion can cause them to suffer. However, if it leads to acceptance of the correct religion, and this enables them to experience the joys of everlasting life in heaven, then that suffering seems a small price for them to be compelled to pay, given the potential benefits at stake.

Stakes are lower for religions that believe in reincarnation after death, rather than salvation (such as Hinduism and Buddhism), and there may be more prospect of persuading otherwise intolerant followers of these religions to become more tolerant, if their motivation for intolerance is to enable other people, whose disapproved-of behavior is not currently tolerated, to receive a better reincarnation than they would otherwise receive.[14] However, these are still significant stakes; and, as we saw in Chapters 5 and 7, appeal to these stakes has been used to justify both targeted assassination and larger-scale killing. Some otherwise intolerant Hindus and Buddhists might be persuaded to stand by and allow others to attain a worse reincarnation than they would if they were compelled to behave in a morally upright manner, but, if such Hindus and Buddhists sincerely believe that coercive or violent behavior can make a significant difference to the quality of the reincarnation that others experience, then it may be difficult to convince many of them that they ought to be tolerant and ought to refrain from acting coercively or violently.

In the next chapter I consider some practical measures that liberal democratic states can take to encourage those religious groups that are convinced that their religion justifies violence to refrain from violent actions. I also consider whether and to what extent liberal states can tolerate religious groups residing within their territory, when members of those religious groups hold the view that violent and coercive acts are justified by their religion.

Notes

1. Not all historians go along with this story. Kaplan (2007) emphasizes the extent to which local instantiations of religious tolerance had developed across Europe in advance of the Enlightenment, and the extent to which instances of religious intolerance continued to be manifested during and after the Age of Enlightenment.
2. I will use the words "tolerance" and "toleration" interchangeably.
3. Coercion is a broader category than violence. Some of the overt activities that fall under this category – threatening, bullying, and the like – will generally be unacceptable in liberal states. Other, more covert forms of coercion, such as the use of "social pressure" and emotional manipulation, will be difficult to prevent and may be considered acceptable, in particular contexts, by many liberals anyway. For philosophical discussion of the concept of coercion, see Anderson (2006). For discussion of some of the difficulties involved in identifying actual instances of religious coercion, see Nussbaum (2012, pp. 122–32).
4. For further discussion of this issue, see Walzer (1997) and Ignatieff (2004).
5. Heyd argues similarly (1996, p. 14).

6. I am unconvinced that the clause "situations of diversity" is necessary in this definition. It seems to me that someone in a situation wholly lacking in diversity could disapprove of a practice and yet decide to tolerate that practice. Suppose that I live in a community in which everyone smokes, including me. I could be in this situation, and disapprove of smoking and decide, nevertheless, that smoking should be tolerated (this same point is made in Powell and Clarke (2013 pp. 24–5, note 9)).

7. Indeed, Goethe famously claimed that "to tolerate means to insult" (Forst 2007).

8. But, as we saw in Chapter 1, there is a danger in taking a selective reading of the Bible, which contains many passages that are difficult to square with the view that the Christian religion is a promoter of peace (and by implication tolerance).

9. These two findings are unusual in that both are taken from studies of adolescent or pre-adolescent population samples, rather than studies of adults (Batson 2013, p. 90).

10. For recent discussion of group dynamics, see Kruglanski et al. (2006).

11. However, this persistent conflation can lead psychologists to overlook a possible state of affairs, which is that people can be both prejudiced against, and yet tolerant of, particular out-groups.

12. For a careful discussion of the normative dimensions of studies of tolerance and intolerance, see Thurow (2013).

13. My investigations into the social psychological literature on religion, tolerance, and intolerance suggest that it is probably not easy to promote tolerance effectively, at least amongst the religious. One strategy that might work is for governments to promote a questing attitude towards religion, which, as we saw, correlates consistently with religious tolerance. There is a danger, however, that this approach could alienate religious fundamentalists, who might suppose that a government program to promote a questing attitude to religion was directed at undermining particular forms of religious fundamentalism. If so, it could backfire, making religious fundamentalists less tolerant than they are currently.

14. Are Eastern religions more tolerant than Western ones? For recent discussion of this complicated issue, see Flanagan (2013).

9

Reducing Religious Violence

Religion, Violence, Justification, and Motivation

We saw in the previous chapter that people who believe that their religion justifies acts of violence are unlikely to be persuaded to refrain from violent action by being presented with arguments in favor of religious tolerance. In this chapter, I consider other possible ways in which religious justifications for violence, which also motivate violence, might be undermined, or overridden, so as to reduce violence. The suggestions I will offer are tailored to liberal democratic state governments. In liberal democratic states, justificatory arguments conducted in the public sphere matter. They often have an impact on policy, and occasionally result in a change of government. In states that are not liberal and democratic, arguments between members of government, conducted behind closed doors may matter, but arguments carried out in the public sphere are usually of limited importance. Furthermore, in non-liberal democratic states, governments often do not feel the need to try to undermine or override arguments that they do not agree with. They can safely ignore arguments and can suppress the activities of arguers. Although I will offer a number of suggestions, I make no claim to comprehensiveness. This is not a general discussion of conflict resolution.[1] Nor is it a general discussion of the resolution of religiously motivated conflicts.[2] I will be concerned with a specific range of circumstances: those involving violent behavior that is motivated by justificatory appeals to religion.

Some instances of violence that are publicly justified by appeal to non-religious concerns can actually be motivated by religion. For example, a twenty-first-century religious leader may be motivated by religion to

The Justification of Religious Violence, First Edition. Steve Clarke.
© 2014 John Wiley & Sons, Inc. Published 2014 by John Wiley & Sons, Inc.

encourage violence against heretical groups in order to prevent the spread of heresies. Perhaps, like Aquinas, the religious leader may worry that people who accept heresies will be denied entry into heaven. However, recognizing that this medieval line of justification for violence (discussed in Chapter 5) is unlikely to persuade many people to avoid heresies in the twenty-first entury, that leader may instead decide to appeal to the potential threat that heretical groups pose to the security of local communities so as to publicly justify violent action against those groups. Recent instances of violence against members of the Ahmadi community in Pakistan appear to follow something like this pattern. Ahmadis consider themselves to be Muslims, but Sunni Muslims often consider them to be heretics.[3] Instances of the violent persecution of Ahmadis in Pakistan have been defended, by some Sunni Muslim Pakistani authorities, on what look like flimsy political grounds[4] and it seems plausible to think such instances of persecution are allowed to occur because these Sunni Muslim Pakistani authorities regard Ahmadis as heretics.[5]

Other instances of violence justified by appeal to religion may not actually be motivated by religion. A leader in a Christian country might invoke a religious concern to publicly justify starting a war with a neighboring Muslim country while actually being motivated by the prospect of incorporating new territory into the Christian country. In such circumstances, where justifications are not motivating, the disputing of justifications will usually have little or no effect on actual behavior. Even if someone were to persuade the leader, in this hypothetical example, that the religious justification offered for war was flawed, the leader's motivation for war would not have been removed. At most, that leader would be prompted to seek a different justification for war. Unless a justification that is acceptable to an authorizing agency is required before a war can be started, and unless an alternative to the religious justification for war on offer proves impossible to come by, demonstrating the inadequacies of the professed religious justification for war is very unlikely to prevent that war.

If Jon Haidt's (2001; 2012) account of moral judgment is correct, then very few of our justifications are also motivations for behavior. In his view, the great majority of motivations for behavior are driven by emotion and intuition, rather than reason, and in most instances justifications are invented after we have already determined, intuitively, what to do. If Haidt is right, then disputing justifications for behavior will hardly ever have a significant effect on that behavior. However, as we saw in Chapter 3, the evidence for Haidt's Social Intuitionist Model (SIM) of moral judgment has been challenged on several fronts, and the relative weight of the contributions of reason and intuition to actual moral judgments is simply unclear. Unless and until decisive evidence for Haidt's social intuitionism comes in, it seems appropriate to continue to treat the moral reasoning that people articulate seriously. There may well be much more scope for our stated justifications for behavior to be motivating than Haidt allows.

There are cases where religious justifications offered for violence seem genuinely motivating of violent behavior. We came across at least a couple of these in Chapter 7. Scott Roeder appears to have sincerely believed that his religion, together with the "justifiable homicide" argument for killing abortion providers, justified his killing of George Tiller (see "The Killing of George Tiller," Chapter 7). Suppose that before Roeder had acted, Christian anti-abortion activists, who did not support the killing of abortion providers, had managed to convince him that his line of justification for killing Tiller was misguided. It is hard to believe that, under those circumstances, Roeder would have gone ahead and killed Tiller. He appeared to lack any other motive, or justification, strong enough to drive him to kill Tiller. It might be supposed that this killing could have been motivated by an overwhelming emotional reaction, to encountering a figure widely hated by conservative Christians, and that Roeder did not require a clearly specified reason to be motivated to kill him. However, there were thousands of other conservative Christian anti-abortion activists who participated in the 1991 Summer of Mercy protests in Wichita, and who picketed Tiller's clinic. All of these activists were outraged by Tiller's ongoing provision of abortions, but none of them was driven by their emotions to make a serious attempt to kill Tiller.[6] So, it seems reasonable to think that the emotions that Tiller stirred up in Roeder would not have been sufficient to motivate his killing of Tiller.

Another case in which it seems clear that a religious justification offered for violence was also motivating was the case of Christopher Turgeon and Blaine Applin's killing of Dan Jess (see "The Gatekeepers and Deific Decree," Chapter 7). Turgeon and Applin thought of themselves as loyal soldiers serving God in a just war against the US government, which, they believed, was under the control of a satanic secret society. They also believed that Jess was an agent of the US government. In their eyes, they were soldiers who had been given a legitimate order, by their commanding officer (God), to kill an enemy agent during a war. Suppose that someone had managed to convince Turgeon and Applin that the US government was not, in fact, under the control of agents of Satan. If so, then Turgeon and Applin would have been deprived of a necessary component of their justification for violence. If a satanic secret society does not control the American government, then there would be no reason for The Gatekeepers – and God – to be at war with the government, and Turgeon and Applin would have lacked a justification, as well as a motive, to kill any agent of the US government, including Jess.

It might be supposed that Turgeon had an additional motive for killing Jess. After having left The Gatekeepers, Jess was reported to have referred to Turgeon as a "false prophet," calling into question Turgeon's credibility as a religious leader. Perhaps the story about a war against the US government was an elaborate ruse designed to obscure Turgeon and Applin's actual motive for killing Jess, and Turgeon and Applin were really motivated by a desire to get rid of a critic. But it is hard to see this desire as a sufficient motive for the drastic measure of killing Jess. Leaders of small religious groups are often denounced by rivals and by apostates, and most of these leaders do not attempt to kill those who denounce them. Furthermore, Turgeon was putting his credibility as a Christian minister at risk by killing Jess. If it came to be widely believed that the leader of The Gatekeepers had responded to criticism by killing the critic in question, then it would have become much harder for The Gatekeepers to recruit followers, and they would have risked further defections. By killing Jess, Turgeon and Applin also put themselves at risk of getting caught and receiving lengthy prison sentences. Indeed, they were caught and given lengthy prison sentences. It makes much more sense for them to be willing to bear this risk if they genuinely believed that they were at war with a government under the control of Satan, rather than if they were merely trying to suppress criticism. As soldiers fighting for God, against a government under the control of a supernatural being as powerful as Satan, their futures were in jeopardy whether or not they attempted to eliminate a particular enemy agent. However, if Jess were merely a critic of Turgeon, unconnected to Satan, then they could easily have ignored him and gotten on with their lives and ministry, and their futures, as well as the future of The Gatekeepers, would not have been jeopardized.

Undermining Religious Justifications for Violence

In both "The Killing of George Tiller" and "The Gatekeepers and Deific Decree," it looks as if stated justifications for violence are also motivating. If these justifications were undermined, to the satisfaction of those who accepted them, then motivations for acting violently would have been taken away and violence averted. So, in at least some cases, we can prevent violence from taking place by undermining justifications for it. What can we do to undermine religious justifications for violence?

Undermining Religion

One approach is to try to undermine religion altogether. If people are not religious, then they do not formulate religious justifications for violence, and so these cannot motivate them. New atheists, such as Dawkins (2006) and Dennett (2006), offer arguments aimed at persuading people to abandon their religion. If religion has evolved, as I argued in Chapter 2 (and as both Dawkins (2006) and Dennett (2006) accept), then, most likely, it will be difficult to persuade people to abandon their religion, regardless of the strength of the arguments in favor of doing so.[7] Evolved forms of behavior typically become entrenched in the populations in which these have evolved, and are unlikely to be easy to do away with.[8] If religion is adaptive, as I also argued in Chapter 2 (contra Dawkins (2006) and Dennett (2006)), then we should think carefully before trying to do away with religion. As an adaptation, religion has conferred evolutionary advantages on humans in the past, and we should not even try to give these up without being extremely clear about the compensating advantages that can reasonably be expected to result from doing so.[9]

Undermining Confidence in Religious Beliefs

We saw in the previous chapter that Pierre Bayle (1685) appealed to the virtue of epistemic humility to develop an argument for religious tolerance. If the religious can be persuaded to try to exemplify the virtue of epistemic humility then they may be persuaded to accept that there is some chance that their own religion is false and another true. If so, then they may also be persuaded that there is some chance that any religious justification for violence, which they are inclined to accept, may be based on false premises and may, therefore, be ill-formed. All things being equal, increased doubt about the reliability of religious justifications for violence should lead to a reduction in instances of violence that are motivated by such justifications.

Are many religious believers likely to be persuaded to become more epistemically humble and accept that their favored religion may not be true? Some may be persuaded to do this. However, religious groups often regard their key beliefs as being based on privileged sources of evidence that are not open to doubt. Many religions hold that their core doctrines have been revealed to them by an infallible supernatural being (or beings), such as the Judeo-Christian God. These doctrines are then collected in sacred texts. Some religious believers may be persuaded to admit that it is possible that the sacred texts of their religion contain inaccurate representations of the word of their deity or deities. However, many believers will regard it is as sinful to allow that there is any doubt about the accuracy of their sacred texts and will not be willing to contemplate this possibility.

Although it may be unrealistic to expect many devout religious believers to doubt core religious doctrines specified in sacred texts, there are nevertheless some prospects for reducing instances of violence by encouraging the religious to doubt those justifications for violence that they are inclined to accept. Some components of religious justifications for violence are premised on beliefs that are not core religious doctrines and are not stipulated in sacred texts. It is probably unrealistic to suppose that The Gatekeepers could be induced to doubt that there is a cosmic war going on between God and Satan, or to doubt that they ought to serve God in that cosmic war. However, it might be possible to persuade them that the United States government is not under the control of Satan and that, therefore, they ought not to attempt to kill agents of the government.

Trying to Keep Religion out of the Public Sphere

Another possible approach to undermining justifications for religious violence that are motivating would be to try to persuade religious leaders to go along with the reasoning of scholars such as Audi (2011) and refrain from invoking religious doctrines in public policy debates and in the formulation of legislation ("the public sphere"). A commitment to keeping religion out of the public sphere would undercut some motivations for religious violence. As we saw in Chapter 7, one of al-Qaeda's goals is to impose shariah law on everyone, everywhere, and they believe that they are justified in using violent means to achieve this goal. If al-Qaeda were to be persuaded to keep religion out of the public sphere, then they would no longer aim to reform the public sphere in line with shariah law and an important line of justification that they currently have for violence would be undercut. Arguments for keeping religious doctrines out of the public sphere share many of the same limitations as arguments for religious tolerance, discussed in the previous chapter. It is easy enough to see why those who are committed to liberal democracy might be persuaded to try to keep religion out of the public sphere (and might also be persuaded to tolerate religious differences).[10] However, it is hard to see why people who are committed to promoting theocratic forms of government, such as members of al-Qaeda, would ever be persuaded to agree to keep religion out of the public sphere.

Offering Incentives

A way to try to persuade religious groups to refrain from violence is to offer them incentives to do so. If these incentives are judged, by religious groups that are liable to commit acts of violence, to be more attractive than whatever benefits they expect to result from violent action, then, all things being equal, they will be effective in persuading those religious groups to refrain from violence, at least while such incentives are available to them. There are various incentives that could be offered to religious groups to persuade them to refrain from violence. Some of these will be problematic for liberal states to offer. For example, a liberal state could offer potentially violent religious groups a privileged role in the formation of legislation, and this may be effective at persuading them to refrain from violence. However, granting particular religious groups a privileged role in the formation of legislation would undermine state neutrality between competing religious groups, and so undermine a key liberal value. Also, it would cause resentment amongst other (both religious and non-religious) groups who would have a comparatively less significant say in the formation of legislation. A liberal state could also offer to pay potentially violent religious groups to refrain from violence, and this might be an effective way of persuading at least some of them to refrain from violence. However, this would create a perverse incentive: other groups would be motivated to generate arguments justifying violent action to try to extract payment from the state too. There is one incentive that liberal state governments can offer – and already do offer – that is not problematic for them to offer, and which is attractive to many religious groups. This is the opportunity to make converts. I will say more about this incentive in the next section of this chapter.

Is it overly optimistic to suppose that religious groups holding the conviction that violent action is currently justified by their religion might be persuaded to defer violent action over long periods of time (perhaps indefinitely)? Examination of the actual behavior of violent religious groups suggests that they do defer violent action when their leaders come to the conclusion that they can achieve their key goals more effectively by non-violent means instead. According to Svensson and Harding, of the thirty-seven armed conflicts with a religious dimension that have taken place in Asia since 1946, thirty have now ended (2011, pp. 133–4). Svensson and Harding studied eight of these Asian conflicts that have ended in some detail. They found that three ended because religious goals were achieved.[11] The other five ended without religious goals being achieved. In none of these five cases were religious demands abandoned, or even compromised. Instead, rebel groups with religious goals that had been acting violently, or had supported violence, came to accept that the violent means they were employing, or had supported, to achieve their key goals were ineffective. So, they began to pursue these same goals by non-violent means instead (Svensson and Harding 2011, pp. 145–6).

Cosmic War, the Afterlife, and the Opportunity to Make Converts

Followers of many (but not all) religions are motivated to make converts. From the point of view of such religious groups, the liberal state is, in effect, an intellectual free market in which they can compete with followers of other religions to make converts. Many religious groups are intolerant of other religions and might well be prepared to use overtly coercive means to ensure that others take up their religion and to ensure that those who currently accept their religion do not abandon it. However, in liberal states, such religious groups are typically prevented from using overtly coercive means to attain these ends. Liberal state governments usually conceive of themselves as neutral umpires, who retain coercive powers – channeled through legal systems and backed up by police forces and armies. They typically consider that they have a duty to use these powers to prevent individuals and groups residing within liberal societies from behaving violently and from using overtly coercive means to suppress the practices of other individuals and groups.[12] So, liberal state governments take it upon themselves to prevent religious groups residing within their borders from using overtly coercive means to make conversions and prevent defections.

Many of those religious groups that hold that violent actions are justified by their religion can benefit from "playing by the rules," which are enforced in liberal states, and forgoing the use of violence and overt coercion. Such groups may hold that the best possible state is a theocratic state that favors their religion and suppresses other religions. However, a liberal state will be preferable, from their point of view, to theocratic states that favor a rival religion, and in which it would be difficult or impossible for them to make converts. It will also be preferable to non-religious autocratic states (such as the former Soviet Union) that can be expected to make it difficult for them to make converts. The opportunity to make converts, which the liberal state can provide, will be attractive to many religious groups that believe they are involved in a cosmic war. It will also be of particular interest to those religious groups that are concerned to improve the quality of people's afterlives.

Cosmic Warriors and the Opportunity to Make Converts

Religious groups that believe they are caught up in a cosmic war often also believe that this war is being played out over very long periods of time, perhaps over many centuries, or even over the entirety of human history. It may not be crucial, from their point of view, for them to act violently now, or at any time soon. So, they may be willing to defer violent action for long periods of time (perhaps indefinitely) if offered appropriate incentives. Cosmic warriors usually value the opportunity to attract new recruits for the war effort by making converts to their religion. This opportunity will be especially valuable to them if they also believe that their chances of success in the cosmic war that is being waged depend, at least in part, on attracting new recruits who are willing to serve in that cosmic war. The liberal state can provide religious groups with the opportunity to recruit new members. However, if religious groups try to use overtly coercive and violent means to attain their ends, then the governments of liberal states may well feel justified in suppressing the activities of those groups. This will most likely harm their chances of attracting new recruits. The opportunity to make new recruits, coupled with the threat that the liberal state will try to deprive them of this opportunity if they act violently, gives "cosmic warriors" a motive to defer violent action.

Afterlife Beliefs and the Opportunity to Make Converts

Religious groups that are concerned with the afterlives of others, and who hold that this concern justifies violent action, can benefit from the intellectual free-market conditions of the liberal state, which gives them the opportunity to make converts. The ideal state, from their point of view, might well be a theocratic state in which people are forcibly prevented from acting in ways that could lead to them being denied the opportunity of eternal life in heaven, or some other desirable afterlife. However, a liberal state in which such religious groups are able to make voluntary conversions, and thereby enable improvements to the afterlives of others, will be preferable to many other possible states in which they lack this opportunity. The opportunity to make converts – and thereby enable improvements to the afterlives of those converts – coupled with the threat that they will lose this opportunity if they act violently gives these religious groups a motive to refrain from acting violently.

Avoiding Conflicts over Sacred Values

As we have seen, liberal states may be able to persuade potentially violent religious groups that aim to prosecute cosmic wars, as well as ones that aim to enable more people to attain a better afterlife, to defer violent action. In effect, they can offer these groups a trade: refrain from acting violently and we will give you the opportunity to make converts. This strategy is unlikely to work when sacred values are at stake. As we saw in Chapter 6, sacred values are considered, by those who hold them, to be values that should never be compromised. Offers of incentives to compromise sacred values are liable to be taken as insults by those who endorse such values and are often, therefore, counterproductive. If religious groups who hold that an immediate violent response is required when their sacred values are violated come to believe that their sacred values have been violated, then they will not agree to refrain from violence, regardless of the incentives on offer to persuade them to do so.[13] It may seem that there is nothing that can be done to dissuade those who hold sacred values, and believe that they are justified in acting violently when their sacred values have been violated, from acting violently under those circumstances. However, psychologists and negotiation studies researchers have suggested a few strategies to reduce the likelihood of conflicts over sacred values and to enable compromises. The most important of these is "reframing."

Reframing Sacred Values

Some forms of sacred space, especially sacred lands, often have ill-defined boundaries; and vagueness over where these boundaries are can sometimes be exploited to enable conflicts to be avoided (Sosis 2011).[14] The area surrounding the holy cities of Mecca and Medina in Arabia, which is sacred for Muslims, is an example of a sacred space that has ill-defined boundaries. On a narrow construal, the sacred territory is the Hijaz, a region in western Saudi Arabia. On a very broad construal it is the entire Arabian Peninsula. As we saw in Chapter 7, Osama bin Laden objected to the presence of non-Muslims in Yemen and Kuwait on the grounds that these places are parts of Islamic sacred territory in which religions other than Islam should not be practiced. Potentially, at least, bin Laden could have been persuaded to set aside his objection to the presence of non-Muslims in Yemen and Kuwait, by being persuaded to accept a narrower construal of the sacred area surrounding the holy cities of Mecca and Medina. Over time, someone can shift between different views about where the boundaries of a sacred space are, and all the while continue to treat that space as sacred.

As we have seen, the sacred values of a religion can give rise to claims of rights to control sacred places that overlap with the rights claims of another religion. The strategy of reframing can sometimes enable such competing claims to be reconciled. As we saw in Chapter 6, both Jews and Muslims consider Jerusalem (Al-Quds) to be a holy city, and members of both groups believe that they have a sacred right to control it; a right which ought not be waived, regardless of the incentives on offer to do so. It may seem that ongoing conflict between Israel and Palestine over the future control of Jerusalem is inevitable. However, if both Israeli Jews and Palestinian Muslims were to agree to reframe their respective conceptions of Jerusalem/Al-Quds, then a compromise could be possible. For example, if Israeli Jews were to re-conceive of sacred Jerusalem as West Jerusalem and Palestinian Muslims were to re-conceive of sacred Al-Quds as East Jerusalem – and both sides were to make appropriate arrangements to allow the other side to control and access buildings and other sites that are sacred to them, but which happen to be located in the territory that is to be ceded to the other side – then a lasting compromise over the future of Jerusalem could be reached (Atran 2010, p. 383).

Competing and incompatible sacred value claims may possibly be reconciled. However, this is unlikely to happen unless all involved parties agree to interpret their own sacred values flexibly, and unless all coordinate their interpretations. A good way to encourage religious groups to interpret sacred values flexibly is to demonstrate that other parties to negotiations are willing to interpret their own sacred values flexibly. In their study of the sacred values of interested parties in the Israel–Palestine dispute, specifically those residing in the West Bank and Gaza (discussed in Chapter 6),

Ginges et al. (2007) found that opposition to compromises involving sacred values lessened when the other side in a negotiation demonstrated that they were willing to interpret their sacred values flexibly for the sake of peace. For example, a group of Palestinian students who participated in the study was asked to consider a symbolic "sweetener" to a proposed "two state" deal, involving Palestinians giving up claims to sovereignty over East Jerusalem. In this case, it was proposed that Israel would formally abandon claims to possess a sacred right to the West Bank (which some Israelis claim as a part of a broader sacred right to the Land of Israel). Amongst the Palestinian students who were asked to contemplate this scenario, opposition to a possible compromise involving Palestinians abandoning claims to have a sacred right to control East Jerusalem was significantly reduced when Israelis were shown to be willing to interpret their own sacred values flexibly, so as to enable compromise. Levels of support for violence were also reduced (Ginges et al. 2007, p. 7359).

Prioritizing Sacred Values

Another suggestion to try to reduce the likelihood of violent responses to violations of sacred values is to encourage religious groups with multiple sacred values to prioritize those sacred values that serve to deter violence over other sacred values. Most religious groups hold that particular places, such as buildings and areas of land, are sacred. Many religious groups also take the view that life is sacred and that they should not kill. A religious group confronted by a violation of a sacred building, or sacred territory, may hold that their religion obliges them to respond to such a violation by attempting to kill the violators. But what if their religion also tells them that human life is sacred and that they should never take a human life? That religious group is faced with a dilemma which could be resolved in at least two ways. The first is to interpret the stricture against killing laid down by their religion narrowly, as referring, for example, only to innocent people, or only to people who have not violated sacred values. A narrow interpretation allows them to offer a justification for a violent response toward those who have violated their sacred territory, while also enabling them to remain committed to the (narrow) view that life is sacred. The second way for them to resolve the dilemma is to interpret the sanctity of life broadly, as forbidding all killing, and to hold that responses to violations of sacred territory should be non-violent. Religious groups that take this second route can still make efforts to deter future violations of sacred territory. They can organize non-violent protests in order to discourage further violations, for example. However, they cannot act violently against those who violate their sacred values, as they are foresworn not to risk violating the (broadly interpreted) sanctity of life. To the extent that outsiders can influence how religious groups decide to reconcile their commitment to respond to violations of sacred territory with their commitment to respect the sanctity of life, then those outsiders can affect the likelihood that religious groups will or will not respond violently to violations of sacred values (Sosis, Phillips, and Alcorta 2012, pp. 248–9).

Rituals, Threats, and the Sacred

Some religious believers treat particular subjects as sacred while other followers of the same religion do not. Forty-six percent of a sample group of 601 Israeli settlers living in the West Bank held that it is impermissible for Israel to give up control of any part of the Land of Israel, regardless of the benefit of doing so. However, the other 54 percent of that sample group did not consider the Land of Israel to be sacred territory (Ginges et al. 2007, p. 7358).[15] What are the factors that lead one follower of a religion to treat a particular subject as sacred while another follower of the same religion does not? As we saw in Chapter 6, Sheikh et al. (2012) found evidence that participation in religious rituals can make it more likely that participants will treat the values incorporated in those rituals as sacred. They also found evidence that religious rituals are more effective at creating a sense of the sacred when a particular group perceives itself to be under threat. It is probably impractical to try to persuade religious groups not to conduct rituals. However, we can do a lot to alleviate their sense of threat. If Sheikh et al. (2012) are right, then Palestinians who feel less threatened by Israel (and other powers) will be less likely to think of the subjects of their rituals as sacred; and so are more likely to be amenable to compromises over the future of these. Similarly, Israelis who feel less threatened by Palestinian organizations and their allies will be less likely to think of the subjects of their rituals as sacred; and so are more likely to be amenable to compromises.

Despite the aforementioned possibilities for encouraging compromises and reducing the likelihood of conflict over sacred values, sacred values remain the greatest conceptual obstacle to the reduction of violence that is justified and motivated by religion. Sacred values can sometimes be interpreted in ways that reduce the likelihood of violence, and enable compromises, but such interpretations may not always be possible. In any case, there is no guarantee that those who hold sacred values will agree to interpret these in ways that are conducive to the reduction of violence and to the enabling of compromises, even when they can do so. Vagueness over the location of the boundaries of sacred spaces can be exploited to enable conflicts over these spaces to be avoided. But there is no guarantee that those who hold that such spaces are sacred will agree to accept accounts of where the boundaries of these sacred spaces are in ways that can enable conflicts to be avoided. There is no guarantee that religious groups with multiple sacred values can be persuaded to prioritize those values that serve to deter violence over other sacred values; and there is no guarantee that members of religious groups who experience a reduced sense of threat will refrain from treating a value as sacred, and, therefore, not subject to compromise. However, as was noted in Chapter 6, sacred values are not currently well understood and an improved understanding may enable us to see new ways to encourage compromises in disputes over sacred values, as well as new ways to reduce the likelihood of violent reactions to violations of sacred values.

Tolerating Violent Religious Groups

Can those of us who reside in liberal states afford to tolerate religious groups whose members believe that they are justified in acting violently on behalf of their religion? Under some circumstances the answer to this question is going to be no, because some liberal states will lack the capacity to prevent particular religious groups from acting violently towards other groups and individuals residing within their territory, and will also lack the ability to persuade these religious groups to refrain from violence. In other circumstances the answer to this question is going to be yes. Some religious groups are minor and their tendency to act violently towards others can be thwarted by the state. And, as we have seen, some religious groups can be persuaded to refrain from violent action, even when they believe that such action is justified. In order to decide whether or not particular religious groups, whose members believe that they are justified in acting violently on behalf of their religion, can be tolerated, governments of liberal states need to invest time and resources in understanding the core doctrines of such religious groups, as well as understanding how these are being interpreted. Only then will they be in a position to assess whether or not these groups are genuinely willing, as many are, to defer violent action for long periods of time, or perhaps indefinitely.

Another concern that governments of liberal states should attend to is that, as well as acting violently against individuals and other groups residing within the liberal state, religious groups may be motivated to attempt to overthrow the liberal state and replace it with a theocratic state. Some members of particular religious groups may believe that they have a significant chance of overthrowing a particular liberal state. If so, then the incentives that liberal states can offer may be insufficient to induce them to refrain from violence. A religious group contemplating the opportunity to make converts by using non-coercive means and "playing by the rules" within a liberal state may be unmoved by this opportunity if they believe that they can make more converts by overthrowing that liberal state. They may calculate that their chances of being able to overthrow that state are good enough to make an attempt at doing so worth risking.[16]

It might be supposed that the only religious groups that would try to overthrow the state are numerically significant, powerful religious groups, but this is not the case. As we saw in Chapter 7, even relatively insignificant groups residing in liberal societies, such as Aum Shinrikyo in Japan, may calculate that they have a good chance of overthrowing the state. The lesson for governments of liberal states trying to decide whether or not to try to tolerate potentially violent religious groups is that they need to understand the doctrines and the overall worldview of particular religious groups, in detail, before deciding whether or not it is practicable to try to tolerate those groups.

Concluding Remark

In this book I have been concerned to understand how justifications of violent acts undertaken in the name of religion proceed. It might be thought, given the diversity of religions to be found in the world, that there would not be any useful generalizations that can be made about religion and its relationship to the justification of violent action. However, as I have shown, there are underlying patterns to be discerned in the apparently diverse justifications of violent action offered in the name of religion. Very many of these are either appeals to cosmic war, to the afterlife, or to sacred values. Understanding this can help us to develop strategies to override or undermine religious justifications for violence, including the strategies discussed in this chapter.

My overall approach to understanding religion is naturalistic. I have drawn on recent work in psychology, cognitive science, neuroscience, and evolutionary biology to characterize religion. I am hardly alone in taking such an approach to understanding religion. However, many scholars who adopt naturalistic approaches to the understanding of human behavior – including violent behavior undertaken in the name of religion – fail to take stated justifications for behavior seriously. Some of these scholars, such as Jon Haidt (2012), offer theoretical considerations that help us to make sense of their failure to engage with stated justifications of behavior. Others do not, but simply proceed as if it is reasonable to assume that the consideration of stated justifications for behavior is unnecessary when seeking to understand human behavior. I have discussed Haidt's reasoning and sought to cast doubt on the theoretical basis he offers for ignoring stated justifications for moral behavior (in Chapter 3). More significantly, I have shown how an examination of an important class of stated justifications for action – justifications of violent action that appeal to religion – can help us to understand an important form of human behavior – violence undertaken in the name of religion. Additionally, I have suggested ways in which this understanding can be deployed to help change some of that behavior.

Notes

1. There is a lot written about conflict resolution. A good entry point into this literature is Ramsbotham, Woodhouse, and Miall (2005). For recent philosophical discussion of conflict and its resolution, see Margalit (2010).

2. For discussion of the resolution of religiously motivated conflicts, see Appleby (2000), Gopin (2000) and Toft, Philpott, and Shah (2011).

3. For examples of anti-Ahmadi material on the Internet, making the case that Ahmadis are heretics, see: http://www.anti-ahmadiyya.org/en/ and http://alhafeez.org/rashid/ (accessed March 14, 2013).

4. See, for example, Sloan (2012).

5. It is currently illegal in Pakistan for Ahmadis to refer to themselves as Muslims.

6. Like Roeder, Shelley Shannon has offered a version of the "justifiable homicide" defense of her 1993 attempt to kill Tiller, which is reproduced on the Army of God website: http://www.armyofgod.com/ShelleyForce.html (accessed February 18, 2012).

7. It is not clear that new atheist arguments for abandoning religion are particularly strong. At any rate, there is no shortage of theists who provide responses to these (e.g., Reitan 2008).

8. Could education make people more likely to form beliefs on the basis of reasoned argument than they would otherwise, and more likely, therefore, to reject religion, as some new atheists hope? If arguments for atheism were compelling, then, for reasons suggested in Chapter 3, in discussion of Haidt's Social Intuitive Model of Moral Judgment, it must be allowed that it is possible that education might lead more people to embrace atheism. However, this may be a distant possibility. For further discussion, see McCauley (2011, pp. 244–52).

9. However, an argument for the conclusion that a key evolutionary advantage conferred on us by religion in the past may no longer be of advantage to us is presented in Clarke, Powell, and Savulescu (2013, pp. 271–2).

10. For an argument for the conclusion that democracies should not restrict religion from the public sphere, see Trigg (2007).

11. For example, conflict between the Indonesian government and the Gerakan Aceh Merdeka effectively ended in part because Aceh (in North Sumatra) was granted increased political autonomy and the right to implement shariah law (Svensson and Harding 2011, p. 140).

12. For a recent philosophical discussion of liberal state neutrality, see Gaus (2009).

13. However, if values that are presented as being sacred are actually pseudo-sacred, then the offer of incentives may make compromise possible. See Chapter 6 for discussion of the distinction between sacred and pseudo-sacred values.

14. This strategy is unlikely to be viable if sacred territory is clearly delineated by geography. For example, if an entire island is construed as sacred territory by a religious group, and if that group accepts the normal definition of "island" – a piece of land entirely surrounded by water – then there is little or no prospect of any territory on the island being construed as non-sacred by that group.

15. Similarly, 54 percent of 719 Palestinian students reported that they considered Al-Quds to be sacred but 46 percent did not (Ginges et al. 2007, p. 7358).

16. For discussion of how such calculations might be modeled, see Clarke (2012).

References

Alexander, Richard D. 1987. *The Biology of Moral Systems*. New York: Aldine de Gruyter.

Alexandra, Andrew. 2003. "Political Pacifism." *Social Theory and Practice*, 29: 589–606.

Alexandra, Andrew. 2006. "On the Distinction between Pacifism and Pacificism." In *Pazifismus: Ideengeschichte, Theorie und Praxis*, edited by Barbara Bleisch and Jean-Daniel Strub, pp. 107–24. Bern: Haupt.

Allport, G.W. 1966. "Religious Context of Prejudice." *Journal for the Scientific Study of Religion*, 5: 447–57.

Allport, G.W., and Kramer, B. 1946. "Some Roots of Prejudice." *Journal of Psychology*, 22: 9–30.

Amundsen, Darrel W. 1989. "Suicide and Early Christian Values." In *Suicide and Euthanasia*, edited by Baruch A. Brody, pp. 77–153. Dordrecht: Kluwer.

Anderson, Scott. 2006. "Coercion." In *Stanford Encyclopedia of Philosophy*, http://www.seop.leeds.ac.uk/entries/coercion/ (accessed April 28, 2012).

Andújar, Eduardo. 1997. "Bartolomé de Las Casas and Juan Ginés de Sepúlveda: Moral Theology versus Political Philosophy." In *Hispanic Philosophy in the Age of Discovery*, edited by Kevin White, pp. 69–87. Washington: Catholic University of America Press.

Angell, Marcia. 1982. "The Quality of Mercy." *New England Journal of Medicine*, 306: 98–99.

Anscombe, G.E.M. 1981. "War and Murder." In *Moral Problems*, edited by James Rachels, pp. 269–83. New York: Harper & Row.

Appiah, Anthony Kwame. 2006. *Cosmopolitanism: Ethics in a World of Strangers*. New York: Norton.

Appleby, Scott R. 2000. *The Ambivalence of the Sacred: Religion, Violence, and Reconciliation*. Lanham, MD: Rowman & Littlefield.

The Justification of Religious Violence, First Edition. Steve Clarke.
© 2014 John Wiley & Sons, Inc. Published 2014 by John Wiley & Sons, Inc.

Aquinas, St. Thomas. 1265–1274. *Summa Theologica*, http://www.intratext.com/IXT/ENG0023/ (accessed December 9, 2012).

Ariely, Dan. 2008. *Predictably Irrational: The Hidden Forces that Shape Our Decisions*. New York: HarperCollins.

Artemov, Sergei and Fitting, Melvin. 2011. "Justification Logic." In *Stanford Encyclopedia of Philosophy*, http://plato.stanford.edu/entries/logic-justification/ (accessed January 9, 2013).

Associated Press. 2010. *Judge Bars Lesser Charge in Abortion Doc Death*. MSNBC.com, January 28, http://www.msnbc.msn.com/id/35103652/ns/us_news-crime_and_courts/t/judge-bars-lesser-charges-abortion-doc-death/ (accessed June 1, 2012).

Astill, James and Bowcott, Owen. 2002. "Fatwa is Issued on Nigerian Journalist." *The Guardian*, November 27, http://www.guardian.co.uk/world/2002/nov/27/jamesastill.owenbowcott (accessed November 28, 2012).

Atran, Scott. 2002. *In Gods We Trust: The Evolutionary Landscape of Religion*. New York: Oxford University Press.

Atran, Scott. 2010. *Talking to the Enemy: Faith, Brotherhood, and the (Un)Making of Terrorists*. New York: HarperCollins.

Atran, Scott and Axelrod, Robert. 2008. "Reframing Sacred Values." *Negotiation Journal*, 24: 221–46.

Audi, Robert. 1971. "On the Meaning and Justification of Violence." In *Violence*, edited by Jerome A. Shaffer, pp. 45–101. New York: David McKay.

Audi, Robert. 2011. *Democratic Authority and the Separation of Church and State*. New York: Oxford University Press.

Augustine, St. 1871. *City of God*, translated by Marcus Dods. Edinburgh: T & T. Clark.

Aulisio, Mark P. 1995. "In Defense of the Intention/Foresight Distinction." *American Philosophical Quarterly*, 32(4): 341–54.

Austin, J.L. 1956–7. "A Plea for Excuses." *Proceedings of the Aristotelian Society*, 57: 1–30.

Avalos, Hector. 2005. *Fighting Words: The Origins of Religious Violence*. Amherst: Prometheus Books.

Axelrod, Robert. 1997. "The Dissemination of Culture: A Model with Local Convergence and Global Polarization." *Journal of Conflict Resolution*, 41: 203–26.

Bagley, Will. 2002. *Blood of the Prophets: Brigham Young and the Massacre at Mountain Meadows*. Norman: University of Oklahoma Press.

Bainton, Roland H. 2005. *Hunted Heretic. The Life and Death of Michael Servetus: 1511–1553*. Rhode Island: Blackstone Editions.

Banerjee, Neela. 2008. "Soldier Sues Army, Saying his Atheism Led to Threats." *New York Times*, April 26, http://www.nytimes.com/2008/04/26/us/26atheist.html?pagewanted=all&_r=0 (accessed November 9, 2012).

Baron, Jonathan and Ritov, Ilana. 2009. "Protected Values and Omission Bias as Deontological Judgments." In *Moral Judgment and Decision Making: The Psychology of Learning and Motivation, Vol. 50*, edited by Daniel M. Bartels, Christopher W. Bauman, Linda J. Skitka, and Douglas L. Medin, pp. 133–67. San Diego: Elsevier.

Baron, Jonathan and Spranca, Mark. 1997. "Protected Values." *Organizational Behavior and Human Decision Processes*, 70: 1–16.

Barrett, H. Clark. and Kurzban, Robert. 2006. "Modularity in Cognition: Framing the Debate." *Psychological Review*, 113: 628–47.

Barrett, Justin. 2004. *Why Would Anyone Believe in God?* Walnut Creek, CA: AltaMira Press.

Barrett, Justin. 2009. "Cognitive Science, Religion, and Theology." In *The Believing Primate*, edited by Jeffrey Schloss and Michael Murray, pp. 76–99. Oxford: Oxford University Press.

Barrett, Justin and Nyhof, Melanie A. 2001. "Spreading Non-natural Concepts: The Role of Intuitive Conceptual Structures in Memory and Transmission of Cultural Materials." *Journal of Cognition and Culture*, 1: 69–100.

Bateson, Melissa, Nettle, Daniel, and Roberts, Gilbert. 2006. "Cues of Being Watched Enhance Cooperation in a Real-World Setting." *Biology Letters*, 2: 412–14.

Batson, C. Daniel. 1976. "Religion as Prosocial: Agent or Double Agent?" *Journal for the Scientific Study of Religion*, 15: 29–45.

Batson, C. Daniel. 2013. "Individual Religion, Tolerance, and Universal Compassion." In *Religion, Intolerance and Conflict: A Scientific and Conceptual Investigation*, edited by Steve Clarke, Russell Powell, and Julian Savulescu, pp. 88–106. Oxford: Oxford University Press.

Batson, C. Daniel., Schoenrade, P., and Ventis, W.L. 1993. *Religion and the Individual: A Social-Psychological Perspective*. New York: Oxford University Press.

Baumeister, Roy, F. 2001. *Evil: Inside Human Violence and Cruelty*. New York: Freeman/Holt.

Baumeister, Roy, F. and Campbell, W. Keith. 1999. "The Intrinsic Appeal of Evil: Sadism, Sensational Thrills, and Threatened Egotism." *Personality and Social Psychology Review*, 3(3): 210–21.

Bayle, Pierre. 1685 [1987]. *Philosophical Commentary*, edited and translated by A.G. Tannenbaum. New York: Lang.

Bazerman, Max H., Tenbrunsel, Ann, and Wade-Benzoni, Kimberly. 2008. "When 'Sacred' Issues are at Stake." *Negotiation Journal*, January, 113–17.

BBC. 2011. Profile: Timothy McVeigh, http://news.bbc.co.uk/2/hi/americas/1321244.stm (accessed November 12, 2012).

Bealer, G. 1998. "Intuition and the Autonomy of Philosophy." In *Rethinking Intuition: The Psychology of Intuition and Its Role in Philosophical Inquiry*, edited by M.R. DePaul and W. Ramsey, pp. 201–39. Lanham, MD: Rowman & Littlefield.

Beckers, R., Goss, S., Deneubourg, J.L., and Pasteels, J.M. 1989. "Colony Size, Communication and Ant Foraging Strategy." *Psyche*, 96: 239–56.

Bedi, Rahul. 2009. "Indira Gandhi's Death Remembered." BBC News, November 1, http://news.bbc.co.uk/2/hi/south_asia/8306420.stm (accessed November 26, 2012).

Bellah, Robert. 2011. *Religion in Human Evolution: From the Paleolithic to the Axial Age*. Cambridge, MA: Harvard University Press.

Benatar, David. 1998. "Corporal Punishment." *Social Theory and Practice*, 24(2): 237–60.

Bentham, J. 1789 [1961]. *An Introduction to the Principles of Morals and Legislation*. Garden City: Doubleday.

Berdan, Francis, F. 2005. *The Aztecs of Central America: An Imperial Society*, 2nd edn. Belmont CA: Thomson Wadsworth.

Berger, Peter L. 2006. *The Osama bin Laden I Know: An Oral History of Al Qaeda's Leader*. New York: The Free Press.

Bering, Jesse M. 2002. "Intuitive Conceptions of Dead Agents' Minds: The Natural Foundations of Afterlife Beliefs as Phenomenological Boundary." *Journal of Cognition and Culture*, 2(4): 263–308.

Bering, Jesse M. 2011. *The God Instinct: The Psychology of Souls, Destiny, and the Meaning of Life*. London: Nicholas Brearley.

Bering, Jesse M. and Bjorklund, David F. 2004. "The Natural Emergence of Reasoning about the Afterlife as a Developmental Regularity." *Developmental Psychology*, 40: 217–33.

Bering, Jesse and Johnson, Dominic D.P. 2005. "Oh Lord … You Perceive my Thoughts from Afar: Recursiveness and the Evolution of Supernatural Agency." *Journal of Cognition and Culture*, 5(1–2): 118–42.

Berker, Selim, 2009. "The Normative Insignificance of Neuroscience." *Philosophy and Public Affairs*, 37(4): 293–329.

Berns, Gregory S. and Atran, Scott. 2012. "The Biology of Cultural Conflict." *Philosophical Transactions of the Royal Society B*, 367: 633–9.

Berns, Gregory S., Bell, Emily C., Capra, Monica, Prietula, Michael J., Moore, Sara, Anderson, Brittany, Ginges, Jeremy, and Atran, Scott. 2012. "The Price of Your Soul: Neural Evidence for the Non-Utilitarian Representation of Sacred Values." *Philosophical Transactions of the Royal Society B*, 367: 754–62.

Blackmore, Susan. 1999. *The Meme Machine*. Oxford: Oxford University Press.

Blackmore, Susan. 2010. "Why I No Longer Believe Religion is a Virus of the Mind." *The Guardian*, Thursday, September 16, http://www.guardian.co.uk/commentisfree/belief/2010/sep/16/why-i-no-longer-believe-religion-virus-mind (accessed August 18, 2011).

Bloom, Paul. 2004. *Descartes' Baby*. New York: Basic Books.

Bloom, Paul. 2010. "How Do Morals Change?" *Nature*, 464: 490.

Boehm, Christopher. 2012. *Moral Origins: The Evolution of Virtue, Altruism and Shame*. New York: Basic Books.

Bohman, James. 1998. "The Coming of Age of Deliberative Democracy." *The Journal of Political Philosophy*, 6: 400–25.

Boone, Jon. 2012. "Pakistani Girl Accused of Qu'ran Burning could Face Death Penalty." *The Guardian*, August 19, http://www.guardian.co.uk/world/2012 /aug/19/pakistan-christian-tensions-quran-burning-allegations (accessed November 26, 2012).

Bourguignon, Erika. 2004. "Possession and Trance." In *Encyclopedia of Medical Anthropology*, edited by C.R. Ember and M. Ember, pp. 137–45. Philadelphia: Springer.

Bowman, Matthew. 2012. *The Mormon People*. New York: Random House.

Boyer, Pascal. 2001. *Religion Explained*. London: Random House.

Boyer, Pascal: 2005. "A Reductionistic Model of Distinct Modes of Religious Transmission." In *Mind and Religion: Psychological and Cognitive Foundations of Religiosity*, edited by H. Whitehouse and R.N. McCauley, pp. 3–29. Walnut Creek, CA: AltaMira Press.

Boyer, Pascal and Ramble, Charles. 2001. "Cognitive Templates for Religious Concepts: Cross-Cultural Evidence for Recall of Counter-Intuitive Representations." *Cognitive Science* 25: 535–64.

Brandt, R.B. 1972. "Utilitarianism and the Rules of War." *Philosophy and Public Affairs*, 1(2): 135–65.

Bray, Michael. 1994. *A Time to Kill: A Study Concerning the Use of Force and Abortion*. Portland, OR: Advocates for Life.

Breecher, Bob. 2007. *Torture and the Ticking Time Bomb*. Oxford: Blackwell.

Brockway, R.W. 1978. "Neanderthal 'Religion'." *Studies in Religion*, 3: 317–21.

Brooks, Juanita. 1950. *The Mountain Meadows Massacre*. Stanford: Stanford University Press.

Brown, Donald. 1991. *Human Universals*. New York: McGraw-Hill.

Bufacchi, Vittorio. 2004. "Why is Violence Bad?" *American Philosophical Quarterly*, 41(2): 169–80.

Cady, Duane L. 2010. *From Warism to Pacifism: A Moral Continuum*, 2nd edn. Philadelphia: Temple University Press.

Carrasco, David. 1998. *Daily Life of the Aztecs: People of the Sun and Earth*. Indianapolis: Hackett.

Cavanaugh, William, T. 2009. *The Myth of Religious Violence*. Oxford: Oxford University Press.

Chaiken, S. and Trope, Y. eds. 1999. *Dual-processing Theories in Social Psychology*. New York: Guilford.

Chidester, David. 1988. *Salvation and Suicide: An Interpretation of Jim Jones, the People's Temple and Jonestown*. Bloomington: Indiana University Press.

Chryssides, George D. 2006. "Sources of Doctrine in the Solar Temple." In *The Order of the Solar Temple: The Temple of Death*, edited by James R. Lewis, pp. 117–31. Aldershot: Ashgate.

Churchill, Ward. 2007. *Pacifism as Pathology: Reflections on the Role of the Armed Struggle in North America*. Oakland, CA: AK Press.

Churchland, Patricia S. 2011. *Braintrust: What Neuroscience Tells Us about Morality*. Princeton: Princeton University Press.

Cladis, Mark S. 1912 [2001]. Introduction to *The Elementary Forms of Religious Life*, by Emile Durkheim, translated by Carol Cosman, vii–xxxv. Oxford: Oxford University Press.

Clarke, Steve. 2007. "The Supernatural and the Miraculous." *Sophia*, 46: 275–83.

Clarke, Steve. 2008. "SIM and the City: Rationalism in Psychology and Philosophy and Haidt's Account of Moral Judgment." *Philosophical Psychology*, 21: 799–820.

Clarke, Steve. 2009. "Naturalism, Science and the Supernatural." *Sophia*, 48: 127–42.

Clarke, Steve. 2010. "On New Technologies." In *The Cambridge Handbook of Information and Computer Ethics*, edited by Luciano Floridi, pp. 234–48. Cambridge: Cambridge University Press.

Clarke, Steve. 2012. "Coercion, Consequence and Salvation." In *Scientific Approaches to the Philosophy of Religion*, edited by Yujin Nagasawa, pp. 205–23. Basingstoke: Palgrave Macmillan.

Clarke, Steve and Roache, Rebecca. 2012. "Introducing Transformative Technologies into Democratic Societies." *Philosophy and Technology*, 25: 27–45.

Clarke, Steve, Powell, Russell, and Savulescu, Julian. 2013. "Religion, Intolerance and Conflict: Practical Implications for Social Policy." In *Religion, Intolerance and Conflict: A Scientific and Conceptual Investigation*, edited by Steve Clarke, Russell Powell, and Julian Savulescu, pp. 266–72. Oxford: Oxford University Press.

CNN. 2007. "Iran Vows not to 'Retreat One Iota' in Nuclear Pursuit," February 22, http://edition.cnn.com/2007/WORLD/meast/02/21/iran.nuclear/ (accessed December 3, 2013).

Coady, C.A.J. 2008. *Morality and Political Violence*. Cambridge: Cambridge University Press.

Coady, C.A.J. 2013. "Religious Disagreement and Religious Accommodation." In *Religion, Intolerance and Conflict: A Scientific and Conceptual Investigation*, edited by Steve Clarke, Russell Powell, and Julian Savulescu, pp. 180–200. Oxford: Oxford University Press.

Coady, David, ed. 2006. *Conspiracy Theories: The Philosophical Debate*. Aldershot: Ashgate.

Coates, James. 1991. *In Mormon Circles: Gentiles, Jack Mormons and Latter-day Saints*. Reading, MA: Addison-Wesley.

Cohen, Andrew J. 2004. "What Toleration Is." *Ethics*, 115: 68–95.

Cohen, Emma E.A., Ejsmond-Frey, Robin, Knight, Nicola, and Dunbar, R.I.M. 2010. "Rowers' High: Behavioural Synchrony is Correlated with Elevated Pain Thresholds." *Biology Letters*, 6: 106–8.

Cole, W. Owen. 2004. *Understanding Sikhism*. Edinburgh: Dunedin Academic.

Cosmides, L. and Tooby, J. 1994. "Origins of Domain Specificity." In *Mapping the Mind: Domain Specificity in Cognition and Culture*, edited by L.A. Hirschfeld and S.A. Gelman, pp. 85–116. New York: Cambridge University Press.

Cosmides, L. and Tooby, J. 2005. "Neurocognitive Adaptations Designed for Social Exchange." In *The Handbook of Evolutionary Psychology*, edited by D.M. Buss, pp. 584–627. Hoboken, NJ: John Wiley & Sons.

Court of Appeals Washington, Division 1. 2003. *State v. Applin. No 49454-6-1*. May 5.

Cowan, Douglas E. and Bromley, David G. 2008. *Cults and New Religions: A Brief History*. Oxford: Blackwell.

Cowell, Alan. 2002. "Religious Violence in Nigeria Drives Out Miss World Event." *The New York Times*, November 23, http://www.nytimes.com/2002/11/23/world/religious-violence-in-nigeria-drives-out-miss-world-event.html (accessed November 28, 2012).

Coyle, John Kevin. 2009. *Manicheanism and its Legacy*. Brill: Leiden.

Cummins, D.D. 1996. "Evidence for the Innateness of Deontic Reasoning." *Mind and Language*, 11: 160–90.

Cushman, Fiery and Greene, Joshua D. 2012. "Finding Faults: How Moral Dilemmas Illuminate Cognitive Structure." *Social Neuroscience*, 7(3): 269–79.

Davis, Winston. 2000. "Heaven's Gate: A Study of Religious Obedience." *Nova Religio: The Journal of Alternative and Emergent Religions*, 3(2): 241–67.

Dawkins, Richard. 1976. *The Selfish Gene*. Oxford: Oxford University Press.

Dawkins, Richard. 2006. *The God Delusion*. London: Bantam.

De Dreu, Carsten K.W., Greer, Lindred L., Handgraaf, Michel. J.J., Shalvi, Shaul, Van Kleef, Gerben A., Baas, Matthijs, Ten Velden, Femke S., Van Dijk, Eric, and Feith, Sander W.W. 2010. "The Neuropeptide Oxytocin Regulates Parochial Altruism in Intergroup Conflict Among Humans." *Science*, 328: 1408–11.

Dehghani, M., Iliev, R., Sachdeva, S., Atran, S., Ginges, J., and Medin, D. 2009. "Emerging Sacred Values: Iran's Nuclear Program." *Judgment and Decision Making*, 4(7): 930–3.

Demiéville, Paul. 2010. "Buddhism and War." In *Buddhist Warfare*, edited by Michael K. Jerryson and M. Juergensmeyer, pp. 17–57. New York: Oxford University Press.

Dennett, Daniel. 2006. *Breaking the Spell: Religion as a Natural Phenomenon*. New York: Viking.

De Roover, J. and Balagangadhara, S.N. 2008. "John Locke, Christian Liberty and the Predicament of Liberal Toleration." *Political Theory*, 36(4):523–49.

Desjardins, Michael. 1997. *Peace, Violence and the New Testament*. Sheffield: Sheffield Academic Press.

DiAngelo, Rio. 2007a. "Rio's Statement: The Sole Survivor of Heaven's Gate, in his own Words." *LA Weekly*, March 21, http://www.laweekly.com/2007-03-22 /news/rio-s-statement/ (accessed December 9, 2012).

DiAngelo, Rio. 2007b. *Beyond Human Mind: The Soul Evolution of Heaven's Gate*. Beverly Hills, CA: Rio DiAngelo.

Donahue, M.J. 1985. "Intrinsic and Extrinsic Religiousness: Review and Meta-analysis." *Journal of Personality and Social Psychology*, 48: 400–19.

Drescher, Seymour. 2009. *Abolition: A History of Slavery and Antislavery*. Cambridge: Cambridge University Press.

Dunbar, R.I.M. 2013. "The Origin of Religion as a Small-Scale Phenomenon." In *Religion, Intolerance and Conflict: A Scientific and Conceptual Investigation*, edited by Steve Clarke, Russell Powell, and Julian Savulescu, pp. 48–66. Oxford: Oxford University Press.

Duncan, Craig, 2007. "The Persecutor's Wager." *Philosophical Review*, 116: 1–50.

Dundas, Paul. 2002. *The Jains*, 2nd edn. London: Routledge.

Dupue, R.A. and Morrone-Strupinsky, J.V. 2005. "A Neurobiological Model of Affiliative Bonding: Implications for Conceptualizing a Human Trait of Affiliation." *Behavioral and Brain Sciences*, 28: 313–95.

Durkheim, Emile. 1912 [2001]. *The Elementary Forms of Religious Life*. Oxford: Oxford University Press.

Edmonds, David. 2009. "Matters of Life and Death." *Prospect Magazine*, http://www.prospectmagazine.co.uk/tag/trolleyology/ (accessed December 9, 2012).

Edwards, Michael. 2012. "Pakistan Drops Blasphemy Case against Girl." ABC News, November 20, http://www.abc.net.au/news/2012-11-20/pakistan-drops-case-against-girl-accused-of-blasphemy/4382724 (accessed November 26, 2012).

Ehrenreich, Barbara. 2006. *Dancing in the Streets*. New York: Henry Holt.

Eliade, Mercia. 1959. *The Sacred and the Profane: The Nature of Religion*. Orlando: Harcourt.

Eller, Jack David. 2010. *Cruel Creeds, Virtuous Violence: Religious Violence Across Culture and History*. New York: Prometheus Books.

Ethics and Religious Liberty Commission of the Southern Baptist Convention. 1994. *The Nashville Declaration of Conscience*, http://erlc.com /documents/pdf/declaration_of_conscience.pdf (accessed May 31, 2012).

Exline, Julie Juola, Yali, Ann Marie, and Sanderson, William, C. 2000. "Guilt, Discord and Alienation: The Role of Religious Strain in Depression and Suicidality." *Journal of Clinical Psychology*, 56(12): 1481–96.

Faulkner, Jason, Schaller, Mark, Park, Justin. H., and Duncan, Lesley. A. 2004. "Evolved Disease-Avoidance Mechanisms and Contemporary Xenophobic Attitudes." *Group Processes & Intergroup Relations*, 7(4): 333–53.

Fiala, Andrew. 2010. "Pacifism." In *Stanford Encyclopedia of Philosophy*, http://plato.stanford.edu/entries/pacifism/ (accessed October 30, 2012).

Fine, Cordelia. 2006. "Is the Emotional Dog Wagging its Rational Tail, or Chasing it? Reason in Moral Judgment." *Philosophical Explorations*, 9: 83–98.

Firestone, Reuven. 1999. *Jihad: The Origins of Holy War in Islam*. New York: Oxford University Press.

Flanagan, Owen. 2013. "The View from the East Pole: Buddhist and Confucian Tolerance." In *Religion, Intolerance and Conflict: A Scientific and Conceptual Investigation*, edited by Steve Clarke, Russell Powell, and Julian Savulescu, pp. 201–20. Oxford: Oxford University Press.

Fodor, Jerry. A. 1983. *The Modularity of Mind*. Cambridge, MA: The MIT Press.

Fodor, Jerry. A. 2001. *The Mind Doesn't Work that Way: The Scope and Limits of Computational Psychology*. Cambridge, MA: MIT Press.

Foot, Phillipa. 1967. "The Problem of Abortion and the Doctrine of Double Effect." *Oxford Review*, 5: 5–15.

Ford, Norman. M. 1988. *When Did I Begin? Conception of the Human Individual in History, Philosophy and Science*. Cambridge: Cambridge University Press.

Forst, Rainer. 2007. "'To Tolerate Means to Insult': Toleration, Recognition, and Emancipation." In *Recognition and Power: Axel Honneth and the Tradition of Critical Social Theory*, edited by B. Van den Brink and D. Owen, pp. 215–37. Cambridge: Cambridge University Press.

France, Peter. 1998. *Hermits: The Insights of Solitude*. Santa Ana, CA: Griffin.

Frank, Robert. 1988. *Passions within Reason: The Strategic Role of the Emotions*. New York: W.W. Norton.

Freud, Sigmund. 1927 [2008]. *The Future of an Illusion*, translated by J.A. Underwood and Shaun Whiteside. London: Penguin.

Friedman, Devin. 2010. "Savior vs. Savior." *Gentleman's Quarterly*. February, http://www.gq.com/news-politics/big-issues/201002/abortion-debate-george-tiller-scott-roeder (accessed May 31, 2012).

Galtung, Johan. 1969. "Violence, Peace and Peace Research." *The Journal of Peace Research*, 6: 167–91.

Gandhi, M.K. 1920. "Editorial." *Young India*. 3(8): August, http://www.saadigitalarchive.org/item/20111027-432 (accessed March 25, 2013).

Gandhi, M.K. 1948. *Gandhi's Autobiography: The Story of my Experiments with Truth*, translated by M. Desai. Washington, DC: Public Affairs Press.

Gaus, Gerald F. 2009. "The Moral Foundations of Liberal Neutrality." In *Contemporary Debates in Political Philosophy*, edited by Thomas Christiano and John Christman, pp. 81–98. Chichester: Wiley-Blackwell.

Genovese, Eugene. 1967. *The Political Economy of Slavery*. New York: Vintage.

Gensler, Harry J. 2013. *Ethics and the Golden Rule*. New York: Routledge.

Gervais, Will and Norenzayan, Ara. 2013. "Religion and the Origins of Anti-Atheist Prejudice." In *Religion, Intolerance and Conflict: A Scientific and Conceptual Investigation*, edited by Steve Clarke, Russell Powell, and Julian Savulescu, pp. 126–45. Oxford: Oxford University Press.

Gert, Bernard. 2004. *Common Morality: Deciding What to Do*. Oxford: Oxford University Press.

Gibson, James. L. 2005. "On the Nature of Tolerance: Dichotomous or Continuous." *Political Behaviour*, 27(4): 313–23.

Ginges, Jeremy, Atran, Scott, Medin, Douglas, and Shihaki, Khalil. 2007. "Sacred Bounds on Rational Resolution of Conflict." *PNAS*, 104(18): 7357–60.

Godfrey-Smith, Peter. 2009. *Darwinian Populations and Natural Selection*. Oxford: Oxford University Press.

Goldenberg, Jamie L. 2005. "The Body Stripped Down: An Existential Account of the Threat Posed by the Physical Body." *Current Directions in Psychological Science*, 14(4): 224–8.

Goodin, Robert. E. 2006. *What's Wrong with Terrorism?* Cambridge: Polity Press.

Goody, Jack. 1961. "Religion and Ritual: The Definitional Problem." *British Journal of Sociology*, 12(2): 142–64.

Gopin, Marc. 2000. *Between Eden and Armageddon: The Future of World Religions, Violence, and Peacemaking*. New York: Oxford University Press.

Gould, S.J. and Lewontin, R.C. 1979. "The Spandrels of St. Marcos and the Panglossian Paradigm: A Critique of the Adaptationist Programme." *Proceedings of the Royal Society of London B*, 205: 581–98.

Graham, Jesse and Haidt, Jon. 2010. "Beyond Beliefs: Religions Bind Individuals into Moral Communities". *Personality and Social Psychology Review*, 14: 140–50.

Grayling, A.C. 2011. *The Good Book: A Secular Bible*. London: Bloomsbury.

Greeley, A.M. and Hout, M. 1999. "Americans' Increasing Belief in Life after Death: Religious Competition and Acculturation." *American Sociological Review*, 64: 813–35.

Greene, Joshua D. 2008a. "The Secret Joke of Kant's Soul." In *The Neuroscience of Morality: Emotion, Brain Disorders and Development*, edited by W. Sinnott-Armstrong, pp. 35–79. Cambridge, MA: MIT Press.

Greene, Joshua D. 2008b. "Reply to Mikhail and Timmons." In *The Neuroscience of Morality: Emotion, Brain Disorders and Development*, edited by W. Sinnott-Armstrong, pp. 105–17. Cambridge, MA: MIT Press.

Greene, Joshua D. 2013. *Moral Tribes: Emotion, Reason and the Gap between Us and Them*. New York: Penguin Press.

Greene, Joshua D., Cushman, Fiery A., Stewart, Lisa, E., Lowenberg, Kelly., Nystrom, Leigh E., and Cohen, Jonathan D. 2009. "Pushing Moral Buttons: The Interaction between Personal Force and Intention in Moral Judgment." *Cognition*, 111: 364–71.

Greene, Joshua D., Summerville, R. Brian., Nystrom, Leigh E., Darley, John M., and Cohen, Jonathan D. 2001. "An fMRI investigation of Emotional Engagement in Moral Judgment." *Science*, 293: 2105–8.

Greer, T., Berman, M., Varan, V., Bobrycki, L., and Watson, S. 2005. "We are a Religious People; We are a Vengeful People." *Journal for the Scientific Study of Religion*, 44(1): 45–57.

Grundy, Kenneth W. and Weinstein, Michael A. 1974. *The Ideologies of Violence.* Columbus: Merrill.

Gunitskiy, Seva. 2002. *In the Spotlight: Kach and Kahane Chai.* Washington, DC: Center for Defense Information, October 1, www.cdi.org/terrorism/kach.cfm (accessed May 15, 2012).

Guthrie, Stewart E. 1993. *Faces in the Clouds: A New Theory of Religion.* Oxford: Oxford University Press.

Guthrie, Stewart. E. 1996. "The Sacred: A Sceptical View." In *The Sacred and its Scholars*, edited by Thomas A. Idinopoulos and Edward A. Yonan, pp. 124–38. Leiden: E.J. Brill.

Haidt, Jon. 2001. "The Emotional Dog and its Rational Tail: A Social Intuitionist Approach to Moral Judgment." *Psychological Review*, 108: 814–34.

Haidt, Jon. 2003. "The Emotional Dog does Learn New Tricks (A Reply to Pizarro and Bloom, 2003)." *Psychological Review*, 110: 197–8.

Haidt, Jon. 2012. *The Righteous Mind: Why Good People are Divided by Politics and Religion.* New York: Pantheon/Knopf.

Haidt, Jon, Björklund, Frederik, and Murphy, Scott. 2000. "Moral Dumbfounding: When Intuition Finds No Reason." Unpublished manuscript, http://commonsenseatheism.com/wp-content/uploads/2011/08/Haidt-Moral-Dumfounding-When-Intuition-Finds-No-Reason.pdf (accessed April 4, 2012).

Haldane, John and Lee, Patrick. 2003. "Aquinas on Human Ensoulment and the Value of Life." *Philosophy*, 78: 255–78.

Hall, John, R. 2002. "Mass Suicide and the Branch Davidians." In *Cults, Religion and Violence*, edited by David G. Bromley and J. Gordon Melton, pp. 149–169. Cambridge: Cambridge University Press.

Hall, John R. 2003. "The Apocalypse at Jonestown." In *Cults and New Religious Movements: A Reader*, edited by Lorne L. Dawson, pp. 186–207. Oxford: Blackwell.

Hamilton, W.D. 1964. "The Genetic Evolution of Social Behaviour, Parts 1 and 2." *Journal of Theoretic Biology*, 7: 1–52.

Hammerstein, Peter. 2003. "Why is Reciprocity So Rare in Social Animals?" In *Genetic and Cultural Evolution of Cooperation*, edited by P. Hammerstein, pp. 83–93. Cambridge, MA: MIT Press.

Hanselmann, M. and Tanner, C. 2008. "Taboos and Conflicts in Decision Making: Sacred Values, Decision Difficulty, and Emotions." *Judgment and Decision Making*, 3(1): 51–63.

Haraldsson, Erlendur. 2006. "Popular Psychology, Belief in Life after Death and Reincarnation in the Nordic Countries, Western and Eastern Europe." *Nordic Psychology*, 58(2): 171–80.

Hardin, Russell. 2003. "The Free Rider Problem." In *Stanford Encyclopedia of Philosophy*, http://plato.stanford.edu/entries/free-rider/ (accessed August 5, 2013).

Harding, Susan. 2005. "Living Prophecy at Heaven's Gate." In *Histories of the Future*, edited by Daniel Rosenberg and Susan Harding, pp. 297–320. Durham: Durham University Press.

Hare Robert, D. 1999. *Without Conscience: The Disturbing World of the Psychopaths among Us*. New York: Guilford Press.

Harris, E. and McNamara, P. 2008. "Is Religiousness a Biocultural Adaptation?" In *The Evolution of Religion: Studies, Theories, and Critiques*, edited by L. Bulbulia, R. Sosis, E. Harris, R. Genet, C. Genet, and K. Wyman, pp. 79–85. Santa Margarita, CA: Collins Foundation Press.

Harvey, Peter. 2000. *An Introduction to Buddhist Ethics: Foundations, Values and Issues*. Cambridge: Cambridge University Press.

Hassner, Ron E. 2006. "Fighting Insurgency on Sacred Ground." *The Washington Quarterly*, 29(2): 149–66.

Hauerwas, Stanley. 1984. *Should War be Eliminated: Philosophical and Theological Investigations*. Milwaukee: Marquette University Press.

Hawthorne, Christopher. 2000. "Deific Decree: The Short, Happy Life of a Pseudo-Doctrine." *Loyola of Los Angeles Law Review*, 33: 1755–811.

Heatherington, Paul, ed. 2005. *The Diaries of Donald Friend*, Vol. 3. Canberra: The National Library of Australia.

Henrich, Joseph. 2009. "The Evolution of Costly Displays, Cooperation and Religion: Credibility Enhancing Displays and their Implications for Cultural Evolution." *Evolution and Human Behavior*, 30: 244–60.

Henrich, Joseph, et al. (thirteen other authors). 2010. "Markets, Religion, Community Size, and the Evolution of Fairness and Punishment." *Science*, 327: 1480–4.

Hewstone, M., Rubin, M., and Willis, H. 2002. "Intergroup Bias." *Annual Review of Psychology*, 53: 575–604.

Heyd, David. 1996. "Introduction." In *Toleration: An Elusive Virtue*, edited by D. Heyd, pp. 3–17. Princeton: Princeton University Press,

Hine, Virginia, H. 1969. "Pentecostal Glossolalia: Toward a Functional Interpretation." *Journal for the Scientific Study of Religion*, 8(2): 211–26.

Hobbes, Thomas. 1651 [1962]. *Leviathan*, edited by Michael Oakeshott. Oxford: Blackwell.

Hodge, K. Mitch. 2011. "Why Immortality Alone Will Not Get Me to the Afterlife." *Philosophical Psychology*, 24(3): 395–410.

Hoffman, Frank and Rosencrantz, Gary S. 2002. *The Divine Attributes*. Oxford: Blackwell.

Holland, Barbara. 2004. *Gentlemen's Blood: A History of Dueling*. New York: Bloomsbury.

Hongo, Jun. 2011. "Aum May be Gone in Name but Guru Still has Following." *The Japan Times*, November 22, http://www.japantimes.co.jp/text/nn20111122a2.html (accessed August 30, 2012).

Hooker, Brad. 2012. *Introduction to Ethical Theory*. Oxford: Blackwell.

Hume, David. 1748 [1999]. *An Enquiry Concerning Human Understanding*, edited by Tom Beauchamp. Oxford: Oxford University Press.

Hume, David. 1778 [1983]. *The History of England from the Invasion of Julius Caesar to the Revolution in 1688*, 6 Vols. Indianapolis: Liberty Fund.

Ibrahim, Raymond, ed. 2007. *The Al Qaeda Reader*. New York: Doubleday.

Ignatieff, Michael. 2004. *The Lesser Evil: Political Ethics in an Age of Terror*. Edinburgh: Edinburgh University Press.

Ingram, Catherine J.E., Mulcare, Charlotte A., Itan, Yuval, Thomas, Mark G., and Swallow, Dallas M. 2009. "Lactose Digestion and the Evolutionary Genetics of Lactase Persistence." *Human Genetics*, 124: 579–91.

International Campaign for Tibet. 2013. "Self-immolations by Tibetans." http://www.savetibet.org/resources/fact-sheets/self-immolations-by-tibetans/ (accessed August 28, 2013).

Jackman, Mary R. 1977. "Prejudice, Tolerance, and Attitudes Toward Ethnic Groups." *Social Science Research*, 6: 145–69.

Jakobsen, J.R. and Pellegrini, A. 2003. *Love the Sin: Sexual Regulation and the Limits of Religious Tolerance*. New York: NYU Press.

Jefferis, Jennifer L. 2011. *Armed for Life: the Army of God and Anti-abortion Terror in the United States*, Santa Barbara: Praeger.

Jenkins, Stephen. 2010. "Making Merit through Warfare According to the Ārya-Bodhisattva-gocara-upāyavisaya-vikurvana-nirdésa Sūtra". In *Buddhist Warfare*, edited by Michael K. Jerryson and M. Juergensmeyer, pp. 59–75. New York: Oxford University Press.

Jenkins, Stephen. 2011. "It's Not So Strange for a Buddhist to Endorse Killing." *The Guardian*, May 11, http://www.guardian.co.uk/commentisfree/belief/2011/may/11/buddhism-bin-laden-death-dalai-lama (accessed December 11, 2012).

Jerryson, Michael. 2010. "Introduction". In *Buddhist Warfare*, edited by Michael K. Jerryson and M. Juergensmeyer, pp. 3–16. New York: Oxford University Press.

Johnson, Dominic D.P. 2005. "God's Punishment and Public Goods." *Human Nature*, 16(4): 410–46.

Johnson, Dominic D.P. and Bering, Jesse. 2006. "Hand of God, Mind of Man: Punishment and Cognition in the Evolution of Cooperation." *Evolutionary Psychology*, 4: 219–33.

Johnson, Dominic D.P. and Kruger, Oliver. 2004. "The Good of Wrath: Supernatural Punishment and the Evolution of Cooperation." *Political Theology*, 5: 159–76.

Johnson, Dominic, D.P. and Reeve, Zoey. 2013. "The Virtues of Intolerance: Is Religion an Adaptation for War?" In *Religion, Intolerance and Conflict: A Scientific and Conceptual Investigation*, edited by Steve Clarke, Russell Powell, and Julian Savulescu, pp. 67–87. Oxford: Oxford University Press.

Johnson, Dominic, D.P. and Tierney, Dominic. 2011. "The Rubicon Theory of War: How the Path to Conflict Reaches the Point of No Return." *International Security*, 36: 7–40.

Johnson, James Turner. 1984. *Just War Tradition and the Restraint of War: A Moral and Historical Inquiry*. Princeton: Princeton University Press.

Johnson, James Turner. 1997. *The Holy War Idea in Western and Islamic Traditions*. University Park, PA: Pennsylvania State University Press.

Johnson, James Turner. 1999. *Morality and Contemporary Warfare*. New Haven: Yale University Press.

Jones, E.M. 1967. *The Church-God's Plan for Man: The Teaching of the Second Vatican Council*. London: Burn and Oates.

Jones, James W. 2008. *Blood that Cries Out from the Earth: The Psychology of Religious Terrorism*. Oxford: Oxford University Press.

Joyce, Richard. 2006. *The Evolution of Morality*. Cambridge, MA: MIT Press.

Juergensmeyer, Mark. 2003. *Terror in the Mind of God: The Global Rise of Religious Violence*, 3rd edn. Berkeley: University of California Press.

Juergensmeyer, Mark. 2007. "Gandhi vs. Terrorism." *Daedalus* 136(1): 30–9.

Juergensmeyer, Mark and Kitts, Margo, eds. 2011. *Princeton Readings in Religion and Violence*. Princeton: Princeton University Press.

Kahane, Guy. 2012. "On the Wrong Track: Process and Content in Moral Psychology." *Mind and Language*, 25(5): 519–45.

Kahane, Meir. 1982. *Forty Years*. Jerusalem: Institute of the Jewish Idea.

Kahane, Meir. 2000. *The Story of the Jewish Defense League*. Jerusalem: Institute for Publication of the Writings of Rabbi Meir Kahane.

Kahneman, D., and Frederick, S. 2002. "Representativeness Revisited: Attribute Substitution in Intuitive Judgment." In *Heuristics and Biases: The Psychology of Intuitive Judgment*, edited by T. Gilovich, D. Griffin, and D. Kahneman, pp. 49–81. Cambridge: Cambridge University Press.

Kamm, F.M. 2007. *Intricate Ethics: Rights, Responsibilities, and Permissible Harms*. Oxford: Oxford University Press.

Kant, Immanuel. 1785 [1983]. *Grounding for the Metaphysics of Morals*, translated by J.W. Ellington. Indiana: Hackett.

Kaplan, Benjamin J. 2007. *Divided by Faith: Religious Conflict and the Practice of Toleration in Early Modern Europe*. Cambridge, MA: The Belknap Press.

Kaplan, David E. and Marshall, Andrew. 1996. *The Cult at the End of the World*. New York: Crown Publishers.

Karimi, Faith. 2013. "20 Questions about the Iran Nuclear Deal: What it says, What's at Stake, What's Next." CNN, November 25, http://edition.cnn.com/2013/11/24/world/meast/iran-nuclear-deal-qa/ (accessed December 3, 2013).

Kass, Leon. 1994. *The Hungry Soul*. Chicago: The University of Chicago Press.

Keeley, Brian. 1999. "Of Conspiracy Theories." *Journal of Philosophy*, 96: 109–26.

Keeley, Lawrence H. 1996. *War before Civilization*. Oxford: Oxford University Press.

Keller, Simon. 2013. *Partiality*. Princeton: Princeton University Press.

Kelly, Daniel. 2011. *Yuck!: The Nature and Moral Significance of Disgust*. Cambridge, MA: MIT Press.

Kelsay, John. 2007. *Arguing the Just War in Islam*. Cambridge, MA: Harvard University Press.

Kennan, George F. 1954. *Realities of American Foreign Policy*. Princeton: Princeton University Press.

Kent, Daniel W. 2010. "Onward Buddhist Soldiers: Preaching to the Sri Lankan Army." In *Buddhist Warfare*, edited by Michael K. Jerryson and M. Juergensmeyer, pp. 157–77. New York: Oxford University Press.

Keown, Damien. 1998. "Suicide, Assisted Suicide and Euthanasia: A Buddhist Perspective." *Journal of Law and Religion*, 13: 385–405.

Kertzer, David I. 1998. *The Kidnapping of Edgardo Montara*. New York: Vintage.

Keyes, Charles F. 2007. "Monks, Guns and Peace: Theravāda Buddhism and Political Violence." In *Belief and Bloodshed: Religion and Violence across Time and Tradition*, edited by James K. Wellman, Jr.,, pp. 145–63. Lanham, MD: Rowman & Littlefield.

Kimball, Charles. 2008. *When Religion Becomes Evil: Five Warning Signs*. New York: HarperCollins.

Kirkpatrick, C. 1949. "Religion and Humanitarianism: A Study of Institutional Implications." *Psychological Monographs*, 63, No. 304. Washington: American Psychological Association.

Kitcher, Philip. 2011. *The Ethical Project*. Cambridge, MA: Harvard University Press.

Klein, Colin. 2011. "The Dual Track Theory of Moral Decision-Making: A Critique of the Neuroimaging Evidence." *Neuroethics*, 4(2): 143–62.

Koch, Anne. 1992. "God Sent him Warning of Arson, Says Everett Preacher – Church Leaders Told that Fires were a Call for Sinners to Repent." *The Seattle Times*, Tuesday, November 17, http://community.seattletimes.nwsource.com/archive/?date=19921117&slug=1525112 (accessed December 11, 2012).

Kohlberg, Lawrence. 1969. "Stage and Sequence: The Cognitive-developmental Approach to Socialization." In *Handbook of Socialization Theory and Research*, edited by D.A. Goslin, pp. 347–480. Chicago: Rand McNally.

Krop, Henri. A. 1989. "Duns Scotus and the Jews: Scholastic Theology and Enforced Conversion in the Thirteenth Century." *Nederlands Archief voor Kerkgeschiedenis*, 69: 161–75.

Kruglanski, A.W., Pierro, A., Mannetti L., and De Grada, E. 2006. "Groups as Epistemic Providers: Need for Closure and the Unfolding of Group-centricism." *Psychological Review*, 11: 84–100.

Kvanvig, Jonathan L. 1993. *The Problem of Hell*. New York: Oxford University Press.

Kyaw, Tin Aung. 2013. "Buddhist Monk Wirathu Leads Violent National Campaign against Myanmar's Muslims." *The Huffington Post*, June 25, http://www.huffingtonpost.com/burma-journal/buddhist-monk-wirathu-lea_b_3481807.html (accessed August 28, 2013).

Kymlicka, Will. 1996. "Two Models of Pluralism and Tolerance." In *Toleration: An Elusive Virtue*, edited by David Heyd, pp. 81–105. Princeton: Princeton University Press.

Landsberg, Mitchell. 2011. "Dalai Lama suggests Osama bin Laden's Death was Justified." *Los Angeles Times*, May 4, http://articles.latimes.com/2011/may/04/local/la-me-0504-dalai-lama-20110504 (accessed December 10, 2012).

Lawrence, Bruce, ed. 2005. *Messages to the World: The Statements of Osama Bin Laden*, translated by James Howarth. London: Verso.

Leitenberg, Milton. 1999. "Aum Shinrikyo's Efforts to Produce Biological Weapons: A Case Study in the Serial Propagation of Misinformation." *Terrorism and Political Violence*, 11(4): 149–58.

Leong, Gregory B. 2008. "Revisiting the Deific-Decree Doctrine in Washington State." *Journal of the American Academy of Psychiatry and Law*, 36: 95–104.

Leverick, Fiona. 2007. *Killing in Self-Defence*. Oxford: Oxford University Press.

Levin, S.L. and Sidanius, J. 1999. "Social Dominance and Social Identity in the United States and Israel: In-Group Favoritism or Out-group Derogation?" *Political Psychology*, 20: 99–126.

Levy, Buddy. 2009. *Conquistador: Hernan Cortés, King Montezuma and the Last Stand of the Aztecs*. New York: Bantam.

Levy, Neil. 2006a. "Cognitive Scientific Challenges to Morality." *Philosophical Psychology*, 19: 567–87.

Levy, Neil. 2006b. "The Wisdom of the Pack." *Philosophical Explorations*, 9: 99–103.

Lewens, Tim. 2007. "Cultural Evolution". In *Stanford Encyclopedia of Philosophy*, http://plato.stanford.edu/entries/evolution-cultural/ (accessed April 7, 2012).

Lewis, Bernard. 1998. "Licence to Kill: Usama Bin Ladin's Declaration of Jihad." *Foreign Affairs*, 77(6): 14–19.

Lewontin, R.C. 1970. "The Units of Selection." *Annual Review of Ecology and Systematics*, 1: 1–18.

Lincoln, Bruce. 2003. *Holy Terrors: Thinking about Religion after September 11*. Chicago: University of Chicago Press.

Lloyd, E.A. 1999. "Evolutionary Psychology: The Burdens of Proof." *Biology and Philosophy*, 14: 211–33.

Locke, John. 1689 [1991]. "A Letter Concerning Toleration." In *John Locke: A Letter Concerning Toleration in Focus*, edited by J. Horton and S. Mendus, pp. 12–56. London: Routledge.

Loftus, Jeni. 2001. "America's Liberalization in Attitudes towards Homosexuality, 1973–1998." *American Sociological Review*, 66: 762–82.

MacDonald, Patrick and Tro, Nivaldo J. 2009. "In Defense of Methodological Naturalism." *Christian Scholar's Review*, 37(2): 201–29.

Machery, Edouard. 2007. "Massive Modularity and Brain Evolution." *Philosophy of Science*, 74: 825–38.

Machery, Edouard and Mallon, Ron. 2010. "Evolution of Morality." In *The Moral Psychology Handbook*, edited by John M. Doris and the Moral Psychology Research Group, pp. 3–46. Oxford: Oxford University Press.

Machin, A. and Dunbar, R.I.M. 2011. "The Brain Opioid Theory of Social Attachment: A Review of the Evidence." *Behavior*, 148(9–10): 985–1025 (41).

MacNeill, Allen D. 2004. "The Capacity for Religious Experience is an Evolutionary Adaptation to Warfare." *Evolution and Cognition*, 10(1): 43–60.

Mapes, Mary. 2009. "No Mercy." *The Huffington Post*, May 31, http://www.huffingtonpost.com/mary-mapes/no-mercy_b_209529.html (accessed December 11, 2012).

Marcus, Gary. 2004. *The Birth of the Mind*. New York: Basic Books.

Margalit, Avishai. 2010. *On Compromises and Rotten Compromises*. Princeton: Princeton University Press.

Marietta, Morgan. 2008. "From My Cold Dead Hands: Democratic Consequences of Sacred Rhetoric." *Journal of Politics*, 70(3): 767–79.

Marshall, I. Howard. 2003. "The New Testament does not Teach Universal Salvation." In *Universal Salvation? The Current Debate*, edited by Robin A. Parry and Christopher H. Partridge, pp. 55–76. Carlisle: Paternoster.

Masuzawa, Tomoko. 1993. *In Search of Dreamtime: The Quest for the Origins of Religion*. Chicago: Chicago University Press.

May, Larry. 2005. "Killing Naked Soldiers: Distinguishing between Combatants and Non-Combatants." *Ethics and International Affairs*, 19(3): 39–53.

Mayer, Jean-François. 2003. "'Our Terrestrial Journey is Coming to an End': The Last Voyage of the Solar Temple," translated by Elijah Siegler. In *Cults and New Religious Movements: A Reader*, edited by Lorne L. Dawson, pp. 208–25. Oxford: Blackwell.

Mayer, Jean-François. 2011. "'There Will Follow a New Generation and a New Earth': From Apocalyptic Hopes to Destruction in the Movement for the Restoration of the Ten Commandments of God." In *Violence and New Religious Movements*, edited by James R. Lewis, pp. 191–214. Oxford: Oxford University Press.

McAuley, Denis. 2005. "The Ideology of Osama Bin Laden: Nation, Tribe and World Economy." *Journal of Political Ideologies*, 10(3): 269–87.

McCauley, Robert N. 2011. *Why Religion Is Natural and Science Is Not*. New York: Oxford University Press.

McCauley, Robert N. and Lawson, E. Thomas. 2002. *Bringing Ritual to Mind: Psychological Foundations of Cultural Forms*. Cambridge: Cambridge University Press.

McCullough, Michael E. and Worthington, Everett L. 1999. "Religion and the For-giving Personality." *Journal of Personality*, 67: 1141–64.

McFarland, S.G. 1989. "Religious Orientations and the Targets of Discrimination." *Journal for the Scientific Study of Religion*, 28: 324–36.

McKennie Goodpasture, H., ed. 1989. *Cross and Sword: An Eyewitness History of Christianity in Latin America*. Stanford: Orbis.

Metcalf, Barbara and Metcalf, Thomas R. 2006. *A Concise History of Modern India*. Cambridge: Cambridge University Press.

Meyer, Stephen. 2000. "Qualified Agreement: Modern Science and the Return of the 'God Hypothesis'." In *Science and Christianity: Four Views*, edited by R.F. Carlson, pp. 127–74. Downers Grove: InterVarsity.

Mikhail, J. 2011. *Elements of Moral Cognition: Rawls' Linguistic Analogy and the Cognitive Science of Moral and Legal Judgment*. Cambridge: Cambridge University Press.

Mill, John Stuart. 1859 [1974]. *On Liberty*, edited by G. Himmelfarb. Harmondsworth: Penguin.

Monin, B., Pizarro, D.A., and Beer, J.S. 2007. "Deciding vs. Reacting: Conceptions of Moral Judgment and the Reason-Affect Debate." *Review of General Psychology*, 11: 99–111.

Moore, Rebecca, 2011. "Narrative of Persecution, Suffering and Martyrdom: Violence in People's Temple and Jonestown." In *Violence and New Religious Movements*, edited by James R. Lewis, pp. 95–111. Oxford: Oxford University Press.

Morgenthau, Hans. 1978. *Politics Among Nations: The Struggle for Power and Peace*, 5th edn. New York: Alfred Knopf.

Morris, Grant H. and Haroun, Ansar. 2001. "'God Told Me to Kill': Religion or Delusion?" *San Diego Law Review*, 38: 973–1049.

Muir, Angus M. 1999. "Terrorism and Weapons of Mass Destruction: The Case of Aum Shinrikyo." *Studies in Conflict and Terrorism*, 22(1): 79–91.

Mummendey, A., Klink, A., and Brown, R. 2001. "Nationalism and Patriotism: National Identification and Out-group Rejection." *British Journal of Social Psychology*, 40: 159–72.

Nagel, Thomas. 1991. *Equality and Partiality*. Oxford: Oxford University Press.

Narveson, Jan. 1965. "Pacifism: A Philosophical Analysis." *Ethics*, 75. 259–71.

Navarrete, Carlos David and Fessler, Daniel M.T. 2006. "Disease Avoidance and Ethnocentrism: The Effects of Disease Vulnerability and Disgust Sensitivity on Intergroup Attitudes." *Evolution and Human Behavior* 27(4): 270–82.

Needham, Paul. 2002. "The Discovery that Water is H_2O." *International Studies in the Philosophy of Science*, 16(3): 205–26.

Neusner, Jacob and Chilton, Bruce D. 2009. *The Golden Rule: The Ethics of Reciprocity in World Religions*. London: Bloomsbury.

Newman, Troy. 2009. "Shooting Abortionists Isn't Just Immoral – It's Stupid". *Troy's Blog: Thoughts from Troy Newman – President of Operation Rescue*, July 29, http://www.operationrescue.org/troys-blog/ (accessed May 31, 2012).

Newton, Huey, P. 2009. *Revolutionary Suicide*. New York: Penguin Classics.

Nichols, Shaun. 2007. "Imagination and Immortality: Thinking of Me." *Synthese*, 159(2): 215–33.

Nichols, Shaun and Mallon, Ron, 2006. "Moral Dilemmas and Moral Rules." *Cognition*, 100: 530–42.

Niditch, Susan. 1993. *War in the Hebrew Bible: A Study in the Ethics of Violence.* New York: Oxford University Press.

Niebuhr, Reinhold. 1940 [2011]. "Why the Christian Church is Not Pacifist." Reprinted in *Princeton Readings in Religion and Violence*, edited by Mark Juergensmeyer and Margo Kitts, pp. 45–54. Princeton: Princeton University Press.

Nisbet. R.A. 1993. *The Sociological Tradition*, 2nd edn. New Brunswick, NJ: Transaction.

Norman, Richard. 1995. *Ethics, Killing, and War*. Cambridge: Cambridge University Press.

North, Scott. 2001a. "Jury to See Confession of Killing." *The Herald* (Everett, Washington), April 4, http://wwrn.org/articles/9591/?&place=north-america&section=gatekeepers (accessed December 11, 2012).

North, Scott. 2001b. "Defendant Says He'd Kill Again." *The Herald* (Everett, Washington). May 17, http://www.heraldnet.com/article/20010517/NEWS01/105170751 (accessed December 11, 2012).

Nussbaum, Martha, C. 2012. *The New Religious Intolerance: Overcoming the Politics of Fear in an Anxious Age*. Cambridge, MA: The Belknap Press.

Odone, Christina. 2011. "Charlie Gilmour: Cenotaph Jailing was Prejudice not Justice at Work." *The Telegraph*, July 18, http://blogs.telegraph.co.uk/news/cristinaodone/100097324/charlie-gilmour-cenotaph-jailing-was-prejudice-not-justice-at-work/ (accessed November 26, 2012).

Office of His Holiness the Dalai Lama, 2011. His Holiness Talks about Secular Ethics and Human Development at the University of Southern California, May 4, http://dalailama.com/news/post/672-his-holiness-talks-about-secular-ethics-and-human-development-at-university-of-southern-california (accessed August 28, 2013).

O'Malley, John, W., SJ. 2010. *What Happened at Vatican II?* Cambridge, MA: The Belknap Press.

Orbach, Benjamin. 2001. "Usama Bin Ladin and Al-Qa'ida: Origins and Doctrines." *Middle East Review of International Affairs*, 5(4): 54–68.

Otto, Rudolph. 1923. *The Idea of the Holy: An Enquiry into the Non-Rational Factor in the Divine and Its Relation to the Rational*, translated by John W. Harvey. Oxford: Oxford University Press.

Palmer, Susan J. 1994. "Evacuating Waco." In *From the Ashes: Making Sense of Waco*, edited by James R. Lewis, pp. 99–110. Lanham, MD: Rowman & Littlefield.

Pape, Robert A. 2005. *Dying to Win: The Strategic Logic of Suicide Terrorism*. New York: Random House.

Parfit, Derek. 2011. *On What Matters*. Oxford: Oxford University Press.

Pedahzur, A. and Perliger, A. 2009. *Jewish Terrorism in Israel*. New York: Columbia University Press.

Pedahzur, A. and Ranstorp, M. 2001. "A Tertiary Model for Countering Terrorism in Liberal Democracies: The Case of Israel." *Terrorism and Political Violence*, 13(2): 1–26.

Perlman, Martin. 2002. "Pagan Teleology: Adaptational Role and the Philosophy of Mind." In *Functions: New Essays in the Philosophy of Psychology and Biology*, edited by A.R. Ariew, R. Cummins, and M. Perlman, pp. 263–290. Oxford: Oxford University Press.

Petrovich, L., O'Neill, P., and Jorgensen, M. 1993. "An Empirical Study of Moral Intuitions: Toward an Evolutionary Ethics." *Journal of Personality and Social Psychology*, 64: 467–78.

Pettit, Philip. 1992. "The Nature of Naturalism II." *Proceedings of the Aristotelian Society*. Suppl. Vol. 66: 245–66.

Piaget, Jean. 1932. *The Moral Judgment of the Child*. New York: Harcourt, Brace Jovanovich.

Pizzaro, D.A. and Bloom, P. 2003. "The Intelligence of the Moral Intuitions: Comment on Haidt (2001)." *Psychological Review*, 110: 193–6.

Posner, Richard A. and Rasmusen Eric B. 1999. "Creating and Enforcing Norms, with Special Reference to Sanctions." *International Review of Law and Economics*, 19(3): 369–82.

Powell, Russell and Clarke, Steve. 2012. "Religion as an Evolutionary Byproduct: A Critique of the Standard Model." *British Journal for the Philosophy of Science*, 63: 457–86.

Powell, Russell and Clarke, Steve. 2013. "Religion, Tolerance and Intolerance: Views from Across the Disciplines." In *Religion, Intolerance and Conflict: A Scientific and Conceptual Investigation*, edited by Steve Clarke, Russell Powell, and Julian Savulescu, pp. 1–35. Oxford: Oxford University Press.

Prinz, Jesse. 2006. "Is the Mind Really Modular?" In *Contemporary Debates in Cognitive Science*, edited by R. Stainton, pp. 22–36. Oxford: Blackwell.

Prinz, Jesse. 2012. *Beyond Human Nature: How Culture and Experience Shape our Lives*. London: Allen Lane.

Pyysiäinen, Ilkka and Hauser, Marc. 2010. "The Origins of Religion: Evolved Adaptation or By-product?" *Trends in Cognitive Sciences*, 14: 104–9.

Rainey, Lee Dian. 2010. *Confucius and Confucianism: The Essentials*. Oxford: Wiley-Blackwell.

Ramsbotham, Oliver, Woodhouse, Tom, and Miall, Hugh. 2005. *Contemporary Conflict Resolution*, 2nd edn. Cambridge: Polity.

Raphael, D.D. 1988. "The Intolerable." In *Justifying Toleration*, edited by Susan Mendus, pp. 137–53. Cambridge, Cambridge University Press.

Rathje, W.L. 2001. "Why the Taliban are Destroying Buddhas." *USA Today*, March 22, http://usatoday30.usatoday.com/news/science/archaeology/2001-03-22-afghan-buddhas.htm (accessed December 5, 2012).

Rauscher, Frederick. 2012. "Kant's Social and Political Philosophy." In *Stanford Encyclopedia of Philosophy*, http://plato.stanford.edu/entries/kant-social-political/ (accessed October 29, 2012).

Ravitzky, Aviezer. 1986. "Roots of Kahanism: Consciousness and Political Reality." *The Jerusalem Quarterly*, 39: 90–108.

Rawls, John. 1999. *The Law of Peoples, with the "Idea of Public Reason Revisited"*. Cambridge, MA: Harvard University Press.

Raz, Joseph. 1988. "Autonomy, Toleration and the Harm Principle." In *Justifying Toleration*, edited by Susan Mendus, pp. 137–53. Cambridge: Cambridge University Press.

Rea, Michael C. 2002. *World without Design: The Ontological Consequences of Naturalism*. Oxford: Oxford University Press.

Reader, Ian. 2002. "Spectres and Shadows: Aum Shinrikyo and the Road to Megriddo." *Terrorism and Political Violence*, 14(1): 145–86.

Reavis, Dick J. 1995. *The Ashes of Waco: An Investigation*. New York: Simon & Schuster.

Reed, D.R.C. 1997. *Following Kohlberg: Liberalism and the Practice of Democratic Community*. Notre Dame: University of Notre Dame Press.

Reitan, Eric. 2008. *Is God a Delusion? A Reply to Religion's Cultured Despisers*. Malden, MA: Wiley-Blackwell.

Repp, Ian. 2011. "Religion and Violence in Japan: The Case of Aum Shinrikyo." In *Violence and New Religious Movements*, edited by James R. Lewis, pp. 147–71. New York: Oxford University Press.

Richerson, P. and Boyd, R. 2005. *Not by Genes Alone: How Culture Transformed Human Evolution*. Chicago: University of Chicago Press.

Richert, Rebekah A., Whitehouse, Harvey, and Stewart, Emma. 2005. "Memory and Analogical Thinking in High-Arousal Rituals." In *Mind and Religion: Psychological and Cognitive Foundations of Religiosity*, edited by Harvey Whitehouse and R.N. McCauley, pp. 127–45. Walnut Creek, CA: AltaMira Press.

Ridges, David J. 2007. *Mormon Beliefs and Doctrines Made Easier*. Springville, UT: Cedar Fort.

Risen, James and Thomas, Judy. 1998. *Wrath of Angels: The American Abortion War*. New York: Basic Books.

Robbins, Thomas. 1986. "Religious Mass Suicide before Jonestown: The Russian Old Believers." *Sociology of Religion*, 47: 1–20.

Robertson, James Craigie. 1854. *History of the Christian Church: To the Pontificate of Gregory the Great, A.D. 590*. London: John Murray.

Robertson Smith, William. 1894. *Lectures on the Religion of the Semites*, 2nd edn. London: A&C Black.

Rose, Jenny. 2011. *Zoroastrianism: An Introduction*. London: I.B. Tauris.

Rosen, Steven. 2002. *Holy War, Violence and the Bhagavad-Gita*. Hampton, VA: Deepak Heritage.

Rosenberg, Alexander.1985. *The Structure of Biological Science*. Cambridge: Cambridge University Press.

Ross, W.D. 1930. *The Right and the Good*. Oxford: Oxford University Press.

Rothbard, Murray N. 2002. *The Ethics of Liberty*. New York: New York University Press.

Ruse, Michael. 2001. *Can a Darwinian be a Christian?* Cambridge: Cambridge University Press.

Ryan, Cheyney C. 1983. "Self-Defense, Pacifism and the Possibility of Killing." *Ethics*, 93(3): 508–24.

Sadakata, Akira. 1997. *Buddhist Cosmology: Philosophy and Origins*. Tokyo: Kosei.

Saltzstein, H.D. and Kasachkoff, T. 2004. "Haidt's Moral Intuitionist Theory: A Psychological and Philosophical Critique." *Review of General Psychology*, 8: 273–82.

Samuels, R. 1998. "Evolutionary Psychology and the Massive Modularity Hypothesis." *British Journal for the Philosophy of Science*, 49: 575–602.

Sanderson, S.K. 2008. "Adaptation, Evolution, and Religion." *Religion*, 38: 141–56.

Saroglou, V., Pichon, I., Trompette, L., Verschueren, M., and Dernelle, R. 2005. "Prosocial Behavior and Religion: New Evidence Based on Projective Measures and Peer Ratings." *Journal for the Scientific Study of Religion*, 44: 323–48.

Scanlon, T.M. 2008. *Moral Dimensions: Permissibility, Meaning, Blame*. Cambridge, MA: Harvard University Press.

Scholl, B.J. and Tremoulet, P.D. 2000. "Perceptual Causality and Animacy." *Trends in Cognitive Sciences*, 4: 299–309.

Scott, George. 1974. *The Rise and Fall of the League of Nations*. London: Macmillan.

Selengut, Charles. 2003. *Sacred Fury: Understanding Religious Violence*. Walnut Creek, CA: AltaMira Press.

Shapira, Yitzhak. 2009. *The King's Torah* (unauthorized English translation), http://wakeupfromyourslumber.com/blog/joeblow/english-translations-kings-torah-torat-hamelech-laws-pertaining-relations-between-jews- (accessed May 22, 2012).

Shariff, Azim, F. and Norenzayan, Ara. 2011. "Mean Gods Make Good People: Different Views of God Predict Cheating Behavior." *International Journal for the Psychology of Religion*, 21: 85–96.

Shariff, Azim, F., Norenzayan, Ara, and Henrich, Joseph. 2009. "The Birth of High Gods." In *Evolution, Culture, and the Human Mind*, edited by M. Schaller, A. Norenzayan, S. Heine, T. Kameda, and T. Yamagishi, pp. 119–36. New York: Lawrence Erlbaum Associates.

Sheikh, Hammad, Ginges, Jeremy, Coman, Alin, and Atran, Scott. 2012. "Religion, Group Threat and Sacred Values." *Judgment and Decision Making*, 7: 110–18.

Sidgwick, Henry. 1907. *The Methods of Ethics*, 7th edn. London: Macmillan.

Singer, Peter. 1993. *Practical Ethics*, 2nd edn. Cambridge: Cambridge University Press.

Singer, T., Seymour, B., O'Doherty, J.P., Stephen, K.E., Dolan, R.J., and Frith, C.D. 2006. "Empathetic Neural Responses are Modulated by the Perceived Fairness of Others." *Nature*, 439: 466–9.

Sloan, Stewart. 2012. "Pakistan: Violence against the Ahmadi Community." *Scoop Independent News*, 19 November, http://www.scoop.co.nz/stories/WO1211/S00264/pakistan-violence-against-the-ahmadi-community.htm (accessed February 18, 2013).

Smart, J.J.C. 1956. "Extreme and Restricted Utilitarianism." *Philosophical Quarterly*, 6: 344–54.

Smith, David Livingstone. 2007. *The Most Dangerous Animal*. New York: St. Martin's Press.

Smith, Jonathan Z. 1999. "The Devil in Mr. Jones." In *The Insider/Outsider Problem in the Study of Religion*, edited by Russell T. McCutcheon, pp. 370–89. London: Cassell.

Sober, Elliot and Wilson, David Sloan. 1998. *Unto Others: The Evolution and Psychology of Unselfish Behavior*. Cambridge, MA: Harvard University Press.

Soltani, Khoshrow. 2013, "This is Iran. Everyone is Happy." Al Jazeera, November 26, http://www.aljazeera.com/indepth/opinion/2013/11/iran-everyone-happy-2013112651855730619.html (accessed December 3, 2013).

Somerville, Keith. 2002. "Controversy Over Nigerian Fatwa." BBC News Online, November 27, http://news.bbc.co.uk/2/hi/africa/2519595.stm (accessed November 28, 2012).

Sorabji, Richard and Rodin, David. 2006. *The Ethics of War: Shared Problems in Different Traditions*. Aldershot: Ashgate.

Sosis, Richard. 2005. "Does Religion Promote Trust? The Role of Signalling, Reputation, and Punishment." *Interdisciplinary Journal of Research on Religion*, 1: 1–30.

Sosis, Richard. 2011. "Why Sacred Lands are not Indivisible: The Cognitive Foundations of Sacralising Land." *Journal of Terrorism Research*, 2(1): 17–44.

Sosis, Richard and Bressler, Eric R. 2003. "Cooperation and Commune Longevity: A Test of the Costly Signalling Theory of Religion." *Cross-Cultural Research*, 37: 211–39.

Sosis, Richard, Kress, Howard, C., and Boster, James S. 2007. "Scars for War: Evaluating Alternative Signalling Explanations for Cross-Cultural Variance in Ritual Costs." *Evolution and Human Behavior*, 28: 234–47.

Sosis, Richard, Phillips, Erika, and Alcorta, Candace S. 2012. "Sacrifice and Sacred Values: Evolutionary Perspectives on Religious Terrorism." In *The Oxford Handbook of Evolutionary Perspectives on Violence, Homicide, and War*, edited by T. Shackelford and V. Weeks-Shackelford, pp. 233–53. New York: Oxford University Press.

Sosis, Richard and Ruffle, Bradley. 2003. "Religious Ritual and Cooperation: Testing for a Relationship on Israeli Religious and Secular Kibbutzim." *Current Anthropology*, 44: 713–22.

Sperber, Dan. 1996. *Explaining Culture: A Naturalistic Approach*. Oxford: Blackwell.

Sprinzak, Ehud. 1985. *Kach and Meir Kahane: The Emergence of Jewish Quasi-Fascism*. New York: The American Jewish Committee.

Sprinzak, Ehud. 1991. "Violence and Catastrophe in the Theology of Rabbi Meir Kahane: The Ideologization of Memetic Desire." *Terrorism and Political Violence*, 3(3): 48–70.

Stern, Jessica. 2003. *Terror in the Name of God*. New York: HarperCollins.

Stirrat, R.L. 1984. "Sacred Models." *Man: New Series*, 19(2): 199–215.

Stouffer, S.A. 1955. *Communism, Conformity, and Civil Liberties*. New York: Doubleday.

Stroud, Barry. 2004. "The Charm of Naturalism." In *Naturalism in Question*, edited by M. De Caro and D. Macarthur, pp. 21–35. Cambridge, MA: Harvard University Press.

Sumner, Serian and Keller, Laurent. 2008. "Social Evolution: Reincarnation, Free-riding and Inexplicable Modes of Reproduction." *Current Biology*, 18: R206–7.

Surowiecki, James. 2011. "Dodger Mania." *The New Yorker*, July 11, p. 38.

Svensson, Isak, and Harding, Emily. 2011. "How Holy Wars End: Exploring the Termination Patterns of Conflicts With Religious Dimensions in Asia." *Terrorism and Political Violence*, 23(2): 133–49.

Sylvester, Ron. 2010. "Scott Roeder Gets Hard 50 in Murder of Abortion Provider George Tiller." *Wichita Eagle*, April 1, http://www.kansas.com/2010/04/01/1249310/roeder-to-be-sentenced-thursday.html (accessed December 12, 2012).

Teehan, John. 2010. *In the Name of God: The Evolutionary Origins of Religious Ethics and Violence*. Malden, MA: Wiley-Blackwell.

Teichman, Jenny. 1986. *Pacifism and the Just War*. Oxford: Basil Blackwell.

Tenbrunsel, Ann. E., Wade-Benzoni, Kimberly A., Tost, Leigh P., Medvec, Victoria H., Thompson, Leigh L., and Bazerman, Max, H. 2009. "The Reality and Myth of Sacred Issues in Negotiations." *Negotiation and Conflict Management Research*, 2(3): 263–84.

Tetlock, Philip. E. 2003. "Thinking the Unthinkable: Sacred Values and Taboo Cognitions." *Trends in Cognitive Sciences*, 7(7): 320–4.

Tetlock, Philip E., Kristel, Orie K., Elson, Beth, Green, Melanie C., and Lerner, Jennifer S. 2000. "The Psychology of the Unthinkable: Taboo Trade-Offs, Forbidden Base Rates, and Heretical Counterfactuals." *Journal of Personality and Social Psychology*, 78(5): 853–70.

Tetlock, Philip E., Peterson, Randall S., and Lerner Jennifer S. 1996. "Revising the Value Pluralism Model: Incorporating Social Content and Context Postulates." In *The Psychology of Values: The Ontario Symposium on Personality and Social Psychology*, Vol. 8, edited by Clive Seligman, James M. Olson, and Mark P. Zanna, pp. 25–51. Hillsdale, NJ: Lawrence Erlbaum.

Thomas, Judy. 2009. "Roeder Upset at Operation Rescue." *Wichita Eagle*, July 26, http://www.kansas.com/2009/07/26/905518/roeder-upset-at-operation-rescue.html (accessed December 12, 2012).

Thomson, Judith, J. 1976. "Killing, Letting Die and the Trolley Problem." *The Monist*, 59: 204–17.

Thurow, Joshua. 2013. "Religion, 'Religion', and Tolerance." In *Religion, Intolerance and Conflict: A Scientific and Conceptual Investigation*, edited by Steve Clarke, Russell Powell, and Julian Savulescu, pp. 146–62. Oxford: Oxford University Press.

Tishkoff, Sarah A., et al. (eighteen other authors). 2006. "Convergent Adaptation of Human Lactase Persistence in Africa and Europe." *Nature Genetics*, 39: 31–40.

Toft, Monica Duffy, Philpott, Daniel, and Shah, Timothy Samuel. 2011. *God's Century: Resurgent Religion and Global Politics*. New York: W.W. Norton.

Toner, Christopher. 2005. "Just War and the Supreme Emergency Exception." *The Philosophical Quarterly*, 55: 545–61.

Tooby, J. and Cosmides, L. 1992. "The Psychological Foundations of Culture." In *The Adapted Mind: Evolutionary Psychology and the Generation of Culture*, edited by J. Barcow, L. Cosmides, and J. Tooby, pp. 19–136. Oxford: Oxford University Press.

Trigg, Roger. 2007. *Religion in Public Life: Must Faith Be Privatized?* Oxford: Oxford University Press.

Trigg, Roger. 2012. *Equality, Freedom and Religion*. Oxford: Oxford University Press.

Trivers, Robert. 1971. "The Evolution of Reciprocal Altruism." *Quarterly Review of Biology*, 46: 35–57.

Turiel, Elliot. 1983. *The Development of Social Knowledge*. Cambridge: Cambridge University Press.

Turner, Nancy L. 2006. "Jewish Witness, Forced Conversion, and Island Living: John Duns Scotus on Jews and Judaism." In *Christian Attitudes Toward the Jews in the Middle Ages: A Casebook*, edited by Michael Frassetto, pp. 183–209. London: Routledge.

Tylor, Edward. 1871. *Primitive Culture: Researches into the Development of Mythology, Philosophy, Religion, Art and Custom*. London: J. Murray.

Urban, Hugh B. 2000. "The Devil at Heaven's Gate: Rethinking the Study of Religion in the Age of Cyber-Space." *Nova Religio: The Journal of Alternative and Emergent Religions*, 3(2): 268–302.

Vacandard, E. 2010. *The Inquisition: A Critical and Historical Study of the Coercive Power of the Church*, translated by B.L. Conway. Whitefish, MT: Kessinger.

Victoria, Brian Daizen. 2006. *Zen at War*, 2nd edn. Lanham, MD: Rowman & Littlefield.

Vitebsky, Piers. 2001. *Shamanism*. Norman: University of Oklahoma Press.

Wade, Nicholas. 2009. *The Faith Instinct: How Religion Evolved and Why it Endures*. New York: Penguin.

Wadia, A.R. 1965. "Philosophical Implications of the Doctrine of Karma." *Philosophy East and West*, 15(2): 145–52.

Waldron, Jeremy. 1991. "Locke: Toleration and the Rationality of Persecution." In *John Locke: A Letter Concerning Toleration in Focus*, edited by J. Horton and S. Mendus, pp. 98–124. London: Routledge.

Walker, Ronald W., Turley, Richard E., Jr.,, and Leonard, Glen M. 2008. *Massacre at Mountain Meadows: An American Tragedy*. Oxford: Oxford University Press.

Wallace, Vesna A. 2010. "Legalized Violence: Punitive Measures of Buddhist Khans in Mongolia." In *Buddhist Warfare*, edited by Michael K. Jerryson and M. Juergensmeyer, pp. 91–103. New York: Oxford University Press.

Walter, Tony. 1996. *The Eclipse of Eternity. A Sociology of the Afterlife*. Basingstoke: Macmillan.

Walzer, Michael. 1997. *On Toleration*. New Haven, CT: Yale University Press.

Walzer, Michael. 2000. *Just and Unjust Wars: A Moral Argument with Historical Illustrations*, 3rd edn. New York: Basic Books.

Walzer, Michael 2004. *Arguing About War*. New Haven, CT: Yale University Press.

Ward, Keith. 2006. *Is Religion Dangerous?* Oxford: Lion Hudson.

Watanabe, Manabu. 1998. "Religion and Violence in Japan Today: A Chronological and Doctrinal Analysis of Aum Shinrikyo." *Terrorism and Political Violence*, 10(4): 80–100.

West, Thomas, G. 1997. *Vindicating the Founders: Race, Sex, Class and Justice in the Origins of America*. Lanham, MD: Rowman & Littlefield.

White, Jon Manchip. 1996. *Cortés and the Downfall of the Aztec Empire*, 2nd edn. New York: Carroll & Graf.

Whitehouse, Harvey. 2000. *Arguments and Icons: Divergent Modes of Religiosity*. Oxford: Oxford University Press.

Whitehouse, Harvey. 2004. *Modes of Religiosity: A Cognitive Theory of Religious Transmission*. Walnut Creek, CA: AltaMira Press.

Whitehouse, Harvey. 2013. "Religion, Cohesion, and Hostility". In *Religion, Intolerance and Conflict: A Scientific and Conceptual Investigation*, edited by Steve Clarke, Russell Powell, and Julian Savulescu, pp. 36–47. Oxford: Oxford University Press.

Wiktorowicz, Quintan and Kaltner, John. 2003. "Killing in the Name of Islam: Al Qaeda's Justification for September 11." *Middle East Policy*, 10(2): 76–92.

Williams, Bernard. 1996. "Toleration: An Impossible Virtue." In *Toleration: An Elusive Virtue*, edited by D. Heyd, pp. 19–27. Princeton, Princeton University Press.

Williams, G.C. 1966. *Adaptation and Natural Selection*. Princeton: Princeton University Press.

Wilson, David Sloan. 2002. *Darwin's Cathedral: Evolution, Religion and the Nature of Society*. Chicago: The University of Chicago Press.

Wilson, David Sloan and Wilson, Edward O. 2007: "Rethinking the Theoretical Foundation of Sociobiology." *Quarterly Review of Biology*, 82(4): 327–48.

Wilson, David Sloan and Wilson, Edward O. 2008. "Evolution 'for the Good of the Group'." *American Scientist*, 96: 380–9.

Wilson, Edward O. 1998. *Consilience: The Unity of Knowledge*. London: Little Brown and Company.

Winkelman, Michael. 2010. *Shamanism: A Biopsychosocial Paradigm of Consciousness and Healing*, 2nd edn. Santa Barbara: Praeger.

Winzeler, R.L. 2008. *Anthropology and Religion: What we Know, Think, and Question*. Walnut Creek, CA: AltaMira Press.

Wrangham, Richard W. 2009. *Catching Fire: How Cooking Made Us Human*. New York: Basic Books.

Wrangham, Richard W. and Peterson, Dale. 1997. *Demonic Males: Apes and the Origins of Human Violence*, New York: Houghton Mifflin.

Wright, Robert. 2009. *The Evolution of God*. New York: Little Brown and Company.

Wright, Stuart, A. 2011. "Revisiting the Davidian Mass Suicide Debate." In *Violence and New Religious Movements*, edited by James R. Lewis, pp. 113–31. Oxford: Oxford University Press.

Yoder, John Howard. 1994. *The Politics of Jesus*, 2nd edn. Grand Rapids, MI: Eerdmans.

Yu, Xue. 2010. "Buddhists in China during the Korean War (1951–1953)." In *Buddhist Warfare*, edited by Michael K. Jerryson and M. Juergensmeyer, pp. 131–56. New York: Oxford University Press.

Zagorin, Perez. 2003. *How the Idea of Religious Toleration Came to the West*. Princeton: Princeton University Press.

Zeller, Benjamin. E. 2006. "Scaling Heaven's Gate: Individualism and Salvation in a New Religious Movement." *Nova Religio: The Journal of Alternative and Emergent Religions*, 10(2): 75–102.

Zeller, Benjamin. E. 2011. "The Euphemization of Violence: The Case of Heaven's Gate." In *Violence and New Religious Movements*, edited by James R. Lewis, pp. 173–89. Oxford: Oxford University Press.

Name Index

Subject Index

The Justification of Religious Violence, First Edition. Steve Clarke.
© 2014 John Wiley & Sons, Inc. Published 2014 by John Wiley & Sons, Inc.